APPEASEMENT AND ALL SOULS: A PORTRAIT WITH DOCUMENTS, 1937–1939

APPEASEMENT AND ALL SOULS: A PORTRAIT WITH DOCUMENTS, 1937–1939

edited by
SIDNEY ASTER

CAMDEN FIFTH SERIES
Volume 24

CAMBRIDGE
UNIVERSITY PRESS

FOR THE ROYAL HISTORICAL SOCIETY
University College London, Gower Street, London WC1 6BT
2004

Published by the Press Syndicate of the University of Cambridge
The Edinburgh Building, Cambridge CB2 2RU, United Kingdom
40 West 20th Street, New York, NY 10011–4211, USA
477 Williamstown Road, Port Melbourne, VIC 3207, Australia
Ruiz de Alarcón 13, 28014 Madrid, Spain
Dock House, The Waterfront, Cape Town 8001, South Africa

First published 2004

A catalogue record for this book is available from the British Library

Library of Congress Cataloging-in-Publication Data applied for

ISBN 0 521 84374 X hardback

SUBSCRIPTIONS. The serial publications of the Royal Historical Society, *Royal Historical Society Transactions* (ISSN 0080–4401) and Camden Fifth Series (ISSN 0960–1163), volumes may be purchased together on annual subscription. The 2004 subscription price which includes print and electronic access (but not VAT) is £71 (US$114 in the USA, Canada and Mexico) and includes Camden Fifth Series, volumes 24 and 25 (published in July and December) and Transactions Sixth Series, volume 14 (published in December). Japanese prices are available from Kinokuniya Company Ltd, P.O. Box 55, Chitose, Tokyo 156, Japan. EU subscribers (outside the UK) who are not registered for VAT should add VAT at their country's rate. VAT registered subscribers should provide their VAT registration number. Prices include delivery by air.

Subscription orders, which must be accompanied by payment, may be sent to a bookseller, subscription agent or direct to the publisher: Cambridge University Press, The Edinburgh Building, Shaftesbury Road, Cambridge CB2 2RU, UK; or in the USA, Canada and Mexico; Cambridge University Press, Journals Fulfillment Department, 100 Brook Hill Drive, West Nyack, New York, 10994–2133: USA.

SINGLE VOLUMES AND BACK VOLUMES. A list of Royal Historical Society volumes available from Cambridge University Press may be obtained from the Humanities Marketing Department at the address above.

Printed and bound in the United Kingdom by Butler & Tanner Ltd, Frome and London

CONTENTS

ACKNOWLEDGEMENTS

For permission to examine and quote copyright materials, the author is grateful to the following:

Alexander Murray (Gilbert Murray papers)
Archives and Special Collections Research Centre, Ball State University, A.M. Bracken Library, Muncie, IN (Norman Angell papers)
British Library Board and the Department of Manuscripts, British Library (J.A. Spender papers)
Department of Special Collections and Western Manuscripts, Bodleian Library, Oxford (Lionel Curtis papers)
Dr Jean Toynbee (A.J. Toynbee papers)
Master and Fellows of Trinity College, Cambridge (Walter Layton papers)
Nigel Nicolson and the Library, Balliol College, Oxford (Harold Nicolson diaries)
Professor A.K.S. Lambton and the Department of Manuscripts, British Library (Lord Cecil of Chelwood papers)
Rare Books and Special Collections, Thomas Cooper Library, University of South Carolina (Lord Allen of Hurtwood papers)
Royal Institution of Cornwall and Special Collections, Old Library, University of Exeter (A.L. Rowse diaries and papers)
Royal Institute of International Affairs (Lionel Curtis and Chatham House papers)
Trustees of the Liddell Hart Centre for Military Archives (Sir Basil Liddell Hart papers)

INTRODUCTION

APPEASEMENT AND ALL SOULS COLLEGE

Appeasement and All Souls College, like Neville Chamberlain and Munich, *The Times* and Geoffrey Dawson, or the Astors and the 'Cliveden Set' appear synonymously in any discussion of British foreign policy in the 1930s. They have been firmly associated since 1961 when A.L. Rowse, the historian, poet, and Shakespearean scholar published *All Souls and Appeasement.* Rowse denigrated appeasement as the foreign policy of 'a class in decadence' that reduced Britain to a second-rate power.[1] Rowse asserted that All Souls was an important clearing-house for politicians, academics, intellectuals, and other establishment figures who supported appeasement as the only policy which could attain a settlement with Nazi Germany. The same claims also surrounded the social gatherings hosted by Waldorf and Nancy Astor at Cliveden, their country home in Berkshire, and the close association between *The Times* and the Foreign Office.[2]

Such assertions have subsequently coloured discussions of appeasement and the origins of World War II. In particular, so ingrained has the association between All Souls and appeasement become, that an important reservation offered by Rowse has been ignored. Rowse wrote that several Fellows of All Souls certainly were prime figures in espousing appeasement diplomacy. But, he added, 'it is equally true that a majority of the Fellows, particularly of the younger generation, as we were then, were strongly opposed to the

[1] A.L. Rowse, *All Souls and Appeasement: A Contribution to Contemporary History* (London, 1961), p. 117. The American edition of the book was titled *Appeasement: A Study in Political Decline, 1933–1939* (New York, 1961). The two editions are the same, including pagination, except for some minor variations, as for example at p. 58, fn. 3, and pp. 109–110. The subject appears to have been raised in public first by Robert Boothby, in letters to *The Spectator*, 195 (7, 21 October 1955), pp. 448, 528. He wrote that All Souls had been 'the headquarters of the Establishment during the decade immediately preceding the Second World War; and it would be difficult to overestimate the damage then done to this country at that disastrous dinner table'; cf. Robert Boothby, *Recollections of a Rebel* (London, 1978), p. 24.

[2] Both Norman Rose, *The Cliveden Set: Portrait of an Exclusive Society* (London, 2000), and James Crathorne, *Cliveden: The Place and the People* (London, 1995), pp. 172–178, debunk the allegations attached to Cliveden. On the other hand, Gordon Martel (ed.), *The Times and Appeasement: The Journals of A.L. Kennedy, 1932–1939* (London, 2000) confirms the newspaper's very close ties with the Foreign Office.

whole policy and course of conduct with which our foremost and best-known members were identified'.[3] Rowse then entered into a vitriolic attack against the elder, grandee Fellows of the College. These included Lord Halifax, who succeeded Anthony Eden in February 1938 as Secretary of State for Foreign Affairs; the Chancellor of the Exchequer from 1937 to 1940, Sir John Simon; and the Editor of *The Times*, Geoffrey Dawson, among others in the pro-appeasement lobby. However, the intensity of Rowse's views led him largely to put aside the 'younger generation' who were critical of appeasement.[4]

Another Oxford manifestation, 'Salter's Soviet',[5] formally called the All Souls Foreign Affairs Group, stood between Rowse's elder grandees involved in appeasement diplomacy and the younger, anti-appeasement generation. Its existence as an unofficial 'Brains Trust', focusing on British foreign policy towards Italy, Germany, Spain, and the threats to Britain's Far East empire and interests was not common knowledge. From December 1937 to August 1938 the group met either at All Souls College, or occasionally in London at the Temple chambers of Sir Harold Nicolson and Sir Norman Angell, 4 King's Bench Walk. Between meetings, individual members corresponded and consulted. Their memoranda on foreign policy were, on occasion, sent to the Foreign Office and to the editors of leading newspapers and weeklies. In later years, the group's activities were first made public by Sir Arthur Salter in his memoirs.[6] This was subsequently treated in the memoirs and biographies of several other members.[7]

The documentation detailing the activities of the All Souls Foreign Affairs Group is not to be found in any one archive. None of the

[3] Rowse, *All Souls and Appeasement*, pp. v–vi, 113. Among the latter he listed: Richard Pares, Geoffrey F. Hudson, A.H.M. Jones, A.H. Campbell, Ian Bowen, Isaiah Berlin, Douglas Jay, Quentin Hogg, Dick Latham, and Harry Davis.

[4] For a useful corrective on the subject of the All Souls' 'grandees', see D.J. Wenden, 'Appeasement and All Souls', 1990 Chichele Lecture, Oxford. On the other hand, Rowse's papers contain his too candid and outspoken pen portraits, 'Brief lives of the Fellows of All Souls', including all of the Fellows who participated in the Foreign Affairs Group: Adams, Curtis, Hodson, Hudson, Salter, and Woodward. See EUL MS 113/1/2/4 (I–IV), main diary, manuscript sequence. For Rowse on Radcliffe-Brown, see EUL MS 113/2/5/8, manuscript transcripts from notebooks and typescripts.

[5] Sir Basil Liddell Hart, *The Memoirs of Captain Liddell Hart*, II (London, 1965), p. 150. The first contemporary use of this phrase appears in Curtis to Ivison S. Macadam, 2 March 1938, ms. Curtis 12, fo. 39.

[6] Arthur Salter, *Memoirs of a Public Servant* (London, 1961), pp. 259–260. There is also a fleeting reference in Rowse, *All Souls and Appeasement*, p. 59.

[7] See, for example, Arthur Marwick, *Clifford Allen: The Open Conspirator* (London, 1964), pp. 176–178; Liddell Hart, *Memoirs*, II, pp. 149–150; Martin Gilbert, *Plough My Own Furrow: The Story of Lord Allen of Hurtwood as Told Through His Writings and Correspondence* (London, 1965), pp. 399–405; Arthur Salter, *Slave of the Lamp: A Public Servant's Notebook* (London, 1967), pp. 131–132; and Arnold J. Toynbee, *Acquaintances* (London, 1967), p. 133.

participants appear to have preserved a complete set of records, despite having the secretarial services of Christina Hole.[8] Minutes were kept of the meetings and these, along with occasional discussion papers, were circulated among the group. However, an exact record of all those who attended a particular meeting is not always possible to collate. Few sets of minutes include the names of discussants, and Harold Nicolson's unpublished diaries, a primary source, do not regularly name all those who were present. Later recollections faltered on either leading or occasional members. In 1961 Sir Basil H. Liddell Hart compiled a list[9] that included the following, besides himself, who participated: W.G.S. Adams, Lord Allen of Hurtwood, Sir Norman Angell, William Arnold-Forster, Alfred Barratt Brown, Lionel Curtis, H.A.L. Fisher, H.V. Hodson, Geoffrey Hudson, Sir Walter Layton, Harold Macmillan, Gilbert Murray, Sir Harold Nicolson, Alfred Reginald Radcliffe-Brown, A.L. Rowse, Sir Arthur Salter, Arnold Toynbee, and E.L. Woodward.[10] Salter later added the name of Guy Wint, his talented young secretary at the time and the person who prepared the minutes, to the list of participants. From internal evidence, Lord Arnold, a pacifist who advocated an isolationist foreign policy,[11] must also be included.

The All Souls Foreign Affairs Group thus included some twenty-one individuals, eight of whom were Fellows of the College. Salter and Nicolson were the conveners, with meetings chaired by Allen. The inner core of members, those attending most regularly and acting as the 'Brains Trust', included the two convenors, Allen, Angell, Hudson, Liddell Hart, Murray, Arnold-Forster, Rowse, Toynbee, and Wint. However, Salter was undoubtedly the driving force behind the discussion group. In October 1934 he had been appointed Gladstone Professor of Political Theory and Institutions at All Souls College. He then won a seat as an Independent MP for Oxford University at the 27 February 1937 by-election. From this vantage point, Salter strove to foster a unique aspect of All Souls that he called the 'bridge

[8] Christina Hole (1896–1985), the noted authority on English folk customs and folklore, and prolific author of such books as *Traditions and Customs of Cheshire* (London, 1937); *English Folklore* (London, 1940); *Witchcraft in England* (London, 1945); and *British Folk Customs* (London, 1976).

[9] For a list of participants, and the extensive correspondence and consultations which led to its compilation, see Liddell Hart papers, LH5/1, LH 1/614; and Liddell Hart to Rowse, 20 October 1961, Rowse papers, EUL MS 113/1/temp/box 166.

[10] See Appendix for short biographical portraits of all the participants. 'I *did* try to get a suitable representative of the *Left*, but the Labour Party at that time was very suspicious of all-party or no-party meetings and persuaded those I tried to get to decline'; Salter to Liddell Hart, 13 February 1967, Liddell Hart papers, LH 5/1.

[11] See for example, notes by Lord Arnold, in PRO, FO371/21232, W4100/1412/50; and his speech in *Parliamentary Debates, House of Lords*, fifth series, CIV, 3 March 1937, cols 505–509.

between the academic and the public life'.[12] With his combination of patience and prodding, he launched seminars, off-the-record meetings and lobbying groups. The All Souls Foreign Affairs Group must be placed in the last of these.

Salter explained the circumstances which had motivated him to form the All Souls Foreign Affairs group in December 1937:

> The reason why I proposed the meetings was that I found myself in grave doubt [...] as to the course of policy to support and advocate, a doubt extending to some of the gravest issues presenting themselves; and in consulting others who started with a similar general outlook I found they were all experiencing equal, though not identical, anxieties. I hoped that we might help each other in clearing our minds and in solving the individual problem presenting itself to each of us as to his own line of conduct.[13]

Salter might also have been driven by another experience. *The Next Five Years: An Essay in Political Agreement* had been published on 26 July 1935, to widespread approval. The foreword included a list of more than 150 signatories, who endorsed the book but who had 'different political associations, and divergent views as to ultimate doctrine and policy'. They were agreed, however, on an 'attainable programme of action' to be implemented over the next five years. The section on foreign policy argued the case for 'Anglo-American co-operation and the strengthening of the collective peace system'. It is significant that five of the six individuals who actually drafted the book in 1935, Salter himself, Allen, Arnold-Forster, Barratt Brown, and Macmillan, were brought together in 1937.[14] At the outset it was not evident whether the meetings would be only for discussion or aim at a publication.

Later in life, Salter reflected on the group and its relation to Oxford life:

> Outside Oxford itself the present image, both in the rest of England, in America and elsewhere, is distorted by a disproportionate emphasis on the association for two or three years of less than a half-dozen of Fellows with the policy of appeasement of Hitler in a College in which many Fellows, like Amery for example, were strongly opposed to that policy. Any such emphasis

[12] 'All Souls – college affairs', n.d., Salter papers.

[13] Salter, 'Notes on foreign policy', 8 March 1938, Liddell Hart papers, LH5/1.

[14] *The Next Five Years: An Essay in Political Agreement* (London, 1935), pp. v–x, 1, 215–307. Geoffrey Crowther was the sixth member of the drafting committee. In addition, Angell, Curtis, Fisher, Layton, and Murray were also among the signatories. The Next Five Years Group formally disbanded on 25 November 1937. See Arthur Marwick, 'Middle opinion in the thirties: planning, progress and political "agreement"', *English Historical Review*, 79 (1964), pp. 293–295, and Thomas C. Kennedy, 'The Next Five Years Group and the failure of the politics of agreement in Britain', *Canadian Journal of History*, 9 (1974), pp. 45–68.

> is fantastically unjust to the College as a mirror of its true character and influence.[15]

Salter began to organize the All Souls group in December 1937, with the first meetings held on Saturday and Sunday, 18 and 19 December. Three major questions were addressed: 'What is our power?', 'Where is the first challenge likely to occur?', and 'What steps should be taken to meet the challenge?' The members divided the world between League and anti-League powers. Among the latter were Germany, Italy, and Japan, with the likely support of Austria, Hungary, and Bulgaria. Yugoslavia, Poland, Turkey, and Greece were deemed 'uncertain quantities'. It was assumed that British policy could not be based for the time being on American assistence. With regard to the military balance of power, it was strongly felt that in the first weeks of a war Britain must concentrate on home defence against air attack.

The morning session on Sunday agreed that, while Japan and Italy were dangerous, 'Germany was the centre of the whole problem'. Some contended that the slogan '*Weltmacht oder Niedergang*' reflected Germany's ambitions eventually to target the British empire. Others regarded Germany as being content with a greater *Reich*, and then seeking '*Grund und Boden*' in eastern Europe. All agreed, however, that 'the German state of mind was one that might lead to a general war'. As to 'What should be done?' two alternatives were envisioned: further concessions to Germany, or the 'Fabian policy' of playing for time, avoiding confrontations with the expectation that fascism and Nazism would fizzle out. It was agreed that the former was 'futile' while the latter was 'too negative'.

A search for a more constructive approach led to some agreement that 'British policy towards Germany should be one of firmness followed by conciliation'. The framework of 'a general settlement' was then sketched out. Britain would offer Germany the *Anschluss*, recognize Germany's right to possess colonies, and its economic primacy in eastern Europe. In return, Germany would provide assurances not to undermine democratic institutions in eastern Europe, agree to an armaments limitation scheme which would give her 'preponderance but not supremacy' in Europe, and not support Italian ambitions in the Mediterranean and in Africa. The meetings concluded 'that, even if Germany declined the terms offered, the

[15] 'The future of All Souls', 1962, Salter papers.

approach would have been worth making, as putting us right with our own public opinion'.[16]

On 20 December, Curtis revealed that it was Nicolson who had primarily advocated the view that Germany sheltered aggressive world-wide ambitions. Curtis was not impressed, as he believed that British objectives 'should be to change the militaristic outlook in Germany [which] we have created.[17] In the interim, the record of the meetings was shown to Anthony Eden, the Secretary of State for Foreign Affairs, who generally concurred with the analysis.' What the Foreign Secretary had picked up on was the group's agreement on 'the desirability of a firm stand at some stage against aggression; to be followed by the offer of generous terms for a general settlement'. However, there was little expectation that any policy-maker would condone 'vigorous action' in the Far East.[18]

The All Souls Foreign Affairs Group next met on Saturday 15 January 1938, and now included Murray, Layton, Adams, Rowse,[19] and Woodward. With the knowledge that the 'affirmation of strength' in the Far East was impossible without firm American support, the group questioned what policy should there be pursued? Any boycott of Japanese goods or League of Nations intervention raised the spectre of war. The only feasible policy, therefore, was to hasten the shipment of supplies to China, institute a boycott against oil, and abandon Hong Kong if it were attacked. Turning next to the question of relations with Germany, one participant supported the Foreign Office view that any '"head-on" collision' with the Axis should be avoided, while playing for time, 'even at the cost of certain immediate sacrifices', and avoiding the impression of trying to encircle Germany. Others argued that the Foreign Office must improve relations with the USSR, in order to resist any German drive to the east. As well, trying to play for time was regarded as too negative. As a consequence, discussion turned to the possibility of organizing 'a positive peace-group', based on 'a constructive economic policy'. The scheme included the building of a new economic order, associated with the League of Nations, and strong enough to be attractive to Germany and Italy. Those critical

[16] Conference on Foreign Affairs, 18–19 December 1937, (Document 'A') Liddell Hart papers, LH5/1; Conference on Foreign Affairs, 18–19 December 1937, (Document 'B'), Liddell Hart papers, LH5/1.

[17] Curtis to Brand, 20 December 1937, ms. Curtis 11, fos 168–170, Curtis to Allen, 20 December 1937, ms. Curtis 11, fo. 171.

[18] Conference on Foreign Affairs, All Souls, 15–16 January 1938, Nicolson diaries; Conference on Foreign Affairs, 18–19 December 1937, (Document 'B') Liddell Hart papers, LH5/1.

[19] Rowse's engagement diaries confirm his attendance at the All Souls meetings on 15–16 January, 26 February, 16 March, and 24 April 1938; see EUL MS 113/2/6.

of this idea pointed out that 'economics depended on power' and was thus not an alternative to a traditional balance-of-power policy.

On Sunday morning, 16 January, the agenda turned from resistance to conciliation. Could Germany could be trusted with the organization of a British-style commonwealth in south-eastern Europe? Did Britain still have the power to enforce its traditional balance of power policy in Europe? In tackling these questions, policy options appeared very limited. It was agreed that any direct overtures to Germany would be taken as a sign of weakness. The problem, unresolved by the end of the day, was to discover what concessions could be made to Germany which would be 'neither dishonourable [...] nor disastrous'.[20]

Afterwards Liddell Hart noted with approval 'the way so many individual viewpoints converged towards a common view of the main elements of the problem'. Salter stressed what he called the 'real value' of the meetings.[21] On the other hand, Curtis criticized Nicolson's attitude of trying to weaken Germany at all costs. 'The rest of them, with their minds concentrated on collective security, again talked as though they were prepared to plunge the world in war in order to assert it.' He continued to press the All Souls proposal for the neutralization of Czechoslovakia.[22] Murray, writing to Liddell Hart, noted that 'the advocates of conciliation at any price had their full fling, and on the whole did not get to any result, except perhaps about the neutralization of Czechoslovakia'. Liddell Hart replied: 'the only security is collective'.[23]

Salter regarded the next meeting of the group at All Souls, on 6 February 1938, as 'the final meeting [...] on which the utility of these discussions will largely depend'.[24] However, the recent purge of the German high command and foreign ministry occasioned gloom.[25] The agenda was given over to a paper, known as 'Document C', by Lord Allen, the most persistent advocate of Anglo-German reconciliation. This sketched out a foreign policy for Britain which combined 'a display of strength with an outline of proposals to

[20] Conference on Foreign Affairs, All Souls, 15–16 January 1938, Liddell Hart papers, LH5/1; notes, 6 pp., attached to entry of 15–16 January 1938, Nicolson diaries. Several days later, Arnold-Forster, described as 'Lord Cecil's right-hand man', was in Oslo as a representative of the International Peace Campaign. He was reported to be in favour of a boycott of Japan. See British Legation, Oslo, to Foreign Office, 25 January 1938, FO371/22562, W1313/1067/98.

[21] Liddell Hart to Salter, 17 January 1938; Salter to Liddell Hart, 18 January 1938, Liddell Hart papers, LH5/1.

[22] Curtis to Dawson, 17 January 1938, ms. Curtis 12, fos 10–13.

[23] Murray to Liddell Hart, 17 January 1938; Liddell Hart to Murray, 19 January 1938, Liddell Hart papers, LH5/1.

[24] Salter to Liddell Hart, 18 January 1938, Liddell Hart papers, LH5/1.

[25] Entry of 6 February 1938, Nicolson diaries.

meet legitimate grievances and claims'. Allen proposed increasing economic pressure on Japan, the continuation of non-intervention in Spain, stepping up rearmament, even while encouraging any movement toward disarmament, and the storage of food and other commodities. His central theme was 'collective action against aggression'. Thus, the League would be retained with its current members and covenant, the League covenant would be disassociated from the International Labour Organization statutes, and the war-guilt clause would be eliminated from the Treaty of Versailles. Austria and Germany would be permitted to unite. He proposed that Czechoslovakia should adopt a cantonal system to deal with minority problems and become a neutral state. Economic policy would move towards larger trading blocs, possibly linked with the League of Nations. Finally, Allen wished to encourage the Prime Minister and Foreign Secretary to 'affirm their willingness to enter at any time upon negotiations for a comprehensive settlement'.[26] Participants were then invited to make revisions, with subsequent drafts to be co-ordinated by Wint.

The Foreign Affairs Group next met at All Souls on 26 February 1938. Layton, Arnold-Foster, Allen, Salter, Curtis, Murray, Rowse, and Nicolson debated the questions of whether the final document would be for private or public circulation, and would it propose amendments or alternatives to government policy? Some argued in favour of a comprehensive 'collective peace system'. Others contended that criticism would make the work of the government more difficult. It was finally agreed that one of the members would prepare a draft document, to be considered at the next meeting.

The discussion then turned to the news of Eden's resignation as Foreign Secretary on 20 February 1938. The short-term issue of Anglo-Italian relations was separated from the long-term ones of collective security and policy towards Germany. On the former, it was agreed that in a deal with Mussolini 'he could offer words and we must give deeds'. On the latter issues, some argued for a clear understanding in advance between Britain, France, and the USSR. Such a step would act as a 'possibly decisive deterrent' to German action, and ensure that the USSR would not return to isolation. Others regarded Germany and Italy as unstable regimes. If war could be avoided, both would collapse. 'The policy therefore suggested was one of minimum commitment east of the Rhine', the minutes recorded, with the implication that it would be 'disproportionate' to endanger the empire on the issue of Czechoslovakia. A basis for a settlement,

[26] 'Document C', enclosure in Wint to Nicolson, 12 February 1938, Liddell Hart papers, LH5/1.

which garnered some approval, rested on encouraging a cantonal system in Czechoslovakia, an open-door policy in the British Empire, and recognizing that German economic hegemony in eastern and central Europe was inevitable. The group finally endorsed a concerted effort to improving air-raid protection and home defence.[27]

The race for consensus to enable publication encouraged Wint to weigh in. He feared that the critical tone of the All Souls document was 'extremely dangerous' and might even make war 'more likely'. He proposed to Curtis that Allen prevail upon Lord Lothian to advise the group on alternative policies before it proceeded.[28] Curtis needed no encouragement. Indeed, he used the opportunity to unburden himself of several concerns. He wrote to Allen on 28 February 1938, enclosing the letter from Wint. Curtis observed that he respected Wint's judgement and added that the last meeting had been 'somewhat darkened by the atmosphere' created by Rowse and Hudson. Curtis went on to emphasize his own view 'that sanctions and collective security are the cause of the present confusion rather than the cure for it'. He agreed that Lothian should be brought in to temper the views of 'people like Arnold-Forster and Rowse with a flame in their minds', and to discuss the proposed publication. Allen's reply reinforced the compliment paid to Wint and continued: 'Speaking in the strictest confidence I was sorry when Salter (without consulting me) brought Rowse into our discussions [. . .]. Men like Rowse [. . .] take a certain pleasure in trying to prove other people to be either knaves or fools.' Allen wrote that he would consider an invitation to Lothian, that he would never be a signatory to any document which would derail the government's peace efforts, and intended to pursue his 'transitional policy'. What most worried him, however, was that the next meeting would leave him 'almost single-handed in resisting the ferocity, however sincere, of men like Rowse and Arnold-Forster'.[29]

The objective of the scheduled meeting of 16 March 1938, if consensus emerged, had been to discuss the publication of a statement. Prior to that, however, on 8 March, Curtis, Murray, Nicolson, Salter, and Allen met at Chatham House to pore over a draft memorandum prepared by Toynbee for a speech he was to deliver there on 10 March. Toynbee was concerned with the consequences to Britain if she gave up the League. Would Britain sink to the position of a second-rate power like Holland or be destroyed in the

[27] Entry of 26 February 1938, Nicolson diaries; Foreign Affairs Group, Meeting of 26 February 1938, Liddell Hart papers, LH 5/1.

[28] Wint to Curtis, 28 February 1938, ms. Curtis 12, fo. 32. The original is in the Lord Allen of Hurtwood papers, University of South Carolina, Columbia, SC.

[29] Allen to Curtis, 1 March 1938, ms. Curtis 12, fos 36–38.

process? While Toynbee inclined to the latter view, Salter proposed an intermediate policy. He regarded Russian help as vital in any struggle with Germany. But if Russia was 'out of the picture', he reasoned, 'we must play for time'. He opposed, therefore, any commitments to the Czechs, but favoured 'defending liberty on the Spanish front'. Murray pointed out that he was against 'the war ideology' of the dictator states. Curtis then digressed on the need for air-raid protection. Nicolson cut to the heart of the matter by stating that the real issue was 'between the traditions of our policy (namely to oppose the strong and to protect the weak) and an experiment in a new policy of trying to conciliate the strong'.[30]

Salter's remarks presaged a memorandum, 'Notes on foreign policy', which he completed just prior to departing for New York. The case he advocated, which he admitted was 'a very painful one, but one personally I feel unable to escape', was for 'surrender east of the Holland-France line but not everywhere'. He endorsed many of the prior measures discussed by the group, but he could not escape this conclusion:

> We have not, and cannot in the near future, secure such a combination of strength as will enable us to prevent without war (or probably even to defeat in war) the realization of the central core of Hitler's (and now Germany's) ambition – the association in some form of the Germans in Czechoslovakia and German Austria with the *Reich*.

Salter must have later regretted not settling for the 'cooler reflection' he admitted the situation required.[31]

The sometimes volatile opinions in the group again encouraged Wint to take the lead. On 11 March 1938 he produced an outline for a pamphlet intended to be both clear and popular. The first part contended that 'the collective system can, in present circumstances, assure no *lasting* peace'. The second part focused on the pursuit of peace and the defence of democracy in the British Empire. To achieve these goals, Wint admitted, might involve giving Germany a free hand in eastern Europe. Only such a concession, he stated, would lead to

[30] Christina Hole to Liddell Hart, 1 March 1938, Liddell Hart papers, LH 5/1; Curtis to Ivison Macadam, 2 March 1938, ms. Curtis 12, fo. 39; Murray to Cecil, 4 March 1938, ms. Murray 232, fos 61–62; entry of 8 March 1938, Nicolson diaries.

[31] Salter, 'Notes on foreign policy', 8 March 1938; and pencilled note by Salter attached and dated 8 March 1938, Liddell Hart papers, LH5/1. See also, Salter to Curtis, 9 March 1938, Lionel Curtis papers, Royal Institute of International Affairs Archives, Chatham House, London.

'European appeasement', the ability to defend vital interests and the re-establishment of the League system.[32]

Three days after the *Anschluss*, on 16 March 1938, the group reconvened in Norman Angell's chambers at 4 King's Bench Walk, in the Temple. The strategic consequences for France and Britain of an imminent collapse of the Spanish government were first examined. This problem had been discussed at previous meetings and had also formed part of Salter's reasoning in favour of 'surrender east of the Holland-France line'. He had argued that Britain was strong enough to make a stand in Spain. Liddell Hart agreed that a victory for Italy, Germany, and the Nationalists in Spain would be disastrous for British interests. He believed that Chamberlain's policy was 'to put everything off until the Germans are in such a complete position of supremacy that we shall be unable to fight anyhow'. However, until the Spanish situation and the Anglo-Italian negotiations were resolved, it was decided to make no statement about Czechoslovakia.[33] What received final approval was an aide-mémoire, '*for information and comment, but not for publication*', for distribution to newspaper editors. The aide-mémoire argued that, as Franco would always bow to demands for strategic facilities from his benefactors, both Germany and Italy could threaten sea communications in the Mediterranean, France's third land frontier, and the Atlantic route to the Far East. However, the eastern Mediterranean was described as an area where 'geography and sea-power still tell heavily in our favour' and some form of effective action was possible. What this might be was not articulated.[34]

The worsening European situation again resulted in several members of the group circulating written materials, lobbying the government for action, and canvassing opinion across a broad political spectrum. Alfred Barratt Brown, encouraged by Salter's 'restrained' note of 8 March, offered some considerations without, as he put it, 'obtruding my Pacifism'. He criticized those who misinterpreted collective security as action designed to deter a general war, contending that there was insufficient might to 'put force behind law'. Instead, he urged the group to concentrate on 'the methods of political and economic appeasement on which we are all agreed'.[35] Something similar was also pressed by Allen, in an exchange of correspondence with Lord Cecil, a pioneer of the League

[32] Wint to Curtis, 11 March 1938, and enclosure, ms. Curtis 12, fos 58–62.

[33] Foreign Affairs Group, 16 March 1938, Liddell Hart papers, LH5/1; Salter, 'Notes on foreign policy', 8 March 1938, Liddell Hart papers, LH5/1; Christina Hole to Liddell Hart, Liddell Hart papers, LH5/1; entry of 16 March 1938, Nicolson diaries.

[34] Hodson to Liddell Hart, 16, 18 March 1938, and Liddell Hart to Hodson, 17 March 1938, Liddell Hart papers, LH5/1.

[35] Memorandum by Alfred Barratt Brown, n.d., Liddell Hart papers, LH5/1.

of Nations and the 1937 Nobel Peace Prize-winner. Allen warned against an Anglo-French-Soviet declaration in advance to defend Czechoslovakia which would be regarded as an ultimatum in Berlin. Cecil replied that it was dangerous to placate the dictators.[36] Allen continued publicly to campaign in favour of appeasement. 'Let us neither madden dictators with too rigid emphasis upon law', he stated, 'nor woo them with baits and concessions'.[37] Geoffrey Hudson, in a note circulated to the All Souls Group, acknowledged that the British government had no intention of intervening in Spain or defending Czechoslovakia, but believed that the Soviet Union would fulfil the Czech-Soviet pact. The last option might require passage by the Red Army across a reluctant Poland. Was the group ready to condone 'a Russian invasion of Poland in the name of collective security'? Hudson thus advocated a retreat by France and Britain behind the Maginot line, provided Spain could be rescued to form 'a London-Paris-Madrid axis'. He admitted that this was a surrender, yet it offered an opportunity to avoid a war in Europe.[38]

Nicolson had also been attempting to clarify his views on the future of Czechoslovakia. 'What we are trying to get the Prime Minister to do', he wrote on 22 March, 'is to adopt our All Souls formula – namely pressure on the Czechs, to give greater concessions to the Sudeten Germans, coupled with some assurances that if they do that we will protect their frontier'.[39] Although this did not represent the reality, Nicolson went ahead. He had already written to the Permanent Under-Secretary of State, Sir Alexander Cadogan, about the Foreign Affairs Group, and stated that the meetings had 'been of considerable value to us in that they have done much to clear our minds'. Nicolson enclosed the memorandum on Spain and pointed out that Italy and Germany 'were really occupying vital strategical points behind our backs'.[40] 'I [. . .] infer from it that you are in favour of immediate and open intervention by His Majesty's Government on the side of the Spanish Government', Cadogan replied, and pointed out that this was not government policy. Nicolson responded that if there were a chance of an agreement between Franco, Germany, and Italy then Britain and France should occupy Minorca and Ceuta. 'The All Souls Group', he continued, 'consist of such upright gentlemen that to suggest any such

[36] Allen to Cecil, 19 March 1938; Cecil to Allen, 22 March 1938, in Gilbert, *Plough My Own Furrow*, p. 399.

[37] Quoted in *ibid.*, p. 395.

[38] Hudson, 'Notes on the European situation', enclosure in Christina Hole to Liddell Hart, 19 March 1938, Liddell Hart papers, LH5/1.

[39] Entry of 22 March 1938, Nicolson diaries.

[40] Nicolson to Cadogan, 21 March 1938, FO371/22641, W4440/83/41. The list of signatories which Nicolson gave to Cadogan left out Hudson and Radcliffe-Brown.

thing in writing would have been agony to their souls, but I quite see that any such action is not within the scope of present policy'.[41]

Acting on the mandate derived from the meeting of 26 February 1938, a member of the group drew up a twenty-eight-page memorandum, 'Foreign policy now'. The document examined collective security, policy with regard to Spain, Italy, Germany, Czechoslovakia, China, and Japan, and rearmament and economic matters. The introduction emphasized that the paper was the outcome of six weekend discussions by individuals 'from different political parties not including the extreme political right or left'. Although the group never had any intention to produce a publication, 'certain conclusions emerged so clearly from our non-partisan discussions [...] that we finally decided to prepare and publish this paper'.

'Foreign policy now' posed the question: 'Somewhere, somehow, some day, a stand will be made. Where? In what conditions? For what cause, and in what company, would British power be used, if it has to be used, in war?' The paper suggested that, in the long term, the reconstruction of a genuine 'collective peace system' dedicated to 'certain standards of peaceful behaviour' was still desirable. A series of precise propositions outlined how this might be realized. The paper then examined some of the short-term problems facing the country, including the question, 'For what purpose shall this nation's power and influence be used?' The answer was unequivocal. 'It is in Spain, rather than in Czechoslovakia, that British power – which is still in the main naval power – can be brought to bear most effectively.' The possible contribution offered by forthcoming Anglo-Italian negotiations for European conciliation led to this view: 'The blindest of all errors would be to attempt to buy a brief respite for ourselves by encouraging the allied dictators to direct their next explosion eastwards, southwards, anywhere rather than westwards, in return for such concessions on our part as would sustain their aggressive power.' As for the ongoing Czech-German crisis, the paper suggested that sympathy towards legitimate German grievances was now 'academic'. 'The lesson of the Austrian *Putsch* is that we must hang together or we shall be hanged separately.' Additionally, the analysis of rearmament, international economic policy, and comments on China and Japan restated areas of previous agreement. Finally, the British government was again urged to rearm for purposes of 'collective defence', improve London's air defences, and hasten the storage of food and other essential commodities.[42]

[41] Cadogan to Nicolson, 2 April 1938, FO371/22641, W4440/83/41; Nicolson to Cadogan, 4 April 1938, FO371/22642, W4471/83/41.

[42] 'Foreign policy now', n.d. [*19 March 1938*], Liddell Hart papers, LH5/1.

When the group next met on 23 March 1938 its main concern was the anticipated government statement on foreign policy. Participants acknowledged that the European situation remained dangerous. With regard to 'Foreign policy now', it was suggested that if France were involved in war because of Czechoslovakia, Britain could not stand by. Therefore, 'the best course would be for us to join in a pledge to Czechoslovakia, in the hope that this would itself prevent the outbreak of war'. Others suggested that Britain's commitment to France be conditioned by a scheme for guaranteed and non-guaranteed frontiers. Finally, the raison d'etre of the group itself was raised, with some wishing to continue with a publication, while others held that the group's real function was to act as a 'Brains Trust'.[43]

During the meeting on 31 March 1938, in Angell's chambers in the Temple, that inconclusive tone and divisiveness resurfaced. A participant described the government's foreign policy as one of crisis avoidance and risk-taking, to minimize the chances of war breaking out 'as the result of drift'. Criticism of the government would only lead to the dictators exploiting the situation. Another participant suggested that 'If we advertized more clearly that we stand for law, individualism, etc., we should be able to mobilize behind us a great force of good will and thus increase our prestige.' The 'alarming prospects' for European affairs were again inconclusively examined. The pessimists pointed to a future Nazi-fascist domination of the continent. But could some rallying point be given to public opinion which would not condone war 'in the defence of international law'. Some suggested a national appeal based on 'the defence of democracy'. Others entertained the notion of dropping the coercive functions of the League of Nations. The group 'agreed that it would welcome an initiative by the Government offering to make sacrifices in the cause of general appeasement, thus demonstrating that we did not merely stand for the status quo'. It was finally decided to continue work on a statement. Although concerned about the 'inconclusive' discussion, Nicolson wrote in his diary that 'our main line is that a purely negative policy gets us nowhere and that there must be some more constructive drive'.[44]

The conclusion of the Anglo-Italian agreement on 16 April 1938, which envisaged trading British recognition of Italy's conquest of Abyssinia for the withdrawal of Italian volunteers from Spain, and the upcoming meeting of Parliament on 26 April, prompted the next meeting of the group at All Souls on 24 April. The minutes detail the urgency to take into account 'considerations of relative strength

[43] Foreign Affairs Group, meeting of 23 March 1938, Liddell Hart papers, LH5/1.

[44] Foreign Affairs Group, meeting of 31 March 1938, Liddell Hart papers, LH5/1; entry of 31 March 1938, Nicolson diaries.

and vulnerability', and the necessity for diplomacy to be directed 'not to resistance to aggression, but to appeasement and the finding of a modus vivendi with the aggressor states'.

It was more difficult to translate this into 'a middle policy between resistance and retreat'. The preconditions to avoiding a war were 'the incorporation of all important irredentist communities within the *Reich*', the acquisition by Germany of colonies, the likely disappearance of Czechoslovakia, and a League bereft of any coercive functions. London's vulnerability to air attack remained a particular concern. Finally, the idea was aired about exploring 'private and unofficial contact with Germany', a task for which some members were considered 'peculiarly fitted'. Before concluding, the group decided to press on with a draft statement for publication.[45]

Even after eight meetings and a mounting body of paperwork, unanimity was as elusive as ever. However, Allen agreed to produce 'a clarifying statement of policy', despite hesitations about the short time-frame and the fact, he noted, that it 'suffers from my attempt to meet points of view which are not entirely my own'.[46] By 10 May 1938 he completed a twenty-nine-page document, titled 'A peace policy for the immediate present'. Allen argued that the state of European affairs demanded 'an effort towards appeasement, even perhaps accepting certain breaches in morality such as that which occurred in Austria, as we make this new attempt to rebuild a system of international collaboration'. But he asked whether it was right that British lives should be lost 'and Europe involved in a ghastly catastrophe to sustain the existing integrity' of Czechoslovakia? Britain 'must hold out the hand of reconciliation even to the lawbreaker'. For Allen this meant support for the new Anglo-Italian agreement, recognition of Italian sovereignty in Abyssinia, and the negotiation of 'a new peace settlement' with Germany. This would include the elimination of the war-guilt clause, 'colonial reconstruction', the recognition of Germany's 'special claims' in Czechoslovakia, its return to a League of Nations, and a covenant dedicated to 'social justice and economic welfare'. Allen concluded with a scenario for his 'transitional policy' which, he wrote, combined rearmament, further military co-operation with France, and economic co-operation with the United States with 'vigorous efforts towards appeasement'. If all this ended in failure, he

[45] Christina Hole to Liddell Hart, 1 April 1938, Liddell Hart papers, LH5/1; Foreign Affairs Group, 24 April 1938, Liddell Hart papers, LH5/1. A meeting tentatively scheduled for 10 April appears to have been cancelled. See Christina Hole to Liddell Hart, 1 April 1938, Liddell Hart papers, LH5/1.

[46] Note by Allen to members of the Foreign Affairs Group, n.d., Liddell Hart papers, LH5/1; Allen to Curtis, 10 May 1938, ms. Curtis 12, fo. 13b.

concluded 'we and other democratic nations will at least have gathered strength and restored a better moral foundation for a conflict if it should in the end be forced upon us'.[47]

What was termed 'a special whip' accompanied the notice of the next meeting scheduled for All Souls on 15 May 1938. No minutes of the discussion survive. However, Nicolson afterwards noted that 'There is really a split between the realists and the moralists'.[48] Murray wrote, affirming Nicolson's impression that the group again displayed 'a tendency to split, Allen taking the line that the way to peace is to satisfy Germany; most of us thinking that resistance, and the maintenance of international law, more important'.[49] Toynbee, in fact, had not been able to attend the meeting, and refused to associate himself with the memorandum. which he regarded as a recipe for failure as well as 'morally wrong'. Of the two choices facing Britain, either abdicating its great-power status or joining the future battle against the European dictatorships, with the outcome being a 'world dominion' won by North America, he preferred the former. 'I am afraid my conclusion is gloomy', he wrote, 'but I have no belief at all in the possibility of "getting by" as the Americans say, in the next act of the tragedy'.[50] These observations were brought to the meeting and, according to Liddell Hart, caused a stir. He, Murray, and Nicolson agreed with Toynbee's views, while Curtis, 'remarked that twenty years of peace were worth any price'.[51] Allen replied to Toynbee on 17 May 1938, suggesting that the majority of participants agreed generally. He pointed out that in preparing the document he had put aside his pacifism, and continued: 'I am willing to take risks with morality during the transitional period in the hope – perhaps a vain one – that events will play into our hands'.[52] He doubted that an agreed document could be formulated.

To break the log-jam, on 20 May 1938 Allen wrote to the Liberal journalist, J.A. Spender. After describing the meetings of a 'distinguished group of international thinkers', he suggested that a statement was needed to assist public opinion and various peace

[47] 'A peace policy for the immediate present', by Lord Allen of Hurtwood, with a covering note 'To those who have taken part in the discussion of foreign affairs at All Souls College', 10 May 1938, Liddell Hart papers, LH5/1. Salter also attempted something along similar lines: see Salter to Allen, 4 May 1938, Allen papers. Of related interest is a memorandum by Arnold-Forster, 'The Anglo-Italian agreement', May 1938, Cecil add. ms. 51140, fos 97–105, British Library, London.

[48] Entry of 15 May 1938, Nicolson diaries.

[49] Murray to Edwyn Robert Bevan, 1 June 1938, ms. Murray 233, fo. 3.

[50] Toynbee to Allen, 11 May 1938, Liddell Hart papers, LH1/698.

[51] Liddell Hart to Toynbee, 25 May 1938, Liddell Hart papers, LH1/698.

[52] Allen to Toynbee, 17 May 1938, in Gilbert, *Plough My Own Furrow*, pp. 400–401.

organizations, to restrain the opposition and to lobby the government. Allen admitted that the group had been unable to reach any consensus, and this had led to the suggestion to reach outside the group for a redraft of the document for publication. He proposed a meeting, which would include Salter, to discuss the document.[53]

Allen followed up on this initiative by embarking on a letter-writing campaign to private correspondents,[54] the *Manchester Guardian*, and *The Times*. He lobbied for a dual policy: 'conciliation and revision of the *status quo* on the one hand; the display of strength to protect lawful procedure on the other hand'.[55] Murray was not impressed with this round of activity. 'Allen's nerves are evidently upset', he noted.[56] Indeed, Murray now showed little patience with Allen, whom he regarded as 'taking the line that the way to peace is to satisfy Germany'.[57]

After the cancellation of a meeting at All Souls, planned for 5–6 June 1938, two papers were circulated on 29 June to the group. The first, a note by Hudson on the Czechoslovak situation, emphasized the many weaknesses and precarious situation of the Czech state. The second was titled 'Memorandum by Mr J.A. Spender'. This argued that the duty of government was 'to mediate and pacify'. Given the limits of British power world-wide, a distinction had to be made 'between what is desirable and what is possible'. Thus Britain should pursue peace with any co-operative government, irrespective of its ideology. Spender finally advised a return in Britain to parliamentary bi-partisanship in foreign policy.[58] Because the next meeting of the group, scheduled for 16 July 1938, was cancelled, the Spender memorandum was never generally discussed. Although Curtis noted his scepticism about whether the All Souls group would ever reach a consensus as a basis for a public document, he acknowledged the wisdom of Spender's effort. Allen thought the document was not 'comprehensive' enough

[53] Allen to Spender, 20 May 1938, Spender add. ms. 46394, IX, fos 103–106, British Library, London.

[54] See, for example, Allen to Lionel Curtis, 8 June 1938, ms. Curtis 12, fo. 162; and the reply in Curtis to Allen, 10 June 1938, ms. Curtis 12, fos 163–164.

[55] *The Times*, 30 May 1938; see also, Gilbert, *Plough My Own Furrow*, pp. 401–403. On Allen's relationship with *The Times* and its editors, see Marwick, *Clifford Allen*, pp. 176–177.

[56] Murray to Wickham Steed, 10 June 1938, ms. Murray 233, fo. 32. See also, Murray to Allen, 24 May 1938, ms. Murray 232, fo. 197.

[57] Murray to Edwyn Robert Bevan, 1 June 1938, ms. Murray 233, fo. 3.

[58] 'Memorandum on Czechoslovakia', 8 June 1938, and 'Memorandum by J.A. Spender', June 1938, enclosures in Christina Hole to All Souls Group, 29 June 1938, Liddell Hart papers, LH5/1.

and looked forward to a meeting with Salter to discuss the future of the All Souls group.[59]

Once again, a desire for some sort of results overtook some in the group. On 4 May 1938 Wint had proposed that the situation in central Europe might be resolved by a British mediator. He thought that Salter might go to Germany carrying a dual message – to warn that Europe was on the brink of war, and to suggest that Germany's grievances could be settled peacefully. Salter refused, and pointed out that such a mission required extensive preparation. The proposal appealed to Allen, however, and he prepared for such a visit to Berlin.[60]

Salter and Allen finally met and they drafted a letter to *The Times*. The covering note suggested that the objective was to unite 'many schools of thought', to avoid demands for unlimited British commitments, and offer 'a practical proposal'.[61] If negotiations failed to resolve the crisis in Czechoslovakia, the signatories to the letter declared themselves ready 'to invite, through some suitable procedure, a third-party opinion as to the best solution'. Allen sent the draft letter to Lord Halifax on 26 July 1938, asking whether the exercise 'would be helpful or at least not harmful'. Halifax's reply the next day was discouraging, stating that 'Lord Runciman's mission to Prague undercut the value of the letter'.[62] The letter was withdrawn, but Allen pressed on with his personal mission. He spoke in the House of Lords on 27 July, emphasizing the need for better Anglo-German relations. He followed this with a visit to Germany and Czechoslovakia from 6 to 15 August, which ultimately proved fruitless.

The question of public, and particularly elite, opinion in the 1930s is one of the least investigated areas of appeasement studies. However, what really propelled public thinking with regard to international affairs into divisions which ran deep into the debate between realism versus morality, and expediency versus principle? It will be suggested here that the experience of the All Souls Foreign Affairs Group vividly demonstrates that the traditional dichotomy between appeasers and resistors is a simplification.[63] A further objective, on the basis of a case

[59] Curtis to Allen, 11 July 1938, ms. Curtis, 12, fo. 219; Allen to Curtis, 13 July 1938, ms. Curtis, 12, fo. 224.

[60] Marwick, *Clifford Allen*, p. 178.

[61] Allen to Nicolson, 20 July 1938, Liddell Hart papers, LH5/1; Allen to Fisher, 20 July 1938, ms. Fisher 77, fo. 30, Bodleian Library, Oxford.

[62] Allen to Halifax, 26 July, enclosing letter to *The Times*; minute by Strang, 27 July 1938; and Halifax to Allen, 29 July 1938, FO371/21730, C7766/1941/18.

[63] William Norton Medlicott, *Britain and Germany: The Search for Agreement, 1930–1937* (London, 1969), p. 32, first suggested that 'the lines of distinction between the popular stereotypes, appeasers (or peacemakers) and warmongers (or resisters), between the doves and the hawks of the1930s, tend to disappear'.

study, is to establish a record of a particular aspect of one Oxford College and thereby to contribute to an understanding of what Salter referred to as the 'true character and influence' of All Souls. The analysis will enable the portrait offered by Rowse in *All Souls and Appeasement* to be assessed and placed in context. Such aims, therefore, illuminate the wider questions of appeasement, public opinion, and the origins of the World War II. An examination of the All Souls Foreign Affairs Group might thus confirm that appeasement was never the one-dimensional phenomenon derided so often by its critics. Rather, it wore many masks, meant different things to different people and at different times. Indeed, it might not be a case of 'appeasement and All Souls', but of appeasement at All Souls.

CHAPTER 1

'A TRANSITIONAL POLICY', DECEMBER 1937–FEBRUARY 1938

In early December 1937 Sir Arthur Salter began to organize the first of the All Souls meetings. By 11 December he had acceptances from Arnold Toynbee, Alfred Barratt Brown, Lionel Curtis, Harold Macmillan, Sir Walter Layton, Lord Allen of Hurtwood, and Basil H. Liddell Hart. Other affirmative replies followed from Lord Arnold, Will Arnold-Forster, Geoffrey Hudson, H.V. Hodson, and A.R. Radcliffe-Brown.[1] *Harold Nicolson also joined the group at its inaugural meetings on Saturday and Sunday, 18 and 19 December. His diaries recorded this.*

Harold Nicolson diaries (Nicolson papers)

Saturday, 18 December 1937

Met by Nigel [Nicolson], who drives with me to All Souls where I go straight into dinner. After dinner we open our discussion on foreign policy, the course of which I shall note in a memorandum to be kept in this diary. Sleep at All Souls. Bitterly cold at night.

Sunday, 19 December 1937

We meet again at 10.30 and continue with an interval at luncheon until 6 pm. I then take the train for London, travelling up with Hodson. In spite of missing my weekend rest which I badly wanted, I feel the visit has been worth it every time.

Monday, 20 December 1937

Write my notes on yesterday's discussion.

The minutes of the meetings were circulated afterwards by Salter.[2]

[1] Salter to Liddell Hart, 11 December 1937, Liddell Hart papers, LH 5/1. In the event, Layton and Allen did not attend.

[2] These were the minutes circulated by Salter with a letter 'A' in the top left-hand corner. Another document, 'Conference on foreign affairs, 18–19 December 1937', was also

Conference on Foreign Affairs (A)
18 and 19 December 1937
(Liddell Hart papers, LH 5/1)

The meeting held three sessions. The first was devoted to the question 'What is our power?'. The second was devoted to the question 'Where is the first challenge likely to occur?'. The third was devoted to the question 'What steps should be taken to meet the danger?'.

[First session]

At our first session we discussed the balance of power. Certain *assumptions* were admitted for the purposes of discussion. These assumptions were:

(1) That for the purposes of this discussion the world could be divided into League and Anti-League powers without examining the nature of that definition.

(2) That Germany, Italy and Japan as the power-elements in the anti-League combine would carry with them Austria, Hungary and Bulgaria.

(3) That Yugoslavia and Poland were uncertain quantities and that, if the League combination showed continued weakness, Turkey and Greece might also become uncertain quantities.

(4) That no British policy could be based upon expectation of American assistance although that assistance (if ever available) would be determinant.

With these assumptions we embarked upon a consideration of the present balance of power. We approached that consideration under two main headings, namely military and economic.

Military considerations

We divided these considerations under two subheadings, namely offensive and defensive, and examined each element of power under those headings.

circulated with a letter 'B' in the top left-hand corner. This contained a more free-form summary of the discussions. As well, the Harold Nicolson diaries include a set of minutes of the discussions. A comparison shows that these are a retyping of documents 'A' and 'B'. This latter set of minutes includes a list of participants as follows: 'Lord Arnold, Sir Arthur Salter, Harold Macmillan, Lionel Curtis, Arnold Toynbee, Arnold-Forster, Norman Angell, Liddell Hart, G.F. Hudson, Barratt Brown, H.V. Hodson, Radcliffe-Brown, Harold Nicolson'.

We also adopted two axioms: namely that

(a) Recent experience had shown that the power of the defensive against the offensive was three to one.
(b) Air bombardment was not in the last resort as determinant as sea power.

We then proceeded to a discussion of the power balance of the several nations with the following conclusions:

GERMANY

(1) *Offence* Difficult against France. Limited as against Czechoslovakia by the possible pressure of Poland on the Silesian Salient.
Army – good: question of reserves.
Navy – supreme in Baltic.
Air – very powerful.
(2) *Defence*
Army – good on Rhine defences.
Navy – supremacy in Baltic.
Air – invulnerability better than ours but worse than that of France.

FRANCE

(1) *Offence* An advance beyond Maginot line might lead them into traps.
(2) *Defence* Maginot line good. Air invulnerability excellent.

ITALY

(1) *Offence* Nuisance value if others engage. Great Mediterranean offensiveness. Subsidiary nuisance value in the Arab world and in East Africa.
(2) *Defence* Nothing against France and ourselves alone. Vulnerability of northern industry and water power.

GREAT BRITAIN

(1) *Offence*
Army – would be occupied by home and Empire defence.
Air – getting powerful.
Navy – Far East: Hong Kong untenable without USA. Mediterranean: untenable as civilian route. Becoming only an area of war. Danger of submarine diminished but that of speed-boat increased.

Conclusions: We should concentrate upon home invulnerability against air attack within the first ten weeks of war.

Second session, Sunday morning

The second discussion centred around the problem, 'where is the attack likely to occur?'.

It was generally admitted that *Germany* was the centre of the whole problem, but it was also recognized that it was unlikely that Germany would wish to provoke a world war during the next two years. Provocation was more likely to come from one of the two satellite states – either Japan or Italy. Germany herself was more likely to obtain control over the economic resources of eastern Europe without resorting to any overt challenge such as might involve France and ourselves. On the other hand it was admitted that from the equipment point of view next summer would be a favourable time for Germany to attack this country.

A discussion took place as to Germany's aims. Two different views were advanced:

(1) That the slogan '*Weltmacht oder Niedergang*' really did reflect the German state of mind and that the German could not conceive of equality between nations but only of supremacy on the part of one. That what the mass of the Germans desired was 'power'. For the moment, that desire might be limited to a wish to dominate eastern Europe. But when once that wish had been realized, it would be followed almost immediately by a temptation to loot the British Empire.

(2) That Germany did not desire a conflict with the sea power of the British Empire and the United States. What she desired was '*Grund und Boden*' in eastern Europe. Nor did she desire to absorb within her boundaries large numbers of Slav citizens. Her ambition would be to incorporate all scattered Germans within her borders and then dominate and control the economic resources of eastern and south-eastern Europe.

Having done this she might well renew her old Berlin–Baghdad ambitions and stretch to the Persian Gulf. But she did not desire to partition British and French colonies in Africa between Italy and herself; nor would she feel happy with oceanic as opposed to territorial lines of communication.

It was generally agreed that whichever of these two forecasts were correct, the fact remained that the German state of mind was one that might lead to general war. A discussion then ensued whether that state of mind was (a) general and (b) durable. Would be possible, for instance, to create a pre-1871 or a 1919 state of mind in Germany? The general agreement was that the present state of mind was something more than a mood, that it was based upon a definite application of the

Hegelian doctrine, and that the mass of the German people had now been 'conditioned' to that doctrine. For the purposes of the discussion it was agreed that we should assume the present state of mind to be general and durable.

The meeting then considered *Italy*. The view was expressed that Mussolini was no longer frightened of this country, but was profoundly impressed by the might of Germany. He might be willing to surrender Austria and the South Tyrol in return for Germany's promise to assist him in a vast Roman Empire from Alexandria to the Equator.

The danger was that Italy cannot afford to wait. It would be to her interest, once she was certain of German support, to provoke a general conflict. On the other hand, Germany had learnt one lesson from 1914, and that was the danger of being involved in dangers by a weaker but ambitious ally. Italy could effect little by herself beyond stirring up trouble in the Arab world and possibly attacking Malta and Tunis. Thus it would be essential for her to obtain her loot by the complete defeat of France and England, which could only be achieved through a world war.

The meeting then considered *Japan*. The view was expressed that the next world war would begin in the Far East, starting with the Japanese attack on Russia and thereby, owing to the anti-comintern pact and the secret military agreement between Germany and Japan, involving Europe. It was recognized, however, that for the moment Japan was weakened by her Chinese conquests and by the tension with the United States. The strategic railway to Lake Baikal would not be completed for at least two years. Thus, by the time Japan was ready to fight Russia, Italy would be at the end of her endurance.

It was pointed out also that the 'Panay' incident had deeply affected American opinion, and especially American naval opinion which was most influential. It had also placed a strain upon the Berlin–Tokyo axis.

It might well be that Hitler would realize that he must now choose between Japan and Russia. It was not impossible that a German–Russian entente could be devised on the basis of a free hand for German in the Danubian basin and a free hand for Russia in the Far East. Hitler's hatred of communism was largely based upon anti-Jewish feeling: in the councils of the Kremlin there were now only two Jews left.

Third session, Sunday afternoon

The question discussed was 'what should be done?'. Two policies were alluded to, namely (a) the policy of Danegeld – or sops to Germany in expectation of her gratitude; (b) the Fabian policy of playing for time, avoiding head-on collisions, and waiting for the fascist and Nazi spirit to ‘burn itself out’.

It was generally agreed that (a) was futile and (b) too negative. Something more constructive was required.

The following considerations were raised:

Spain: It was agreed that Franco’s victory would be disadvantageous to this country. It was true that in the end Franco would wish to rid himself of Italian and German influence and come to us for money. But during this period of pacification, he would still need German and Italian help and would have to buy it by offering submarine bases as well as raw materials. It was thus a British interest that Franco should not win and the grant of belligerent rights should be postponed as long as possible.

Central Europe: The policy of ‘keeping the Germans guessing’ was an unconstructive policy. Obviously we could not commit ourselves to a complete policy to meet every eventuality, but we should be able to narrow the area of uncertainty by telling the Germans what we certainly *should* do, and the Czechs what we certainly should *not* do.

Our attitude to the *Anschluss* should certainly be defined, and efforts should be made to assure Czechoslovakia, Yugoslavia, and Romania of our continued interest. These efforts might take the form of financial assistance.

Russia: Should we approve of the Franco-Soviet pact or should we encourage a Russo-German detente or even entente?

France: The danger was stressed of a financial collapse in France, leading to internal disorder and even fascism. It was regarded as a direct British interest to prevent that collapse.

Germany: It was pointed that, once you enter the sphere of force, German diplomatic clumsiness is an advantage to her rather than a disadvantage. It was a mistake to ‘wait until Germany made her inevitable blunder’.

Should we adopt the view that Germany is impossible and can only be restrained by force? Such a view was mere determinism leading to war. What, then, should be done?

A possible policy

It was agreed that British policy towards Germany should be one of firmness followed by conciliation. But how were we to show firmness without becoming provocative? What we needed was an affirmation of strength as a prelude or preface to conciliation. But what opportunity had we to affirm strength without provoking violence?

It was agreed that the Far East situation, if rapidly and courageously handled, should provide that opportunity and for the following reasons:

Japan: We were threatened with the creation of a vast yellow Empire which would prove a terrific menace to Malaya, the East Indies, and Australasia. Yet to impose a boycott (even an unofficial boycott) against Japan might not prove efficacious for twelve months and might lead to war. Apart from the possible loss of Hong Kong, such a war would dangerously weaken us in regard to Germany and Italy.

It should thus be an axiom that we should not contemplate such action unless assured of American active support.

USA: The United States administration would find it difficult to give such an assurance in advance. Yet it is more than probable that if we took the initiative the USA would follow. It was felt that this risk was worth taking because:

(a) It would settle the Japanese question.
(b) More importantly, it would provide us with an affirmation of strength as regards Germany and the Berlin–Tokyo axis.
(c) It might encourage Germany to exchange Japanese friendship for Russian friendship.
(d) It would be comparatively acceptable to our own opinion since London would not be bombed.
(e) It would unite us with America.

We might then pass to our policy of conciliation, known as 'a general settlement'.

A general settlement

Such a settlement was outlined as follows:

1. *We offer Germany:*

(1) The *Anschluss*.
(2) An arrangement by which the Sudeten Germans would be granted 'cantonal status' by the Czech government, on condition the latter retained adequate powers for military defence of the Czech state.
(3) Recognition of Germany's right to possess colonies. We should be prepared to extend the Congo Basin system plus the mandate system to all our tropical colonies, Germany to be given a pooled territory in the Cameroons.
(4) A readiness to admit Germany's prior *economic* interests in eastern Europe.

2. *We demand from Germany:*

(1) An assurance that the extension of her influence in eastern Europe will not entail any attack upon the autonomy or democratic institutions of other countries.
(2) An assurance that she would agree to a scheme for the limitation of armaments under which (a) Germany would be the strongest power in Central Europe, but (b) no single power should be strong enough to dominate the collective force of the other powers. In other words, preponderance but not supremacy.
(3) Germany not to support Italian ambitions in the Mediterranean and in Africa.

The meeting was adjourned until 15 January 1938, at 3.30 pm. However, a final talk between some members of the group took place on Sunday.

Conference on Foreign Affairs (B), 18 and 19 December 1937 (Liddell Hart papers, LH 5/1)

Evening session[3]

The proposals for the general settlement were examined in rather more detail. It was pointed out that, even if Germany declined the terms offered, the approach would have been worth making, as putting us right with our own opinion.

It was suggested that, as part of a settlement, Germany should be required to withdraw support from Italy in her endeavours to stir up trouble in the Mediterranean and the Near East.

Colonial questions

The question was raised whether France, owing to the nature of the French colonial empire, would be able to grant Germany the 'open door'. One proposal was that the Congo Basin principle should be extended to all British tropical colonies in Africa; and colonies likely to be most advantageous to Germany from an economic point of view

[3] The minutes of the evening session do not appear in 'Document A' but are a part of 'Document B' and are repeated in the Nicolson retyping of the minutes, inserted as a carbon flimsy in the Nicolson diaries.

should be returned to her to be held on absolutely equal terms with ourselves – this arrangement being conditional on Germany accepting a general settlement. The distinction between colonies class 1 and 2 in Africa might be abolished, and all British non-self-governing colonies in Africa be placed under the mandate system.

Foreign Office

It was asked why we should contemplate with satisfaction the military association of France with the east European countries; and the attitude of the British Foreign Office was further discussed. Its traditional policy was stated to be to prevent the domination of Europe by any single power; and it was pointed out that the policy had been departed from in 1923, when we did not oppose French domination.

Far East

The need for action in the Far East was again stressed, and the question was raised to what extent we should make our policy there conditional upon the attitude of Australia and New Zealand. It was suggested that, in the event of joint Anglo-American action, neither of these countries would be seriously threatened.

Germany's ambitions

It was stressed that Germany's irredentist ambitions should be sharply distinguished from purely expansionist ones; since they were much more passionately supported by the population.

Economic situation in France

Finally, the financial situation in France was discussed, the probable effects on the European system of a new economic crisis there, and the possibility of joint Anglo-American financial assistance to stabilize the French economic situation, and attract back to France the expatriated capital.

The following day, 20 December 1937, Curtis revealed in a private letter the crucial role which Nicolson[4] *had played in emphasizing Germany's aggressive ambitions.*

[4] Nicolson's views at this time can also be studied in his 'Germany and the colonies', *Fortnightly*, 142 (1937), pp. 641–648, where he pointed out that 'concessions can be made only as part of a general settlement'. Likewise, Arnold Toynbee argued in a letter to *The Times*, 28 October 1937, that '[i]ngenious attempts to plant on other people our own share of Germany's bill will recoil on us like a boomerang'.

Curtis to Brand, 20 December 1937 (ms. Curtis 11, fos 168–170)

I spent the weekend at All Souls taking part in a discussion which Salter had organized between various people who wanted to make up their minds what line they ought to take with regard to foreign affairs at the present juncture. Amongst those present were Lord Allen of Hurtwood, Harold Nicolson, Liddell Hart, Hodson, Norman Angell, Toynbee, and Harold Macmillan.

Nicolson led off: to him Germany represented a power which must be regarded as actuated by the motive simply to dominate, and in the last instance to dominate the world. Their youth were inspired by a motive entirely different from that which inspires us, which he described as the heroic motive, to suffer for the sake of power with the glorious ideal of perishing on the battlefield.

As the discussion went on, the motives which inspired the Foreign Office were revealed and clearly emphasized. It was a cardinal principal of Foreign Office policy to keep Germany and Russian estranged. Then I suggested as a possible alternative to this policy that our diplomacy should set out to work to try to bring about arrangements between Germany and the states to the east of her; which would be more mutually satisfactory to both than the status quo, and further suggested that in doing this we should take the line of recognizing that Germany was entitled to special economic privileges in this area, just as we ourselves arrange preferences inside the British Commonwealth. Nicolson objected that this arrangement would so strengthen Germany that she would first dominate Europe and then us and the world.

In the discussions it was admitted that our treatment of Germany after the war had ruined the Weimar Republic and the growth of self-government in Germany, and had brought into existence a form of authoritarian government far more dangerous than that which existed in Germany before 1914. But in Nicolson's view it was no use going back on the past. The character of the present German government must be accepted as it was and it must be dealt with as such. Later in the discussion I felt impelled to say that, as far as I could gather from Nicolson, it was the fixed policy of the Foreign Office to keep Germany and Russia estranged from each other and also to oppose measures calculated to increase the prosperity of Germany and the states to the east of her. Nicolson said quite simply that that was the policy of the Foreign Office and one with which he agreed. I then remarked that I had an instinctive feeling that any British policy was making a fatal mistake, which was either based on keeping two great sections of the human race on bad terms with each other, or was opposed to measures tending to confer greater economic prosperity on any large group of peoples.

Curtis to Allen, 20 December 1937 (ms. Curtis 11, fo. 171)

[...] I confess that the more I think of our discussion at All Souls the more I am appalled by the Foreign Office attitude as revealed by H[arold] N[icolson]. Our acquiescence to the French attitude after the war is to me one of the most catastrophic blunders in history. H.N. admits the blunder and then goes on to insist that the only thing now to do is to repeat it. One is reminded of the French emigrés who, when they got back to power, had learnt nothing and forgotten nothing. Our real objective, I submit, should be to change the militaristic outlook in Germany we have created. I have spent the last thirteen years writing a book in which I have tried to show how, in my view, the present as it stood in December 1936 had arisen out of the whole past from the beginnings of history, and then I have forced myself to think out and see how far that situation ought to be handled by us from the long distance point of view.

Allen to Curtis, 22 December 1937 (Allen papers, box 13, The Next Five Years Group, 1936–1937)

[...] may I say how warmly I echo your words of distress about H[arold] N[icolson] and the Foreign Office attitude. I struggled against it in 1919, have gone on doing so ever since, and have done everything I can both personally with Hitler and in this country to plead during the last three or four years for a change in Anglo-German policy. I venture to enclose a copy of my last speech in the House of Lords. I think there are potent influences now at work to counteract those who wish to pursue once more a mistaken policy.

May I say how deeply indebted we all were to you for joining us in our talk at All Souls. It was not only delightful to have you with us, but a great benefit as well.

I have not read all your three volumes,[5] but I have read a good deal and was deeply moved, as I think many other people have been.

Thanking you for all that you are doing in the way of making us think decently and intelligently.

Salter to Liddell Hart, 23 December 1937 (Liddell Hart papers, LH 5/1)

Thank you very much for your letter and your book[6] which I shall read and greatly value. Your contribution was of the greatest value at Oxford, and we were all extremely grateful to you for coming [. . .].

Murray to Salter, 29 December 1937 (ms. Murray 230, fos 97–101)

I have been doubly regretting that I could not attend your discussion of policy, because I see a great need of a re-statement on the part of the LNU. I have just drafted the enclosed [*not reproduced*] to put before the Executive on January 13, when they meet to discuss the loss of membership [. . .]. My statement of policy is of course very general, and does not go into the immediate practical problems.[7]

Angell[8] to Liddell Hart, 5 January 1938 (Liddell Hart papers, LH 1/16/2)

[. . .] I hope to be able to get down to the next meeting of the Salter-Allen group on the 15th, but it is a little doubtful as I seem to be a good deal out of sorts.

[5] Lionel Curtis, *Civitas Dei*, 3 vols (London, 1934–1937).

[6] Basil Liddell Hart, *Europe in Arms* (London, 1937).

[7] To another correspondent, Murray put it bluntly: 'The greatest issue now is collective security *plus* peaceful change'; Murray to Allen, 13 December 1937, ms. Murray 230, fo. 66. See also Gilbert Murray, 'Sanctions', *Contemporary Review*, 152 (1937), pp. 135–141.

[8] Norman Angell, 'Can aggressor states be checked?', *Contemporary Review*, 152 (1937), pp. 521–529 argued the case for the affirmative. In his letter to the *Manchester Guardian*, 31 January 1938, he urged that effective rearmament must be coupled with clear prior commitments to deter aggression.

The group which met to discuss this impasse at 3.30 p.m. on Saturday, 15 January 1938 also included, for the first time, Murray, Layton, Adams,[9] *Rowse and Woodward.*[10] *Nicolson, as usual, put some notes in his diary.*

Harold Nicolson diaries (Nicolson papers)

Saturday, 15 January 1938

[. . .] on to Salter's rooms at All Souls. Salter, Toynbee, Gilbert Murray, Walter Layton, Allen of Hurtwood, Lionel Curtis, Hodson of the Round Table, Liddell Hart, the Warden of All Souls. We start our discussion at 3.30 and continue to 7.00. We then adjourn for dinner in hall. I sit next to [Isaiah] Berlin and talk to [Reginald] Coupland afterwards, about the Palestine Report. But I am dragged away to the meeting which continues till 11.00. The record is attached.[11]

Sunday, 16 January 1938

[. . .] to All Souls for the continuance of our discussion which goes on till 1.15. Then lunch with Niggs [. . .] at the Randolph and back to All Souls. Leave at 4.00 for London.

[9] In a rare written contribution, W.G.S. Adams, 'Whither England?', *Southern Review*, 3 (1937), pp. 15–27 made a case for the removal of 'legitimate grievances' in international affairs along with a better system of collective security.

[10] Woodward's views at the time can be gauged from his memorandum, 'Germany and Europe', 27 January 1937, FO371/20734, C678/226/18; and his rather gloomy analysis of British foreign policy 'From 1914 till now', *The Spectator*, 161 (1, 8, 15, 22, 29 April 1938), pp. 575–576, 620–621, 664–665, 700–701, 740–741. Woodward concluded that appeasement should not result in 'merely arming the enemies of liberty'.

[11] This consisted of six pages of notes in pencil on a carbon flimsy of the minutes of the previous meetings of 18 and 19 December 1937. These add little to the substance of the circulated record of the conversations, but occasionally serve to identify speakers. Nicolson's notes of those who attended included the name of Toynbee, which was omitted from the copy of the minutes in the Liddell Hart papers. The latter lists the participants as: 'Lord Allen of Hurtwood, Captain Liddell Hart, Sir Walter Layton, Sir Arthur Salter, Mr Lionel Curtis, Professor Gilbert Murray, Warden of All Souls, Mr Rowse, Mr Radcliffe-Brown, Mr Barratt Brown, Mr Hodson, Mr Woodward, Mr Harold Nicolson'.

Meeting at All Souls College, Saturday, 15 January 1938 and Sunday, 16 January 1938 (Liddell Hart papers, LH 5/1)

First meeting, Saturday, 15 January, 3.30

The Far East

The meeting had before them some informal notes of the previous meeting held on December 18 and 19 in which it had been advocated that the Far Eastern situation might constitute that 'affirmation of strength' which appeared to be a necessary prelude to any opening of conciliatory negotiations with Germany.

The meeting were informed that these informal notes had been shown to Mr Anthony Eden who, while expressing general agreement with the diagnosis contained in these notes, stated that it had been made quite clear at Brussels that American opinion was not yet prepared to support the administration in any active policy which might lead to war with Japan.

The meeting felt, therefore, that in view of this information it would not be possible to use the Far Eastern situation as an affirmation of Anglo-American strength. The point was, however, raised that serious people in America had derived the impression that it was the British government who had shown weakness at Brussels and who had in fact sent some message to Washington which had discouraged the administration and assisted the isolationists. It was felt that this impression should be contradicted in some authoritative manner.

Assuming, therefore, that active American assistance could not be relied upon, what should be the Far Eastern policy of His Majesty's Government? It was generally agreed that in view of the extreme sensitiveness of American opinion, we should do everything possible to avoid creating an impression that we were involving the United States on behalf of British Imperial interests. Our line should be solely that we were assisting the Chinese against Japanese aggression. The two main features of this problem were considered:

(a) *A boycott of Japanese goods* It was recognized that an official government boycott would, owing to the uncertainty of American participation, be far too dangerous. It was also agreed that a private boycott (especially one directed against the supply or carriage of oil) would certainly be an effective demonstration, although it would have no decisive influence upon the issue of the war. Would it, however, be legal for a trades union to enforce such a boycott by the strike weapon? Alternatively, would it be possible to organize some League of Nations demonstration on the assumption that American opinion is less suspicious of a general policy based on the Covenant, the Kellogg pact and the Washington treaties, than of a policy which could be identified with purely British interests? The point was also made that the League of Nations might further supply relief measures on behalf of the Chinese. It was generally felt that although Russia would welcome some sort of League mandate for supplying China with munitions, yet the result of League intervention would be an immediate declaration of blockade by Japan and a danger of war. This danger led the meeting to consider:

(b) *The position of Hong Kong* It was questioned whether Japan really desired to take military action against Hong Kong and would not prefer processes of commercial strangulation. It was questionable whether we could afford to divert sufficient forces to the Far East to enable us to defend Hong Kong against Japanese attack. We should thus avoid being manoeuvred into conflict with Japan over the defence of Hong Kong, which would not only be difficult in itself but would give the world an impression that we were defending, not the principle of international law and order, but an isolated Imperial interest.

Singapore, owing to its distance from Japanese bases, was far more defensible and would not oblige us to detach from European waters any essential naval forces.

The general feeling of the meeting was that any overt challenge to Japan would, without the certainty of American assistance, place us in a weak strategical and moral position, and would not therefore constitute that 'affirmation of strength' which we desired to find.

Our policy, therefore, should not be one of official boycott, but:

(a) to facilitate the passage of supplies of all kinds to China, without making a public declaration to that effect.
(b) This could be fortified by a trades-union boycott, especially of oil.
(c) If Hong Kong were attacked we should make no effort to defend it.

Europe

The meeting then discussed the possibility of an agreement with Germany. It was remarked that M. Flandin had returned from his visit to Berlin with the definite impression that Germany would refuse to enter into any system of collective security or disarmament, and that she regarded south-eastern Europe as her own sphere of influence and as one in which the western powers had no say at all.

The comment was made that although M. Flandin's account of his visit might have been exaggerated for political purposes, yet our own Foreign Office were inclined to agree that such, at the moment, was in fact the known policy of Herr Hitler and his advisors. The general Foreign Office view was that the Berlin–Rome–Tokyo triangle represented the most dangerous situation that had faced this country for more than a century, and that the greatest caution must be exercised to avoid any 'head-on' collision. Their own idea was that the triangle, formidable though it was at the moment, was already losing some of its force, or more precisely, its 'simultaneity'. The Japanese adventure had irritated German opinion and was likely to commit Japan so deeply that she might in time become a liability to the triangle rather than an asset. The Foreign Office feeling, therefore, was that we should play for time, even at the cost of certain immediate sacrifices. Thus, although only recently the Foreign Office had been haunted by the spectre of a Russo-German understanding, they now showed some disposition to reconsider this view, since such an understanding would diminish the likelihood of an immediate war. Meanwhile, they were very anxious to do nothing which might create in Germany a feeling of encirclement.

They were well aware of the danger of the small countries being attracted to the German orbit and forming fascist administrations. They did not feel, however, that any British support of the democratic elements in those countries would be anything but a dangerous game to play. They were not unduly alarmed by the armament race since, in the end, our resources were greater than those of Italy and Germany and since, if we were always ready to proclaim an armament holiday, it might be possible that the economic strain upon the less well equipped countries might lead them to alter their present hopeless competition.

The point was raised that the Foreign Office ought to pay more attention to cultivating close relations with Russia, and it was generally agreed that without Russian support the authority of the civilian countries would remain less powerful than that of the military countries. It was agreed that Russia was the only factor which, in co-operation with the western powers, could prevent the domination by Germany of central and south-eastern Europe.

It was pointed out that the policy of playing for time was in fact a purely negative policy and one which might prove incorrect. Ought we not to direct all our efforts to organising a positive peace-group among the powers? There were other methods than purely power methods, such as economic agreements. Thus it might be possible for us to initiate a constructive economic policy. Such a policy was sketched as follows:

(1) *United States*
- (a) A firm determination to conclude a treaty agreement in the face of all vested interests.

(b) A settlement of the American Debt.

(2) *A new League policy* so devised as to rally the smaller powers without frightening Germany or alienating America.

Could this not be done on the purely economic basis, and would it not be possible to create an economic section which would be supported from the main League and with which countries who are not at present members of the League might be induced to co-operate? Thus the Van Zeeland Report could be brought quickly and closely into relation with Geneva. It might be possible to break the vicious political circle by economic negotiations with the democratic powers. To take an extreme case, it would be difficult to induce Germany to modify her exchange-control system without providing her with a large loan, and the provision of such a loan would be attacked in this country as bolstering up the Nazi system. But although such difficulties are obvious and formidable, this does not mean that our economic and financial power should not enable us to take the initiative in forming a group of economic co-operation into which Germany and Italy might eventually be willing to come.

Thus, although it would be a mistake to modify the covenant with some idea of placating Germany and Italy, or attracting the United States, yet it should be possible so to play up the prosperity of the League as to render the League an attractive organization with which non-League powers will eventually desire to co-operate of their own free will. Although it is true that autarchy has created certain vested interests of its own, yet it can never be anything more than a *pis aller* to a free system. The democratic group should not aim at attacking the closed system, but merely at creating a sort of club which will be so prosperous as to attract all others. The creation of such a club would, of course, entail enormously increased vigour on our part. There is, of course, the risk that any such group might be regarded as encirclement, yet if we continue to take no risks we shall only relapse into a negative policy.

In opposition to this view, it was pointed out that, in the last resort, economics depend upon power. The balance of power in Europe could not be adjusted without close collaboration between France, Russia, and Great Britain. The question which the small powers ask themselves is: 'which of these two groups is more likely to give way?'. Obviously they feel at the present moment that our group is more likely to surrender. Only by affirmation of power can we prevent the smaller countries from making their own terms with the military nations. Moreover, the policy of the open door, if applied throughout our colonial possessions, would benefit, not the western democracies but Japan.

It was the general feeling of the meeting that, although an active economic policy based upon expanding 'circles of assistance' for democratic powers might prove a valuable adjunct to political action, yet such a policy contained dangers and difficulties peculiar to itself and, even at the best, could only be an adjunct and not an alternative to the balance of power.

Sunday, January 16, 10 am

It was pointed out that at Saturday's discussion the group had concentrated upon various forms of resisting the pressure of the military powers and it was suggested that we should not discuss problems of conciliation. These problems could best be approached under the following question: 'Is it possible to satisfy German ambition in south-eastern Europe without damaging the vital interests of France, Russia, and Great Britain?'

Few people could consider the Paris settlement as a permanent settlement and from the outset many political thinkers, such as General Smuts, regarded the League of Nations as possessing the functions of a trustee able to make subsequent adjustments. This hope has proved an illusion. Would it not be possible to agree to some formula such as the following?

> That south-eastern Europe needs reorganization. Germany is the only country able and willing to undertake that reorganization. Could not Germany be entrusted with some sort of mission to reorganise south-eastern Europe into some system analogous to the British Commonwealth of Nations?

The first difficulty was naturally the German character and the fact that they possessed no outstanding genius of the type of Bismarck. On the other hand, Germany had no desire to annexe or incorporate these countries: what she wished was to control them.

Would these countries voluntarily join a German combine? There were certain elements of solidarity. The fascists' systems in Poland, Yugoslavia, and Romania might feel that Germany would help them to retain power. Germany would also acquire some sympathy from non-colonial countries such as Poland.

It was admitted that such a policy ran counter to our national tradition, to opposing the dominance of Europe by any single power. But are we today strong enough to maintain that tradition? It would be very difficult for us to preserve both the British Commonwealth and south-eastern Europe, and of the two, the British Commonwealth (in that it is the home of free institutions) is the more important. It was also suggested that our task should be to establish the rule of law and that entailed first collective security, and only after security had been attained could we exercise the truest wisdom and be generous.

The meeting considered the nature of our 'moral position'. Were we not a little inclined in this country to make virtues of our necessities and even to define as 'good', actions which were only expedient? Moreover, the priceless treasure of our Commonwealth of Nations was really based upon the fact that no party to that combination violently wanted the possessions of any other party. When, however, (as in the case of Ulster) there was violent opposition between two members of the Commonwealth, our sweet reasonableness did not always operate. There was always a danger of treating the League of Nations as an ideological disguise for the creation of an armed alliance.

The meeting then considered the application of these questions and principles to concrete facts.

Czechoslovakia

Public opinion in this country would not tolerate going beyond the Leamington speech, or committing us in advance to defend the Czechs by force of arms. If we faced the situation squarely, we must admit that in present circumstances we would not be justified in urging Czechoslovakia to resist a German ultimatum. Yet, although we would not be able to prevent German domination in south-eastern Europe, we might be able to prevent that domination being imposed by violence. It was generally agreed that there was in fact a vital distinction between what happened and how it happened, and that we really were maintaining the theory of law and order if we were able to prevent things happening in the wrong way. Thus, in regard to the Czechoslovak problem, there were certain points in favour of a non-violent solution, namely the consideration that Germany did not wish actually to annexe Czechoslovakia and thereby to incorporate non-Germans within the *Reich*, and might well accept some compromise under which the Germans in Bohemia might achieve some sort of cantonal autonomy. The real difficulty of the Czech problem was not the internal difficulty but the external difficulty. The present power tension in Europe actually centred in Czechoslovakia, and it would be very difficult to induce France or Russia to abandon the Czechs to the Germans. It might be possible to induce Germany to accept a cantonal solution of the *Sudeten* problem, but only by promising her a free hand in south-eastern Europe, and by implying some loosening of the power tension and especially of the Franco-Soviet pact.

The theory was also advanced that it might be possible to neutralize Czechoslovakia, even as Switzerland is neutralized, but it was admitted that such a policy would be the opposite of collective security and might entail a liability without any corresponding asset.

The meeting then discussed the *Anschluss*.

It was generally agreed that, although some action tending towards an *Anschluss* might precede any action against Czechoslovakia, yet in fact Hitler was, for several reasons (Italian and Hungarian feeling, Austrian Catholics, etc.), unlikely to incorporate Austria within the *Reich*.

At the same time, it might be a wise thing to remove the treaty veto on the *Anschluss*. Both technically and diplomatically, this would be a difficult thing to do.

Poland and Romania

Polish policy at present was to defend their neutrality against any form of violence. Thus, the present right-wing government in Poland would not allow the passage of Russian troops across Polish territory, even if asked to do so by the League of Nations.

Similar considerations affected Romania. It was possible that if the Goga government swung further to the right, Romania would tend to swing towards the German orbit. On the other hand, both Poland and Romania might support the scheme for the neutralization of Czechoslovakia.

Hungary

The Hungarians were at present bewildered. German diplomacy at Budapest had not been very tactful, and there was a growing feeling in Hungary that Germany could not give her more than a small slice of Czechoslovakia, and that this would not be a sufficient inducement to justify becoming Germany's vassal. Thus, a movement is growing in Hungary towards better relations with the Czechs and Romanians and this movement constituted a slight diplomatic asset. In the event of war, Hungary would have to take the side of Germany, but she would do so most unwillingly and would therefore assist in any programme likely to postpone hostilities.

The general impression left by the discussion was that the neutralization of Czechoslovakia would be a great step towards general appeasement and might meet with support from Hungary, Poland, and Romania. On the other hand (since it would imply a weakening of the Paris–Moscow axis) it would be strongly opposed by France and Russia. Moreover, if that neutrality were to be guaranteed jointly and severally, British opinion would not approve of the creation of a new Belgium and ensuing responsibilities in central Europe.

Sunday, January 16, 2.30.pm

Yugoslavia

It was agreed that Stoyadinovitch was an unreliable reactionary who had purchased the help of the Catholic Church by alienating the orthodox. The democratic elements were anti-German, but the general trend of the present system was towards Berlin. On the other hand, Yugoslavia was so weakened by internal dissension that she represented no constructive element in any diplomatic pattern.

Russia

It was agreed that Russia was the most vital and at the same time the most uncertain factor in the whole problem. If we were absolutely certain of Russia's armed assistance, then we could take a stronger line against Germany. Conversely, if we were positive that in every circumstance Russia would remain isolated, then the danger of war would be less acute. The difficulty was to estimate what was really happening in Russia. Was Stalin aiming at an agreement with Germany, or did he execute his pro-German generals because he was fundamentally opposed to any such policy? Would it again be a real disaster if Germany and Russia made friends? Or yet again, if we accept the theory that Germany's sole aim is the acquisition of overwhelming power, would she not, if assured of Russian friendship, not merely dominate Europe, but turn against ourselves?

It was mentioned incidentally in this connection that the French mission which visited Russia in 1936 were far less optimistic regarding Russia's military strength. Their material was good, but the commanders were of very low efficiency.

Germany

Must we abandon all hope of a general settlement including disarmament? The general feeling of the meeting was that any direct overtures to the present rulers of Germany would, at least until the armament programme was almost completed, be taken as a sign of panic and weakness. Yet if by evading all 'head-on collisions' we enabled Germany to obtain the resources of south-eastern Europe and to purchase the neutrality of Russia, then her power would become almost invincible.

The problem was to discover what concessions could be made to Germany which would be neither dishonourable in intention nor disastrous in their effects on ourselves. There was some hope that if Germany were entrusted with greater responsibilities in Europe her general policy would become less destructive.

It was agreed, however, that any public statement at this moment in favour of the Franco-Soviet pact would be regrettable in that it would destroy any hope of a scheme for the neutralization of Czechoslovakia.

Italy

As regards policy towards Italy, the meeting discussed whether, in the event of Italy's economic difficulties increasing, the correct line was to withhold assistance, in the hope of forcing Mussolini to terms; or whether there was the danger, if Mussolini's position was allowed to become too acute, of his precipitating European war. The possibility of a compromise over Abyssinia was mentioned, the proposal being to recognize Italian sovereignty over the areas which it actually controlled.

Spain

As regards Spain, there was general agreement on the desirability of postponing the granting of belligerent rights until the evacuation of a substantial number of volunteers. In these circumstances, and as the position of the government appeared to be improving, there was the less cause to urge the expediting of the non-intervention negotiations. It was suggested that we should take a bolder line about food supplies to government territory, and that any official pressure to discourage importers should be discontinued.

Curtis to Geoffrey Dawson, 17 January 1938 (ms. Curtis 12, fos 10–13)

I have just attended another weekend conference at All Souls on foreign affairs in which Lord Allen, Harold Nicolson, Salter, Gilbert Murray, Toynbee, Liddell Hart, and Hodson took part. On Saturday afternoon Salter and Murray said that Eden had addressed some private gathering at which they were present, and in the course of his speech had used words to the effect that people might presently be thankful for the Franco-Soviet pact. They got the impression that Eden himself now strongly approved that pact, but had not yet got the Cabinet united with him.

Harold Nicolson, who more than ever gives the impression that he is closely in touch both with Eden and the Foreign Office, then said that he thought it likely that Eden, backed by Chamberlain, would get the Cabinet united on the subject and make a declaration in favour of the Franco-Soviet pact, very likely during the course of the next session.

The group seemed to me to have swung back to the attitude of mind revealed at the last conference a month before. Nicolson's fundamental attitude is that everything must be done to weaken Germany as the strongest power in Europe. The rest of them, with their minds concentrated on collective security, again talked as though they were prepared to plunge the world in war in order to assert it.

On Sunday morning Toynbee summed up the previous discussion and then Allen asked me to give my views, so I put in a plea for the policy of recognizing Germany's special position in eastern Europe and suggested that we should do our best to keep Germany in paths of moderation, and also use our influence with Czechoslovakia to get her to accept the reconstruction on the Swiss model, which would give the German population on the western extremity the same kind of position as the German-speaking Swiss have in the cantons of Zurich Valais. I further suggested that, following out this Swiss policy, we should see whether Germany and the rest of the great powers could not agree to neutralize Czechoslovakia, as Switzerland had been neutralized.

The reception was not encouraging and I felt like Athanasius. At 11.45 am I had to excuse myself to go to a meeting of the Oxford Preservation Trust. When the meeting was resumed at 2.45 pm I found, to my astonishment, that they had all agreed to adopt and advocate my proposals about Czechoslovakia, which they had decided to describe as the neutralization policy. I said nothing but searched for fleas for fear of disturbing this frame of mind. Then, at the end, Lord Allen said definitely that everyone seemed agreed on the neutralization policy. I then said 'I think then you had better consider what your attitude is going to be with regard to Eden's possible declaration in favour of the Franco-Soviet pact.' To get things clear, I again elicited from Salter, Murray, and Nicolson what they had said before. Nicolson added, what was news to me, that the Foreign Office were dead against the Franco-Soviet pact when it was made; but were now coming round in favour of it.

Faced by this question, they finally agreed, with the exception of Gilbert Murray, that a declaration by Eden on behalf of the British government approving the Franco-Soviet pact would scotch once for all the possibility of the policy in eastern Europe of neutralization of Czechoslovakia and otherwise, which they had approved that morning.

I cannot myself conceive why, at this juncture, Eden and the British government should announce their approval of the Franco-Soviet pact, nor was anyone present, not even Nicolson, able to suggest an explanation. They were simply clear that that was in Eden's mind. If so, then good-bye to any prospect of better understanding with Germany for us, and indeed I should say to the last chance of avoiding a world conflagration.

I felt so disturbed on the subject that I thought of ringing you up last night; but felt I could not talk of it over the telephone. Please destroy this letter when you have read it and don't show it to anyone else. It is enough that you should know that the possibility of this madness is in the air. You, I imagine, if you saw fit, could render such a declaration difficult or impossible by leading articles written in advance. Don't show that you know what I have told you; but on the other hand you might easily draw on Liddell Hart and Hodson separately to talk to you about the conference, the whole object of which is to enable its members to decide what course in foreign affairs to advocate. You could judge from what they told you how far there is any risk of Eden coming out with a declaration in favour of the Franco-Soviet pact on behalf of the British government.

I accepted to join this group merely in the hope of understanding their state of mind. I had not intended to join in the discussions and only did so under strong pressure. To my great surprise yesterday I got the impression that what I had said decisively influenced most of them.[12]

Liddell Hart to Salter, 17 January 1938 (Liddell Hart papers, LH 5/1)

Just a note to express my appreciation in general of a most stimulating weekend, and to thank you in particular for your kindness in letting my boy be present at the discussions [. . .]. I think that something practical emerged from our discussions, while of no less value was the way so many individual viewpoints converged towards a common view of the main elements of the problem.

Murray to Liddell Hart, 17 January 1938 (Liddell Hart papers, LH 5/1)

[. . .] It was an interesting discussion yesterday. I thought the advocates of conciliation at any price had their full fling, and on the whole

[12] For an informative pen portrait of Curtis, see Toynbee, *Acquaintances*, pp. 129–148.

did not get to any result, except perhaps about the neutralization of Czechoslovakia.

Salter to Liddell Hart, 18 January 1938 (Liddell Hart papers, LH 5/1)

Many thanks for your letter. I was extremely glad that you were able to be there and greatly hope you will be able to come again for the final meeting of February 6, on which the utility of these discussions will largely depend – though I think that in any case they will have been of real value [. . .].

Liddell Hart to Murray, 19 January 1938 (Liddell Hart papers, LH 5/1)

[. . .] The discussion was interesting and also very helpful, if not very productive directly. But the more the difficulties and dangers are realized, the more likely is the inevitable revival of the idea that the only security is collective.

Rowse diaries, typescript sequence, 19 January 1938 (Rowse papers, EUL MS 113/2/2/10)[13]

Over the weekend an interesting conference in Salter's rooms on foreign policy, Clifford Allen in the chair, Harold Nicolson, Liddell

[13] The diaries of A.L. Rowse exist in various formats. He edited the original handwritten version for retyping and made further changes to both. The final typescript copy has been used here. Rowse was later to describe Allen as a 'distasteful figure [. . .]. Enjoying invalidism, a fund was raised for his support, which he invested to such good purpose that he was henceforth not a member of the Independent Labour Party but, better, independent financially. This holier-than-thou type was created a Labour peer'; A.L. Rowse, *A Man of the Thirties* (London, 1979), p. 202. See also Rowse's letters to *The Times*, 23 August and 3 September 1937, in which he advocated rearmament and an alliance policy, and 'Reflections on the European situation', *Political Quarterly*, 9 (1938), pp. 334–350. In his 'The present and immediate future of the Labour Party', *Political Quarterly*, 9 (1938), pp. 13–29, he condemned the 'failures, the treachery, the disaster' of the National Government's ministers, who were 'following their class-interests and sacrificing the interests of the country'. Rowse's comments on Allen's personal wealth are disputed in Martin Gilbert to Rowse, 25 August 1967, EUL MS 113/3/temp/box 169.

Hart, Walter Layton, Gilbert Murray, Arnold Toynbee, and others. I felt so weak, and once through sheer high temperature lost my way in an argument I was trying to put: rather humiliating. Interesting to watch Harold Nicolson at close quarters: his industry – he wrote the whole time as well as taking part, having taken on the job of reporting the discussion. For the rest, a sanguine temperament, naively saying 'Anthony told me' this or that; equally obvious was his uncertainty of judgement.

Liddell Hart I thought impressive intellectually – so odd for a soldier, and that fact giving him a great advantage at such a time. Walter Layton and Gilbert Murray impressed in their respective ways. Layton a weighty person, but a bit of a doctrinaire liberal, too regardful of people's susceptibilities. Murray is more of a politician than the world realizes – people think of him more as a saint, an English equivalent to Gandhi; but, sitting by me, he wished to be realistic, yet once or twice giving way to the doctrinaire.

Clifford Allen made a good Chairman – that is evidently his claim – and was treated with evident respect. I didn't wish to speak to him if it could be avoided; but he caught me in a doorway with outstretched hand, which I held merely the fingers of and passed on with the briefest recognition. I never forget 1931, not the people who went wrong in 1931. Allen went out of his way to pay marked attention to whatever I said and was extremely polite.

Murray to Cecil, 19 January 1938 (ms. Murray 231, fos 95–97)

[. . .] The League has been badly defeated. There have been five wars which it has failed to prevent. The anti-League axis is so strong that countries like Belgium, and even Sweden, are giving up their idea of collective security. The idea of 'universality' or overwhelming force have become ridiculous. We are driven back, broadly speaking, on a League of countries that are prepared to live by the rules of the Covenant and to defend one another where militarily possible. That is in itself a great, though limited, ideal. I should like to make an effort to get closer co-operation for the defence of this limited programme among all the L[eague] of N[ations] societies, including Winston's movement, omitting only the pure pacifists. I think on such a programme one could get something like national support for the League [. . .]. Disarmament is the obvious case.

Liddell Hart to Salter, 3 February 1938 (Liddell Hart papers, LH 5/1)

[. . .] there is no chance of my getting to Oxford on Sunday as I had hoped. I am very sorry to notify you of this, as it is a real disappointment to me to miss the opportunity of taking part in the continued discussions.

The next meeting of the group was held on Sunday, 6 February 1938 at 12 noon.[14]

Harold Nicolson diaries (Nicolson papers)

Sunday, February 6, 1938

[. . .] on to All Souls. The meeting is smaller than before – only Gilbert Murray, Salter, Arnold-Forster, and Toynbee plus the unimportant others. We have a paper by Lord Allen which we take as an agenda. We discuss with great gloom the recent purge [*of the high command and foreign ministry*] in Germany and come to the conclusion that it means that Hitler has given Mussolini a free hand in Spain in return for a free hand in Austria. We are very disturbed.

We then go on with the agenda and come to several conclusions but we feel it is all very academic when one thinks of the raging activity of Berlin. We lunch there and we dine there [. . .]. Salter has flu and is very wretched. I expect he will pass it on to all of us. We thus adjourn at 11.00 pm. I shall put our conclusions in this diary when I have drafted them.[15]

Allen had by now emerged as the most persistent proponent of Anglo-German friendship.[16] *The paper which he had prepared for the 6 February 1938 meeting*

[14] Hole to Liddell Hart, 30 January 1938, Liddell Hart papers, LH 5/1.

[15] Entry of 6 February 1938, Nicolson diaries, does not contain any further 'conclusions'.

[16] Allen's views on foreign affairs had been changing. Compare his contributions in *Parliamentary Debates, House of Lords*, fifth series, CVII, 17 November 1937, cols 115–131, and 'A constructive peace policy', *Contemporary Review*, 152 (1937), pp. 11–20, with the earlier *Peace in Our Time: An Appeal to the International Peace Conference of June 16, 1936* (London, 1936), and the chapter, 'A practical peace policy', in *Britain's Political Future: A Plea for Liberty and Leadership* (London, 1934), pp. 107–118. See also Thomas C. Kennedy, '"Peace in our time": the personal diplomacy of Lord Allen of Hurtwood, 1933–1938', in Solomon Wank (ed.),

received a thorough airing. No record of the discussions has survived. However, the results led to several redrafts co-ordinated by Guy Wint, and circulated as 'Document C' on 12 February.

Document C[17]
(Liddell Hart papers, LH 5/1)

Introduction

A. The proposals are intended to represent the kind of policy we should like to see followed by the British government in foreign affairs. They are not designed to conform with what we know of the present government's state of mind or to facilitate the propaganda of opposition bodies bringing pressure to bear upon the government of the day.

B. The suggestions are founded upon the basic principle that under existing circumstances the foreign policy of the British government needs to combine a display of strength with an outline of proposals to meet legitimate grievances and claims; and in the belief that we are in danger of losing important allies. The ultimate object is to rebuild a peacekeeping system between the nations.

C. This memorandum therefore deals with two subjects which are distinct and yet interlocked:
   (i) What *form* should the proposals take, and in what form should the display of strength be made?
   (ii) What *procedure* should be followed by the British government in order to make known these proposals and to display that strength?

The proposals: immediate policy

1. *The Far East*

Active co-operation with America is a sine qua non. It should be intimated privately to America that the British government will proceed as far as America in every variety of joint action. Britain

Doves and Diplomats: Foreign Offices and Peace Movements in Europe and America in the Twentieth Century (London, 1978), pp. 217–239.

[17] This version of 'Document C' from the Liddell Hart papers is reprinted without several amendments in a variety of hands.

should additionally make known to America that she thinks it desirable to bring economic pressure to bear upon Japan, provided co-operation with America could be arranged. This pressure should then take the form of the prohibition of financial credits; the refusal to accept exports from Japan; the withholding of munitions and oil.

The despatch of all forms of munitions to China should be allowed. They should be 'slipped in' without any public declarations of policy at the League of Nations or elsewhere.

An unofficial boycott should be organized by private persons and, if possible, by trade unions. Such action would involve less risk of war than governmental sanctions; and would meet with a favourable response from American public opinion.

In the event of an attack on Hong Kong, it is essential that we should not be drawn into fleet action in the China seas: since the distance from our base – Singapore – would put us at a grave disadvantage. Opinion should therefore be prepared for the possible abandonment of Hong Kong – which, if sanctions were successful, would only be temporary. In order to avoid a public outcry for the relief of besieged British subjects, women and children should be evacuated while there is still time: this being technically quite feasible in view of the small British population. (Evacuation of women and children would still leave Japan guessing as to whether we intended to fight: non-evacuation might be taken as a sign that we would in no circumstances risk a war.)

2. *Spain*

Failing foreign intervention on a grand scale, it is clear that Franco can win only by naval blockade. It is of the greatest importance to withhold belligerent rights until the scope of hostilities in Spain has been reduced to genuine civil war.

Having regard to the diminished scale of Italian intervention, our interests would not at present be served by abandonment of non-intervention policy.

We should, however, recognize the possibility of a sudden crisis occurring: and in such circumstances our policy must be based on an estimate of the risks of alternative lines of action.

3. *Rearmament*

A declaration that rearmament would be expedited in every possible way, especially on the defence side, which seems to be behind other parts of the programme, accompanied by a public statement that Britain would always be prepared to cease rearming at any time, provided other countries would do the same, and provided that an arms agreement was accepted which recognized equality for comparable powers in Europe, so that no one country should be able alone to dominate the continent.

A great effort to increase the storage of food and other commodities.

4. *Anglo-American trade negotiations*

Trade and economic negotiations should be expedited with America with a view especially to the amplification of the existing tripartite agreement between Britain, America, and France. Any surrender to vested interests by the government such as to reduce the importance of the treaty would make a deplorable impression in the USA. A private intimation should be given to the American government that we are ready to start debt negotiations when the USA thinks the occasion appropriate.

5. *Van Zeeland Report*

The calling of the conference, as suggested in the Van Zeeland Report, not desirable until a later stage. For economic policy, see paragraph 11.

The proposals: long-term policy

6. *Collective action against aggression*

Reaffirmation that British policy is directed to helping to rebuild a system by which countries provide a collective defence, similar to that of the Covenant. The League to be retained for its present members but this would not exclude the co-operation of other powers on the basis of maintaining law and order.

All suggestions for emasculating the League Covenant by eliminating Article XVI should be avoided. Non-League powers might be asked to discuss to what extent, in case of threat of aggression, or aggression, they would agree to consider action on the lines of Article XI.

An intimation by Britain, in some form, to the effect that she was always prepared to join in making use of every opportunity, where conditions made it possible, to get a preponderance of force behind law, to implement the method of the collective protection of law, either by economic or military joint action, such as was to be seen at Nyon.

7. *League Covenant and Treaty of Versailles*

A declaration in favour of the signing of a new protocol resubscribing the League Covenant and the ILO statutes so that these may become disassociated from the Treaty of Versailles. (See the report of the committee of Jurists). An offer to agree to the removal of the present form of discriminative restriction upon the union of Germany and Austria: but with the recognition that the Austrian problem is not solved thereby. Statement that historical responsibility for the war is in our view not a matter on which it is suitable for the combatants on one side to impose their judgement on the combatants of the other: and that it would therefore be better if that clause were eliminated from the Versailles Treaty, as also any reflections on German colonial administration.

8. *Czechoslovakia*

If and when a general European settlement becomes possible, the solution of the Czechoslovakian question might be contemplated on lines not at present feasible: for example, (a) as regards the minorities' problems, by adopting the cantonal system; (b) as regards reassuring Germany against the use by another power of Czechoslovakia as a bastion for attack, by either the neutralization of Czechoslovakia or the rebuilding of the League system.

9. *Economic policy in central and eastern Europe, etc.*

An offer to join with other League powers in economic facilities to the central, eastern and south-eastern countries of Europe, and in other practicable ways of improving their economic position. Plans for this purpose to be worked out by the BIS in conjunction with the League of Nations: and to be conditional on their tending to an improvement of the general political situation. In the event of an all-round settlement becoming possible, we should not exclude from consideration the possibility of preferential economic arrangements such as would give Germany an economic position in central and south-east Europe superior to that which we ourselves claim.

10. *Revision of frontiers*

Revision of frontiers and minority questions in regard to Hungary and the South Tyrol to be considered in any general settlement.

11. *General economic policy*

The central idea should be that the nations desiring a less controlled economic system should negotiate an extension of their economic interdependence and a relaxation of their economic controls. By such agreement, the nations participating would on the one hand be bound more closely together, on the other hand their economic prosperity, and thus ultimately their strength and resources, would be increased.

To such a bloc, any nation, whatever its political complexion, should be admitted: adhesion would, however, ipso facto involve a more liberal economic policy: and this would run counter, in the nations concerned, to a totalitarian and military organization of their national life.

While no direct advances should be made to Germany, it should be made clear that German participation in the bloc, on the terms described, would be welcomed. It is especially desirable that agreement between the non-dictatorship powers should not seem to be directed against Germany.

The negotiation of the agreements should be linked with the League of Nations, through its Economic Section, and should not be conducted outside the Geneva framework. This would have the effect of linking membership of the League with tangible economic benefits, which would be an advantage in countering the attraction of Berlin for the east European states.

Germany would be unwilling to enter into negotiations directly sponsored by the League. This difficulty might, however, be reduced by giving the Economic Section of the League an independent status, on the lines of the ILO.

12. *Equality of trading opportunity in colonial areas*

An offer to join with other countries in a policy of equal trading opportunity for all non-self-governing colonial territories, at least in equatorial Africa. This would in effect be the extension of the Congo Basin Convention to all colonies in equatorial Africa. Other countries which possess colonies should, however, be required, as a condition, to accord reciprocal treatment.

13. *Colonies*

Britain should offer to extend the Congo Basin regime to other of her tropical African areas, and suggest that other countries should do the same. This regime having been established, and the distinction between Class I and Class II colonies having been abolished, we should invite Germany, when negotiating with her on the question of colonies, to accept a similar principle for the status of colonies. It is, of course, essential that the character of the mandate, and the political situation at the time of the negotiations, should be such as to give reasonable confidence that the conditions aimed at will be achieved: whether or not agreement on the colonial issue forms part of the general settlement. An effort to strengthen the Mandates Commission and its powers.

14. *Arms limitation agreement*

As a condition of a general settlement, an arms limitation agreement: and an understanding that, if one country exceeds its limitations, all other countries should, in consultation with one another, so adjust their programmes that the country setting the pace should be unable to secure the relative advantage which it seeks.

15. *A League or peace system*

The hope to be entertained that, with the conclusion of a general settlement (conferring as it would economic and other advantages), all European signatories would enter some kind of peace system – League or otherwise. As a minimum, agreement to be aimed at by which, in the event of the peace system being broken, countries engage not actively to aid the aggressor country.

Procedure

1. Direct overtures to Berlin, indicating our willingness to discuss above proposals, are at present undesirable, owing to the non-response to previous advances and the present state of mind of the German government. It is important to avoid giving an impression of weakness. The best course is that the Prime Minister and the Foreign Secretary, in speeches to their constituents or to the public, or in replies in Parliament, should – in the context of their general policy, domestic as well as foreign – affirm their willingness to enter at any time upon negotiations for a comprehensive settlement.

2. At the same time, in order to give clearer leadership to the smaller powers, as well as to the British public, opportunity should be taken to emphasize, in official statements, the fidelity of Great Britain to the League method of peace-keeping and peaceful procedure for treaty revision; and also to democratic government; though this should not be done in such a way as to intensify the division of Europe into two camps, fascist and democratic. The stressing of our faith in democracy is of special importance for our relations with the USA.

3. The British government might therefore circulate a despatch to all British ambassadors redefining Britain's attitude to the League system and democracy, and at the same time including a reference to Britain's desire to expedite the process of treaty revision and economic co-operation. This despatch should call upon British ambassadors to

take every opportunity of making this British standpoint known in their respective countries.

Great Britain to develop a wireless *news* service in many foreign languages of a nonchalant character including comparatively little propaganda.

4. The British government to indicate either publicly or privately that, in the event of the proposal for working out a new European peace settlement being agreed to, Britain would favour the setting up of commissions, working not on the basis of bargaining but of fact-finding; and studying simultaneously the various problems concerned, namely:

those dealing with economic proposals;
those dealing with political problems;
those dealing with colonial questions;
those dealing with a peace-keeping system;
those dealing with arms limitation.

Diplomatic exchanges and discussions between governments to deal with all the above problems on the basis of the reports received from these fact-finding commissions, to be followed by a peace conference to embody the decisions in a general settlement.

The unwisdom of a conference being prematurely called to be emphasized.

Nicolson's suggested additions to Wint's redraft of 'Document C' (Liddell Hart papers, LH 5/1)

Alteration no. 1

(Page 1 of Wint's draft: add after words 'grievances and claims'.)

We need an affirmation of strength in order to demonstrate to Germany, Italy, Japan, and the smaller powers that there exists a point at which violence will be checked by force. We need a promise of conciliation in order to prevent the militant powers from acquiring a mood of desperation, and in order to show the world that our policy is something more flexible and creative than a mere defence of the status quo.

Our ultimate object is to recreate a peace-keeping system between the nations. If we are to attain that object we must make it clear in all our actions that our policy aims at the safeguarding of law and order and the sanctity of international treaties. Our policy of recent years has given the impression that we are ready to condone any breach of contract or custom provided it does not damage some direct British interest. This bad example on our part has not only alienated American opinion, but done as much to destroy the League, as have the direct attacks aimed at Geneva by the militant powers.

Alteration no. 2

(Page 1 of Wint's draft: add after 'could be arranged'.)

This pressure might take two forms, official and unofficial. Official action should be limited to discouraging (and where possible preventing) the grant of financial credits to Japan. Unofficial action might take two forms. First, there might be a private boycott of Japanese goods. Secondly, trades-union action might be taken, especially in the form of refusal to handle or carry any war material or oil destined for Japan. It is possible that the trades unions of America, Holland, Scandinavia, and even (in spite of Mr Lyons) Australia might cooperate in such action.

Concurrently assistance, both in food and war material, could unostentatiously be given to China. A definite pronouncement either on the part of the government or from Geneva might precipitate a conflict. For the moment supplies should be allowed to 'dribble in'.

1. *Hong Kong*

It is urgently hoped that Hong Kong will not be allowed to become a hostage to fortune. The Japanese now argue: (a) that we can only defend Hong Kong by detaching from home waters a greater number of ships than we can afford to part with; (b) that our prestige obliges us to defend Hong Kong; and (c) that therefore, whatever happens, we shall not take action likely to expose us to a war with Japan.

Were we to indicate that we are perfectly prepared to base ourselves on Singapore and to face the temporary loss of Hong Kong, the Japanese would be less confident of our abstention. It might have a salutary effect if preparatory steps were taken to evacuate women and children from Hong Kong. Such precautionary measures would leave Japan guessing whether we intended to fight; so long as they believe that we shall cling to Hong Kong at any cost they know that we shall not go to war.

2. *Spain*

Failing the despatch of a vast Italian army, it now appears unlikely that General Franco can impose a decision either by land or air. His one hope of forcing the government to surrender is to blockade them by sea. He can only do so if we accord belligerent rights. We must thus recognize the fact that the grant of such rights may be the determining factor of the civil war. They should be withheld at least until the scope of hostilities in Spain has been reduced to genuine civil war and all foreign auxiliaries (whether combatants or technicians) have been withdrawn.

Alteration no. 3

(Page 4 of Wint's draft: add after 'Versailles Treaty').

An opportunity should also be taken to withdraw the accusation of colonial maladministration which was made against Germany in the note of 16 June 1919, covering the reply of the allied and associated powers to the German counter-proposals.

On 16 February Christina Hole informed members of the group of the next meeting scheduled for 26 February.[18] *There were adequate written materials when the group convened at All Souls at 12 noon on Saturday. Nicolson, as usual, wrote in his diary.*

Harold Nicolson diaries (Nicolson papers)

Saturday, 26 February 1938

[. . .] on to All Souls. Present – Walter Layton, Arnold-Forster, Allen, Arthur Salter, Lionel Curtis, Gilbert Murray. We discuss a final form of our report. We are all agreed that Anthony's resignation means a new course and that we are in danger of a four-power pact.[19] This will

[18] Hole to Liddell Hart, 16 February 1938, Liddell Hart papers, LH 5/1.

[19] In letters to the *Manchester Guardian*, 25 February 1938, both Rowse and Murray aired extremely critical views of Chamberlain and expressed the deepest fears about the consequences of Eden's resignation. For Nicolson, speaking in the Commons, the question was whether policy would be pursued 'on a basis of expediency or on a basis of principle'; *Parliamentary Debates, House of Commons*, fifth series, CCCII, 21 February 1938, cols 99–103. In

mean the isolation of Russia and the possibility of civil disturbances in France and even here. We also agree that Hitler may come to us and say, 'I offer you diminished demands in the colonies, a guarantee of the integrity of the French frontier, in return for a free hand in the East'. In other words a purely western Locarno. This would be very tempting and very dangerous.

Foreign Affairs Group, 26 February 1938 (Liddell Hart papers, LH 5/1)

Saturday 26 February 1938

The meeting began by discussing whether the group should draft a document making proposals for our foreign policy.

There was some uncertainty about the purpose of such a document, whether it should be for publication, or private circulation or simply to enable the group to clarify its views. It was asked whether it would be confined to proposals which the government as at present constituted might conceivably entertain, or whether it should sketch out the policy of an alternative government, supposing the present policy to prove a failure; whether it should say what Halifax might do, or what a Labour government would probably do.

One view was that the public, bewildered by the Eden resignation, was inclined to despair of salvaging a collective peace system. According to this view, the document should show how, working up from the present situation, a collective peace system could be recreated. In any case the public should not be left without a lead. The demand for a general election was, for example, mischievous, was based on an inadequate view of the crisis, and might lead to a disastrous result.

Another view was that it would be undesirable to publish anything which would increase the difficulties of Halifax and the Prime Minister. But it was also suggested that their bargaining position vis à vis Mussolini might be stronger if it was made clear that the British public was ready for an alternative policy in case agreement with Italy proved impossible.

Some held that great caution was needed in anything like propaganda to bring back Eden: for his return would in present

the Lords, Allen observed that Eden had 'an insufficient reason' for resignation; *Parliamentary Debates, House of Lords*, fifth series, CVII, 24 February 1938, cols 906–910.

circumstances be such a challenge to the dictatorships as considerably to increase the danger of war.

Finally it was agreed that one of the members should prepare a draft, which should be considered at the next meeting of the group, and which should take the following form:

Chapter 1	Contrast of the attitude to the League indicated in the Prime Minister's recent speeches and of the policy hitherto pursued. Possible implications of the new orientation.
Chapter 2	Negotiations with Italy. Enumeration of possible Italian demands upon us, and of possible demands by us upon Italy.
Chapter 3	Negotiations with Germany. Possible contents.
Chapter 4	Policy towards France.
Chapter 5	Policy towards Russia.
Chapter 6	Conclusion. Long term aims of our policy and attitude towards the League.

It was stressed that the draft should not be written in general terms, but should make concrete and specific proposals.

The Eden crisis

The discussion then passed to a survey of the situation created by the Eden resignation. The Chamberlain view, it was suggested, was to accept, at least temporarily, the new state of affairs resulting from the failure of the League, and so to model our policy as to minimize the dangers confronting us in a world without collective security. The Eden line, on the other hand, was said to have as guiding principle of all our policy the attempt to recreate conditions favourable to the collective system.

Some members raised the question of whether the Chamberlain policy would require us to defend smaller nations only when our interests were involved, irrespective of the merits of each case; others questioned whether any peaceful revision in Europe, essential for the Chamberlain policy of appeasement, was possible except within the framework of the League system.

It was asked whether the Prime Minister aims at the Stresa front or at the four-power pact.

One interpretation was that hitherto we had been trying to form a bloc of the democratic countries vis à vis Germany and Italy. Now we had decided to approach Germany and Italy direct, and to establish a peace bloc transcending the 'triangle'. It was suggested that, in fact, this might be virtually to enter the Rome–Berlin axis, with France left out.

It was asked why we had changed our policy so precipitately. Had there been real danger of war, or was the whole crisis artificial?

The Eden policy had aimed at preventing the ideological division of Europe. It was asked whether the Chamberlain policy, if it led to our virtually joining the anti-comintern pact, would not precipitate the ideological conflict.

It was suggested that the Chamberlain policy might be considered under two heads. The immediate, and transitory, issue was our relations with Italy. The long-term issue was our attitude towards the collective system and towards Germany.

Negotiations with Italy

Mussolini's demands might include the following:

(1) Granting of belligerent rights to France.
(2) Financial assistance, possibly in the form of government guaranteed credits, which might not need parliamentary sanction.
(3) Recognition of Abyssinia.
(4) Share in the management of the Suez Canal.
(5) Possibly condominium in Aden and Port Said.
(6) Subsequently, if negotiations were widened, naval parity with France.

Mussolini might be prepared to concede the following:

(1) Cessation of agitation in the Near East.
(2) Withdrawal of Italian infantry and evacuation of the Balearics, but possibly not withdrawal of technicians, who were of much greater importance to France than Italian infantry.
(3) Reduction of garrison in Libya.
(4) Possibly an increase in forces stationed near the Brenner.
(5) Possibly an agreement over the fortifications of Pentellaria.

Was there a community of interests between England and Italy sufficient to make agreement possible? England and Italy had no common ground as democracies: but this need not rule out an understanding, provided there was material for a deal.

It was mentioned that the view was held in some circles that Mussolini was, in fact, very apprehensive about a further German advance in Austria. According to this view, Mussolini was a nationalist and fundamentally anti-German: in this respect there was a difference between him and Ciano, who was an 'international fascist', and counted on German support for the maintenance of the regime in the event of the disappearance of Mussolini. Ciano was said to have the support of the younger generation of fascists, who favoured abandoning Italy's interests in central Europe, and concentrating instead on a forward policy in the Mediterranean. The group had no means of testing what truth there was in this account.

In discussion of the possible terms of the agreement, it was suggested that all Mussolini's concessions would be of a transitory nature, ours of a permanent nature; i.e. we should have taken steps which we could not retrace, for example, in financial assistance or recognition of Abyssinia, or the granting of belligerent rights, while Mussolini would merely have suspended operations which he could renew whenever it suited him. Mussolini could offer nothing comparable in permanence to the concessions which we would make to him; he could offer words and we must give deeds.

To meet this difficulty, one proposal was that financial assistance should be postponed, and made conditional on a loyal fulfilment of the spirit of the agreement. This would have the following advantages. Firstly, we should not find ourselves in the position of financing Italian armament before Italy had given proof of a real change of policy. Secondly, if financial arrangements were postponed for the time, they might at a later stage be negotiated through ordinary commercial channels, and would not therefore meet the same public opposition as would credits guaranteed by the government.

The group was in substantial agreement about conceding *de jure* recognition of Italian sovereignty over the parts of Abyssinia which it had effectively occupied. The right of the Emperor to representation at Geneva might, however, be safeguarded.

As regards Spain, there was a discussion whether the granting of belligerent rights would in fact be decisive in Franco's favour, since the republic still had land communication with France. It was pointed out that rail transport was very expensive, and also that land communications south of Barcelona were exceedingly bad. There was general agreement that the granting of belligerent rights should be considered only in the event of an agreement upon evacuation of a very far-reaching character.

Owing to his economic difficulties, an agreement upon Mediterranean disarmament might be to Mussolini's advantage.

The effect of an Anglo-Italian agreement upon France was then discussed. It was remarked that feeling in France had been turning against Italy, owing to the fear of Mussolini's intentions towards the French north African possessions. An Anglo-Italian agreement might therefore intensify the movement in France towards closer relations with Russia, less intimate relations with England.

Germany's attitude to an Anglo-Italian agreement was hard to foresee. If it suspected the re-formation of the Stresa front, it might be inclined to forestall it by expediting its programme in central Europe.

Finally, it was questioned whether the terms obtainable from Italy could be represented in such a way as to satisfy British public opinion.

Collective security and central Europe

Our policy with regard to German action against Czechoslovakia was discussed at length. Two views emerged sharply contrasted with one another. They may be summarized as follows:

The first view This was that we should decide in advance in what circumstances we should be prepared to take action provided that France and Russia would act with us, and should then ascertain from France and Russia whether they would in fact be ready so to act. Following this the three powers should, privately through their ambassadors, notify Berlin what action by Germany they would *certainly* oppose; and should notify Prague in a similar manner of the circumstances in which Czechoslovakia could *certainly not* look for assistance. Thus the powers would (a) be prepared for an emergency, (b) would have placed a possibly decisive deterrent in the way of a gamble by Germany. Policy of this kind would still leave a gap of uncertainty between the kind of action by Germany which would *certainly* mean war, and the kind of action in which we should *certainly not* intervene. As far as the British public was concerned, it should be prepared for the possibility of war over Czechoslovakia, and the fact that we were in intimate military relations with Russia would be made clear. An understanding of so decisive a character between France, England, and Russia would probably revive the League and rally the smaller powers to its support. The effect of American opinion would also be favourable.

Public opinion in England, not only in the Labour Party but also among Conservatives and even in the City, had been disturbed by the Austrian crisis and the Eden crisis, and would probably demand strong action if Germany intervened in Czechoslovakia. The Conservatives as a whole would probably move with opinion. Opinion in France was also moving in favour of a strong policy. If France took the initiative in collective action against Germany, public opinion in this country would probably favour our giving support to France.

The effects of surrender in the past had been disastrous. If Germany was allowed to dominate Czechoslovakia and eastern Europe, its capacity to wage a long war would be greatly increased.

If war resulted, it need not involve conscription. Our contribution would be not by land armies, but economic, naval, and in the air.

It was argued that if the collective principle was not applied in the case of Czechoslovakia, and if a four-power pact was contemplated, Russia would cancel its association with the democracies. For its own security it would then revert to its former policy – so-called Trotskyism – of attempting to cause dissension among the four powers, using as its instrument the comintern. Civil war in France might be one of the results. Finally, should the result be a Russo-German war, this would before long turn into an international class war. In fact, the only means of preventing the ideological conflict so widely feared was to prevent Russia from being driven into isolation. Russian co-operation was also to be retained in case we were to be faced with a 'go south' movement in Japan.

The second view This proceeded from the assumption that the German and Italian regimes were radically unsound and that, if war were avoided, they would eventually collapse or be modified in such a way as to relieve the international situation.

In any case, if Germany succeeded in its penetration eastwards, it would be unwilling to jeopardize its gains there by an attack against the western powers.

The policy therefore suggested was one of minimum commitment east of the Rhine.

It was suggested that it would be disproportionate to hazard the Empire, especially while rearmament was still incomplete, upon an issue rising out of Czechoslovakia. Moreover, in the event of action being taken by France, Germany might undertake to fight a purely defensive war in the west, and not to cross the French frontier: in such circumstances, the British public, and still more the Empire, would probably be very lukewarm about supporting France.

The Franco-Czech pact had been concluded when the League system was still intact and when the Rhineland was demilitarized. These conditions no longer existed, and it would be extremely difficult for France to render military aid.

The danger was stressed of making any hard and fast commitments about action in central Europe. In the unstable conditions of the times, we should be free to deal with each emergency on its merits. If a pledge were given, it would so much increase the danger of war that the government should feel itself obliged to propose conscription.

If Czechoslovakia realised that no aid would be forthcoming from England, it might be more ready to settle its differences with Germany, and thus one of the major causes of friction would be removed. Finally, the analysis (given by the supporters of the first view) of the ultimate effects of a four-power pact was challenged.

Anglo-German negotiations

The group agreed that it was possible to envisage proposals coming from Germany upon the following lines:

(1) Suspension of the colonies claim.
(2) Denunciation of the Franco-Soviet pact.
(3) Pledge by Germany not to cross the French frontier.
(4) Pledge by Germany not to annexe Czechoslovakia, but demand for cantonalization and relatively small rectifications of frontier.
(5) Four-power pact (Russia excluded).

There was some discussion on what should be our reactions to such proposals. It was suggested that to accept them would be to run counter to our traditions of foreign policy; would end the attempt to find an alternative to power politics; would worsen our relations with France and the USA; would create conditions of international anarchy very dangerous to the Empire; and would be regarded with disfavour by public opinion in the dominions.

On the other hand it was suggested that, if Germany desired to negotiate, a basis might be found as follows:

(1) Joint approach to Czechoslovakia to adopt cantonal system.
(2) Open door in the British Empire, as discussed at meeting on February 6.
(3) Germany economic hegemony of central and eastern Europe.

There was some indication that Benes was now prepared to consider a cantonal system.

Home defence

In conclusion, the group agreed that there should be increased pressure for more adequate air protection and home defence generally, and was ready to contemplate some measure of air-defence training on a national basis.

The efforts to reach a consensus for publication was tending to emphasize differences rather than to speed unanimity. On this occasion Guy Wint first broke ranks.

Wint to Curtis, 26 [27] February 1938[20] (ms. Curtis 12, fo. 32)

The publication by the Foreign Affairs Group of the document envisaged yesterday will surely be extremely dangerous. What they have in mind is apparently something similar to the book *The Next Five Years*. It might conceivably have a very considerable influence.

Even if one were not convinced that the Halifax line is the correct one, it is surely taking a terrible responsibility to campaign actively against its success, and this is what a published statement on the lines discussed at the meeting would come very near doing. As one of the speakers said yesterday, if opinion in the country should move radically and Eden be brought back, this would be such a challenge to the dictatorships as to make war infinitely more likely.

In these circumstances, perhaps the group might at least be asked, before proceeding further, to hear the views of the other side. For example, Lord Lothian[21] might be invited to the next session.

Would you consider writing to Lord Allen and suggesting this?

Curtis to Allen, 28 February 1938 (ms. Curtis 12, fos 33–34)

After much cogitation I have come to the conclusion that the best thing I can do under the circumstances is to forward you the enclosed letter from Wint, and to ask you not to let anyone, including Wint himself, know that you have seen it. I have a certain respect for this young man's judgement, more indeed than I have for that of Hudson or Rowse, and found myself always regretting that he was not brought into the discussion as they were. He is singularly free from the streak of fanaticism to which young intellectuals like Rowse and even Hudson are subject. We most of us were at their age. But I felt on Saturday that counsel was somewhat darkened by the atmosphere which Rowse and Hudson created, especially when they tended to represent the Cabinet

[20] The original of this letter was sent to Allen. See Allen papers, box 15, correspondence, 1937–1938.

[21] 11th Marquess of Lothian (1882–1940) private secretary to David Lloyd George, 1916–1921; Secretary of Rhodes Trust, 1925–1939; Chancellor of the Duchy of Lancaster, 1931; Parliamentary Under-Secretary of State for India, 1931–1932; Ambassador to the United States, 1939–1940.

as anxiously hoping for the victory of Franco. I dare say that is true of Duff Cooper,[22] and possibly of Hailsham,[23] but greatly doubt whether it goes further. Also in the mind of Rowse, who is one of my dearest friends, Lothian, who is another of my dearest friends, is Public Enemy Number One. You and I can remember how some people in the early days of August 1914 spoke of Edward Grey as Public Enemy Number One. My feeling is that Wint is right. I suggest that you would be wise, when the first draft of your joint memorandum is finished, to send Lothian a copy, ask him to meet your gathering, and hear what he has to say before you commit yourself to publication. Looking back at our discussions, I now feel that many things were made clearer by the presence of a man like myself who differs from all the rest in thinking that sanctions and collective security are the cause of the present confusion rather than the cure for it. I came after some hesitation simply because it was such a golden opportunity of seeing into the minds and through the eyes of the people who hold views opposite to my own; but looking back at the discussion, I think now you were right in insisting now and then that I should give my unpalatable criticisms. But Lothian can speak with incomparably more knowledge and practical experience than I can, and I feel that people like Arnold-Forster and Rowse, with a flame in their minds, might gain a great deal by meeting him face to face and hearing his criticism of their views.

It has been a great privilege to me to be allowed to listen to these discussions. I doubt whether anyone has learnt so much as I have by listening to them.

Allen to Curtis, 1 March 1938 (ms. Curtis 12, fos 36–38)

I very much appreciate your helpful letter. I too have formed a very high opinion of Wint, and I should like the group to go on using him even though Salter may be away in America.

[22] Alfred Duff Cooper, 1st Viscount Norwich (1890–1954) MP, 1924–1929, 1931–1945; with War Office and Treasury, 1928–1935; Secretary of State for War, 1935–1937; First Lord of the Admiralty, 1937–1938; Minister of Information, 1940–1941; Chancellor of the Duchy of Lancaster, 1941–1943; Ambassador to France, 1944–1947.

[23] Quentin Hogg, 1st Viscount Hailsham (1872–1950) Lord Chancellor, 1928–1929, 1935–1938; Secretary of State for War and Leader of the House of Lords, 1931–1935; Lord President of the Council, 1938.

Speaking in the strictest confidence, I was sorry when Salter (without consulting me) brought Rowse into our discussions, but being a creature who attaches enormous importance to toleration I did not grumble. Groups, such as we have been working in, require essentially for their success a peculiar quality of mind. By that, I mean a combination of immense sincerity founded upon opinions rigidly held, yet with a capacity for restrained expression and a passionate longing to enter into the hearts and minds of those with differing points of view. Men like Rowse are no doubt intellectually very alive, but they want to batter their opponents into submission. They may be willing to engage in intellectual exchanges, but they have never the least intention of modifying their own opinions, and take a certain pleasure in trying to prove other people to be either knaves or fools. Once or twice during the discussion I had thought, as chairman, of being a little formidable, and warning Rowse and others of the convention of intellectual good comradeship under which we ought to be working, but I thought it would be better to be silent rather to be priggish.

As to the possibility of some document being published, you can be quite sure that, so far as I am concerned, I shall never give my consent or my signature to any document that is anti-Halifax and pro-Eden. I have already taken a stand in the House of Lords on this point, and have brought down upon myself one more bout of anger from my friends, but I intend to stand firm, as I am sure you would, under similar circumstances.

Unlike yourself, I do not quite rule out altogether the principle of collective security under present circumstances, but I do believe in what I call a 'transitional policy' in which, whilst not surrendering that principle, we use the League with far more discretion and gentleness than we have done in the past. But nothing would induce me to sign a document which has only one object, namely to destroy the effort of Halifax and the Prime Minister to rebuild the peace of Europe.

I also have a great admiration and personal liking for Lothian, and will think over the wisdom of getting him included in future discussion.

What does worry me, I admit, is the fact that when the draft document comes before us on March 16, Salter will be absent and yourself as well. This will leave me almost single-handed in resisting the ferocity, however sincere, of men like Rowse and Arnold-Forster. I only wish you were going to be with us, for I and the others have gained a great deal from the challenge to our thinking that you have made. As chairman of the discussions I have felt it right to drag you in even when you were sometimes reluctant to intervene. I hope you may feel able to rely upon me doing my best to prevent anything disastrous occurring, and I am most grateful to you for writing as you have done.

Allen to Trevelyan,[24] 28 February 1938
(Allen papers, box 15, correspondence, 1937–1938)

I am quite certain, as I was throughout the whole war when dealing with the Kaiser, that we must never refuse a chance of negotiating a peace settlement. I am equally certain that if we are to attempt this the only hope of success is to do it by unconventional means without stiff penalty conditions, in the hope that a sudden cut through of a tangled situation may create a psychological change favouring peace.

As I find Charlie Buxton[25] saying this week-end, never reject an opportunity of talking peace even with the devil himself [. . .]. I am pretty sure that public opinion will in the end come to see that those of us who are taking this unconventional position are right today as we were in 1914 and again in 1916.

Allen to Wint, 1 March 1938
(Allen papers, box 15, correspondence, 1937–1938)

You were kind enough to say that you would go on helping us with our Foreign Affairs Group. I suggest therefore that you should quickly notify everybody of the date and time of our next meeting, drawing their attention to the urgency which will arise from the fact that we shall have an eventual document before us. I personally am a little bothered as to quite where this document is going to get us, as I have no intention of being associated with any document which makes the work of the Prime Minister and Lord Halifax more difficult. My task as chairman will be greatly increased at our next meeting owing to the absence of Sir Arthur Salter. However, we must jump our

[24] Julian Trevelyan (1910–1988) painter, etcher, and author; numerous one–man exhibitions and several retrospectives; engraving tutor at the Royal College of Art, 1955–1963.

[25] Charles Roden Buxton (1875–1942) MP, 1910, 1922–1923, 1929–1931; Treasurer of the Independent Labour Party; author of *The Alternative to War* (London, 1936).

hurdles when we come to them, as I often find that dangers which one thought were going to occur disappear when the time arrives.

Hole to Liddell Hart, 1 March 1938 (Liddell Hart papers, LH 5/1)

[...] I am asked to say that a document will be submitted to the meeting [*called for 16 March at 11.30 am, in the chambers of Sir Norman Angell, 4 King's Bench Walk, EC4*] for discussion, with a view to publication if this is found to be desirable.

CHAPTER 2

'FOREIGN POLICY NOW', MARCH 1938

It had been intended that the meeting of 16 March 1938 would discuss the question of publishing a statement, if agreement were reached. But given the pace of events in 1938, it was not surprising that individual thinking in the All Souls group was often subject to changes, sometimes dramatic, with regard to international affairs. Several members of the group, including Curtis, Murray, Nicolson, Salter, and Allen agreed to meet at Chatham House on 8 March, there to discuss a draft memorandum prepared by Toynbee for a speech he was to deliver at the same venue two days later.[1]

Curtis to Macadam,[2] 2 March 1938 (ms. Curtis 12, fo. 39)

Through the privilege I have enjoyed in attending 'Salter's Soviet' at All Souls I feel that I can contribute something to Toynbee's paper at 12.45 on 8 March. I have, therefore, cancelled a lunch engagement which I had here, in order that I may be with you.

Murray to Cecil, 4 March 1938 (ms. Murray 232, fos 61–62)

[. . .] It does seem possible that we should get a basis of co-operation between Liberal and Labour in a common support of the League, plus

[1] For Toynbee's speech at Chatham House, which indirectly referred to the All Souls discussions, see 'The issues in British foreign policy', 10 March 1938, Royal Institute of International Affairs Archives, 8/526, Chatham House, London. The revised version appeared in *International Affairs*, 17 (1938), pp. 307–337.

[2] Ivison S. Macadam (1894–1974) Secretary and Director-General, Royal Institute of International Affairs, Chatham House, 1929–1955; Principal Assistant Secretary, Ministry of Information, 1939–1941; Editor, *The Annual Register of World Events*, 1947–1973.

a sort of Five-Years-Plan attitude in Home Affairs [*in the forthcoming Bridgwater by-election*].

I am reading an awfully interesting paper by Arnold Toynbee on the question [of] whether Great Britain, if she gives up the League, will sink peacefully and comfortably to the position of a second-rate power like Holland, or must be destroyed in the process. He inclines to the latter view.

Rowse diary, typescript sequence (Rowse papers, EUL MS 113/2/2/10)

5 March 1938

Liddell Hart has a thought that war may have 'some purpose that is beyond the ambit of human reason, despite its palpable unreasonableness as a way of settling any human issue'.

Last night at dinner, when Woodward and Salter were talking hopelessly about it, I said, 'So long as we retain sovereign capitalist-states, these are the consequences we must expect.' They both protested, Salter no less than Woodward, though he should know better; they are both Liberals. Woodward said, patronisingly: 'Come, come, none of these bad jokes of the 1890s.' I said, 'Unfortunately, they were the realities of the 1930s.' These people do not or will not know what I mean; but all the young men there agreed with me, not with them.[3]

Harold Nicolson diaries (Nicolson papers)

Tuesday, 8 March 1938

There is a meeting at Chatham House to discuss the memorandum prepared by Arnold Toynbee for his speech on Thursday. His main argument is that we are no longer strong enough to maintain

[3] There is a further diary reference to 'these foreign policy conferences of Salter's I have been attending these past few months, a whole group of us, Harold Nicolson, Walter Layton, Gilbert Murray, Liddell Hart and so on', in Rowse papers, EUL MS 113/2/1/10b, manuscript sequence, entry of 14 May 1938.

our nineteenth-century Pax Britannica or to preserve our great possessions. We must therefore either try to remain neutral in an anarchical world or make some determined effort to rebuild the League idea [. . .]. Salter says that between a 100-per-cent League of Nations policy and the policy of allowing ourselves to decline to the status of Holland there is a vast intermediate zone. He believes that we cannot fight Germany without Russian help and that Russia is now out of the picture. We cannot therefore fight for the moment and must therefore play for time. Czechoslovakia is our weak point but Spain is a strong point. He advises us therefore not to commit ourselves too deeply for the Czechs, but to concentrate upon defending liberty on the Spanish front. Gilbert Murray says that has no particular bias against the Nazi ideology as such but that he has a profound hatred of the war ideology which the dictator states possess. Lionel Curtis urges us to bring in a bill for compulsory training in air-raid precautions. He thinks that this would show the world we are prepared to defend ourselves if attacked. I point out that the issue is not only between the League idea and the dictator idea, but that it is an issue between the traditions of our old policy (namely to oppose the strong and to protect the weak) and an experiment in a new policy of trying to conciliate the strong [. . .]. Toynbee [. . .] says he wrote it [*the memorandum*] in order to show the governing classes how the present policy of selfish evasion would place them in an impossible position. Do not let us go one tenth along the road and then turn back.

'Notes on foreign policy' by Salter, 8 March 1938 (Liddell Hart papers, LH 5/1)

Note: This memorandum has been written under great pressure in the last hours before sailing [*to New York*]; and it is likely that, on cooler reflection, I should somewhat change the balance as I should in many respects change the wording and expression. But such as it is I should like the group to read it as a confidential document.

1. As I am unable to be at the March 16th meeting at which the question of publishing a statement (if we can be agreed) will be discussed, I think that I ought to leave a note as to my own opinions as they stand after our earlier meetings (and all that has happened in the meantime).

2. First a word as to my point of departure. The reason why I proposed the meetings was that I found myself in grave doubt (of a

kind I have never felt before the last two years) as to the course of policy to support and advocate – a doubt extending to some of the gravest issues presenting themselves; and in consulting others who started with a similar general outlook I found they were all experiencing equal, though not identical, anxieties. I hoped that we might help each other in clearing our minds and in solving the individual problem presenting itself to each of us as to his own line of conduct.

I believed – and believe – that the essential principles of the League of Nations (collective security and peaceful change) are the only ones upon which anything more than a precarious and short-lived peace can be established. I believe indeed with Lord Lothian, and H.G. Wells and others that ultimately some form of world federation, with the abandonment of national sovereignty, is the only permanent and sure method of avoiding wars. But I have always thought that the most practicable way towards that was by the gradual surrender and subordination of sovereign rights through successive treaties and settlement of disputes, etc., under the League system. The alternative would seem to be a speculative gamble on the seizure of power, after world destruction, by a group of people endowed with the impossible combination of those qualities which bring men to the top at a time of chaos and those which would enable them then to construct a free system of government on federal principles (like Wells's idealized airmen). For if countries will not willingly surrender their sovereign rights by small stages (as through the League) it seems unlikely that they will willingly do so in a single act. There remains, it is true, a more reasonable doubt as to whether the Covenant did not attempt too big a single jump towards something approaching universality, instead of starting with a smaller group (or simultaneously with several such groups) composed of peoples with similar ideas and political systems – an alternative to which (if such a system can now be restored at all) we are being forced – in circumstances of particular difficulty.

But believing in these fundamental principles, I realized also that the inescapable condition of any system of collective security is that the countries who support it (and are willing to do so with the obligations it involves) possess a collective preponderance of strength (which in the last resort they are ready to use) over those who at any period may assail it.

From the beginning, the abstention of the USA, there was the clear possibility that this vital condition would not be capable of realization in all circumstances and in regard to all situations, and that in those cases the application of the full provisions of the Covenant would require modification, or perhaps suspension.

But since the Abyssinian fiasco, preceded by the the advent of the Hitler regime and the secession of Japan, and followed by all the later events with which we are familiar, this question – 'Have the League Powers, or can they quickly secure, a collective preponderance of power sufficient to deter, (or if that is impossible, at least to defeat) aggression?' – is obviously one that needs to be asked in regard to every vital problem of Europe, as well as of other continents.

For two years, therefore, those desiring a League policy have been under the necessity of measuring relative strength closely (with due allowance for the effect on the strength collectively available of a given line of policy).

In such a period as this we must therefore constantly ask: (a) where and how far, having regard to collectively available strength, can we apply a straight League policy?; (b) how can we restore the political conditions under which such a policy can in future be more fully, and more widely, applied?

This second object cannot be relegated to the future. It must always be an element in policy; and on this point the Prime Minister's February 21 speech was especially open to objection.

Successive retreats have destroyed the political conditions required. We must at some point stop the retreat and prepare for advance. But it is essential that the point at which we resist is so chosen that we have the strength to make resistance effective. We may be compelled to retreat further in certain cases, and must choose the point at which we are strongest for our main stand.

3. It is this difficult, but inescapable, necessity of measuring strength that constitutes the basic difficulty of those who start with the League outlook, as defined above, in determining their precise course.

In calculating the strength – material and psychological – of the two main groups, and the attitude of countries whose association is not quite certain, the factors to take into account are very numerous. Individual judgements as to the weight to be attached to each factor, and possibility as to the net result will doubtless differ – the more since much of the essential information required for any exact estimate is not available to us. We can only exchange our individual judgements after our sharing of information of the last few weeks.

My own estimate is this. Taking all the factors (including as an important one our known vulnerability to air attack) into account, I have been of the opinion for more than a year that Great Britain and France with Czechoslovakia have not, and cannot in any near future, secure such a collective preponderance of strength as can be relied upon to deter Germany from insisting on the realization of her more essential ambitions in central Europe (or even with certainty to defeat her and her associates if war results) – unless they can add to their own strength that of another great power. Of these, there are only three that can enter into possible calculations – the USA, Italy, and Russia.

It is not in my view an answer to say – though it is true – that the number of those throughout Europe, west of Russia, who would prefer to be associated with a British-French system exceed those who prefer the association of the German system; nor that – though this is also true – our failure to take a strong collective line in the past has been a principal reason for the successive changes of orientation of Poland – of Yugoslavia – of Romania – of Greece, and now the neutralizing attitude of Holland, Scandinavia, and even Belgium. If countries felt able to determine their attitude by their sympathies rather than their fears, we should have a majority of votes, possibly even a preponderance of strength. But they do not. Whatever line we take I do not believe we can rely upon bringing into effective association with us and a League system (covering armed action, if necessary) any of the smaller countries except Czechoslovakia. If we had another great country on our side, we should doubtless be in a position in which, by pursuing a consistent 'collective' policy we could bring back most, perhaps nearly all, of the smaller countries. But except upon that condition we must, I think, assume only France, Czechoslovakia and ourselves as standing together if we pursue a policy which challenges Germany at the centre of her ambition.

What then of the three great powers whose adherence has been, or is being, sought by one policy or another?

4. There is, of course, the Stresa policy of detaching Italy. This would count two [*sic*] on a division if practicable and would turn the balance against Germany. But it is not, of course, a way of restoring the League system, but rather the opposite, and since Abyssinia and the establishment of the 'axis', I think it is impracticable. The Anglo-Italian negotiations may result in expediting some things Mussolini has anyhow strong reasons for being ready to do – the withdrawal of Italian infantry from Spain, the reduction of Italian troops in Libya. They may result in a little more – in encouraging Italy to exercise some effective influence on Germany to limit her action, at least for the time, in Austria to something like the present position;[4] perhaps even to persuade Hitler to limit his demand in Czechoslovakia (again for the present) to a cantonal arrangement for the *Sudeten Deutsch*. That, however, is the best – and even that is dependent upon the extent to which Hitler is amenable to Mussolini's influence on these issues. To break the axis is beyond any reasonable possibility. (Perhaps the strongest case for attempting Anglo-Italian negotiations is this. There is some danger that Mussolini might precipitate a war in which Germany would join, as Austria did: the negotiations may reduce the

[4] Footnote in the original reads: 'This was written before the present crisis.'

danger and make a war on the issue in which German does not herself wish to risk one less probable.)

5. *The USA* If the USA were on our side, in the same sense as France, of course that would give the preponderance and act as a deterrent. But this is obviously impossible. The USA's position is one of armed isolation, developing into a possible policy of action in the Far East (which in time would neutralize Japan, already perhaps a less powerful support to the axis than if she were less heavily engaged in China). In time and very gradually, given wise policy, there might be something a little better than this – a visible sympathy, so likely to express itself in material aid in case of war that German would take this prospect into account. But that is a long way off. For the time being, and as regards immediate European problems, we must regard the USA as neutral.

6. These are the reasons why, for the last year, I have felt that 'the sum would not come out with a balance on the right side', unless Russia were definitely in among the assets. With Russia fully co-operating and at her full strength, we should have a collective preponderance which might serve as a deterrent, even allowing for the extra element of provocation, of the strengthening of the 'encircling' sentiment in Germany, and of the complications as regards Poland and Romania.

For a long time I thought this was practicable and believed that much more cordial and complete co-operation with Russia was both practicable and desirable – the decisive factor being that, whatever the rigours of her internal system, she was unacquisitive and willing, indeed anxious, to co-operate in a League system.

I still think that co-operation up to a point, and in certain fields, is practicable and desirable; and that every reasonable effort should be made to maintain friendly relations. In particular in the Far East the Russian interests tend to march with our own, and co-operation there may be practicable and desirable.

But the crucial and immediate issue is whether we can stake all upon the certainty of Russian co-operation, and her ability to act with sufficient strength, if we pursue an unreserved League policy in Europe (including Czechoslovakia). Can we pursue a policy which (on the view set out above) would be fatal unless Russia is both reliable enough and strong enough? And we must take into account, of course, the position in Poland, and the 'precipitating' effect on German policy and sentiment of a visibly active policy of increasing the links with, and commitments to, Russia.

Slowly, and very reluctantly, I have personally felt forced to the conclusion that the answer to this question must be 'No'. We cannot interpret precisely the 'purges', but they must indicate a precarious position, a great weakening of the administrative system and of the army. More than that, they make more active co-operation much more difficult in this country, and probably impossible with this government and parliament. And the latest feature in the trials confirms this strongly. The Stalin government have required this time confessions of treachery with Great Britain.

On the whole, I feel forced to conclude that any policy which is only practicable on the basis of increased co-operation with, and commitments to, Russia, and of complete reliance on fully effective armed action by her in case of war, must be rejected.

And the conclusion which follows – a very painful one, but one personally I feel unable to escape is this:

We have not, and cannot in the near future secure, such a combination of strength as will enable us to prevent without war (or probably even to defeat in war) the realization of the central core of Hitler's (and now Germany's) ambition – the association in some form of the Germans in Czechoslovakia and German Austria with the *Reich*.

We may have sufficient bargaining and diplomatic strength (and here conceivably the Anglo-Italian negotiations may be of some service) to restrict the expression of Germany's demand to something short of incorporation in the *Reich*. More than that – and perhaps even that – I do not believe we have the strength to secure.

7. Well, this is the betrayal and breaking up of Czechoslovakia, the one democracy east of Belgium and France; the surrender to brutal force and menace; the admission of one more successful over-riding of law and treaty right.

More than that, Czechoslovakia may fight; France may join her; the war may then sweep into France; we may be forced to fight at once or later, under disadvantageous conditions and having lost the chance of Germany being deterred by the knowledge that we shall fight.

All that is true. All I can say is that I do not believe we can, in any case, deter Germany from insisting, to the point of war if necessary, on a change in the present position of the Germans outside Austria. Even if we can for the moment, the danger will continue and increase, so long as these great masses of Germans remain in other countries under conditions which Germany, rightly or wrongly, regards as intolerable. We may not be able to persuade Czechoslovakia, with or through France, to give way. But the chance of permanently holding back the German demand is even less.

We must also take these considerations into account:

(a) In forming Czechoslovakia the main 'nationality' principle of the treaties was over-ridden by the 'historic' and the 'strategic' claims. The precisely opposite course was taken with Hungary.

(b) The German 'hard-core' demand is in regard to these German peoples; these have (even apart from Hitler and the Nazi policy) a powerful support in German public opinion. The other side of the Nazi creed is that non-Germans are not wanted in the *Reich*. Further ambitions are therefore in a different category.
(c) We must doubtless resist at the appropriate point, on penalty of accepting an extending, and perhaps illimitable, German domination, but we must measure our strength and resist where we are strongest, not wheakest.

In the case of the *Sudeten-Deutsch*, we are at our weakest because:

(i) Czechoslovakia is militarily indefensible through Austria (which we must probably assume is available for the passage of troops).
(ii) Germany is infinitely stronger where land operations are in question, not naval operations (as, e.g. in Spain). And while Czechoslovakia cannot defend herself against invasion through Austria, France can only go to her aid with the terrific disadvantage of an attacking army against the defence in a now fortified Rhineland.
(iii) In addition are all the 'political' considerations suggested in 7 (a), with their effect both in this country and in Germany. Such political considerations are of great importance in choosing the ground on which we should stop our retreat and resist. The method by which pressure will put upon Czechoslovakia and concessions extorted will doubtless be inconsistent not only with the League but with everything upon which international law must be based. And I do not pretend for a moment that we ought not to oppose a collective resistance to the method, and some of the results that will follow – even if we then tried to secure some modifications of the present situation – if we were strong enough.

Nevertheless, it must be recognized that there is a real element of justice in the German aspirations as to Germans outside the *Reich*. And when such nationalist aspirations are deep and general, they make resistance much more difficult – they strengthen the will on the one side and weaken it on the other.

If, of course, we do accept the position, much follows. We must make our position clear to France and Czechoslovakia at once. We may try (conceivably with some aid from Italy) to exercise any influence we can on Germany to limit her demands, e.g. to the cantonal arrangement. But we must also face what I believe to be the fact (and not conceal it from France and Czechoslovakia) that even if she demands incorporation with the *Reich* we cannot resist. We must not give 'moral support' to Czechoslovakia, if by that we mean doing anything that will encourage her to resist. On the contrary we must do the utmost possible in the contrary sense.

8. This means a further surrender: a further increase of prestige to the dictators; a dismemberment (or something like it) of a most remarkable state with immense achievement to its credit. But it does not mean a policy of indefinite surrender. It means concentrating our defence of free systems of government and law where we are strongest – at, that is, west of the line Holland–Belgium–France. Here, I believe, we have still strength to hold, and behind this line we can build up again. Our chance may come as the inherent 'long-run' (but possibly very 'long-run') weaknesses of unfree systems begin to develop.

9. This line of policy – surrender east of the Holland–France line but not everywhere – should express itself in a strengthened policy in Spain. We are probably strong enough there to insist on a fully effective non-intervention policy, including the effective withdrawal not only of infantry, but of technicians, airmen, and gunners, and the stoppage of aeroplanes, submarines, and war material. In that case we must still prevent the fatal blow to our interests, and deadly danger to France, of a fascist Spain. Here, both the geographical and political factors are as much to our advantage as they are against us in central Europe. The sea is vital, and there we have overwhelming strength. There is an open and easy access for civilian supply through France. The Spanish venture is a most serious drain on Mussolini's resources and extremely unpopular in Italy. It is even more unpopular in Germany. No ambition comparable with the German aspiration for the association of Germans outside Germany is involved.

In this country, while there is much pro-Franco sentiment, it is not comparable to the feeling that would obstruct an active association with Russia, and it is weakening as the danger to our imperial interests becomes apparent.

And if non-intervention is made effective, we may well, in the result, help to secure the establishment of a government in Spain that is free – neither fascist nor communist. It is, of course, essential, on this line of policy that, in the negotiations with Italy, we should not be induced to turn (or continue to turn) a blind eye to any form of breach of the non-intervention agreement.

We have a further advantage in this policy in the apparently growing strength of the Spanish government's navy, which may greatly reduce the difficulties attendant upon recognition of belligerency – the objection to which has been that Franco would be able to impose a blockade, which would have to recognized. This he may now be unable to do.

If we are strong enough to stand anywhere it is here. And an effective stand here would do more to turn the tide than an attempt, ultimately abandoned, or resulting in a war, further east.

10. I believe also that we can, and should, pursue the policy proposed at our earlier meetings as regards the Far East – indicating to the USA that we will go as far as they will up to and including economic boycott of Japan (with material aid to China in the meantime), and being prepared to face the temporary loss of Hong Kong if necessary as a part of this policy.

11. The crucial point is this. In view of Germany's present temper and her strength, it seems to me most unlikely that we shall avoid a great European war if we attempt to resist, to the point of war if necessary, the realization of German ambitions as to the *Sudeten Deutsch*. Real as is the risk that, in the alternative, Czechoslovakia will precipitate a war in which France, and then we, will be involved, I believe this to be less and more capable of being dealt with.

And if war comes over Czechoslovakia, under the military conditions already referred to, I believe the issue would be at least doubtful. And in case of defeat, or even of victory, our defence of democracies would probably have failed in its purpose – for democratic systems and perhaps most of our civilization would be destroyed for generations in the process.

At a time when relative strength is so nearly equal, we cannot afford to stake all where the conditions are in every respect the least favourable – military, psychological, and even, in the sense indicated, in some respects (though not, of course, all) moral. An unresolved problem of Germans outside Germany will prevent all European appeasement so long as German aspirations and strength endure.

To oppose ambitions which are in some measure reasonable – even if possible for a time – increases the feeling behind those that are quite unreasonable. But probably even a respite can be secured by concessions. And time is needed for continued efforts at German appeasement, without which no League system for Europe can be rebuilt. Time, if we can secure it, is at least in this sense on our side, that whatever happens – the death of Hitler, a reaction from aggressive excitement due to a kind of fatigue – it can scarcely fail to result in a situation less immediately dangerous to peace than would result from a flat opposition now to a demand upon Czechoslovakia.

12. I agree with the rest of our proposals as to appeasement, 'equality of opportunity' in the colonies with the further colonial policy proposed, the consistent cultivation of close relations with America by every possible method, and the general economic policy suggested

for Europe and elsewhere. But I need not discuss these, beyond this bare mention, in order to indicate that this memo does not purport to be a policy, even in outline, but only an argument on one vital point.

13. I would only say in conclusion that the above general view, whether right or wrong, has been formed after taking into account the factors of weakness in the dictatorship powers: the economic strain (in time likely to be great for Germany, already serious for Italy – though not, I believe, such that she is now on the verge of collapse); the incomplete organization of the German army (but we must remember that in numbers German troops plus Italian equal perhaps twice French plus Czechoslovakian plus ours); the deficiency of German supplies for a long war; the relative weakness of their naval forces; the incomplete training of German pilots (but only temporary – and probably the German air force is in numbers equal to ours and France's together), etc. On the other side is, of course, the civil weakness of France and, as a major factor, our known vulnerability, especially in London.

I also realize fully both the grave disadvantages, extending far beyond the fate of Czechoslovakia, and the serious risk of such a course as I am proposing. The first effect of a substantial success of Germany in Czechoslovakia will, of course, be to increase her prestige, to strengthen fascist forces within each country where the issue between them and those which represent free government is uncertain. It will tend to make that system of government the 'fashion', as parliamentarism was till recently. It will be a big step towards Germany becoming recognized as the dominant power throughout central and south-eastern Europe. It will enable her to utilize this power in economic arrangements which will go far to repair her deficiencies in certain foods and raw materials.

If she successfully consolidates the possibilities of this advantageous position, she may feel strong enough to turn west and at once, or later, feel able to challenge us also by sea, or to acquire what she wishes in other parts of the world by threats to Great Britain. And success may enlarge her ambitions. It is possible, of course, that Russia may disappear out of our orbit altogether and make some kind of accommodation with Germany. These are all possibilities and, if realized, they would create a balance of power and a situation even more adverse to us than the present one. These considerations should perhaps prevail, were not our present situation substantially stronger, and if there were not real possibilities that a measure of satisfaction of her less unreasonable claims will tend to a temper in Germany less dangerous than the present, and that the combination with this of the economic strains that must continue for some time and the inevitable difficulties attendant upon enlarged responsibilities will tend to limit her further ambitions. Even success may create a mood in which Germany will hesitate to stake all she has gained – because she has so much, and so much more, to lose. But in any case the risks of such a course as I now suggest are, of course, very great. I can only say that weighing them against those of the alternative course, which are also extremely grave and which do not allow for the possible alleviation that time (and with time even accidents) may bring, I personally feel that the balance inclines as I have indicated.

The conclusion, which personally I feel increasingly unable to escape, is destructive of so much that all of us have centred our hopes in for so many years, that I have felt myself unable to accept it for long after the time at which I think I should have done, if desires had not biased a cool estimate. But at present, and on such information as I have – admittedly incomplete as regards much that may be essential – I cannot myself come to any other conclusion, and I have felt it my duty to state my opinion, for what it is worth, to the group before I leave.

14. One last remark: on one thing I think we are probably all unanimous. The worst single feature in the whole of our position – and perhaps in the general international position – is our vulnerability against air attack, (and a secondary though very important, point, as regards food supplies). And the one thing on which we can probably all agree is that a great national effort to remove this weakness is what is now most urgently necessary – necessary whatever foreign policy we pursue; even if we can publish nothing on other policy, I suggest we could, and should, publish a declaration upon this. And, personally, I would go so far as to advocate compulsory powers to secure that all are trained and prepared to fulfil the appropriate functions required in case of air attack.

Salter to Curtis, 9 March 1938 (ms. Curtis 12, fo. 53)

[...] I have written a long memo, expressing the same views as at Chatham House yesterday. It is a hastily written document, rushed off in the last hours before sailing: and it is, in its present form, highly unsuitable not only for publication but even for any general circulation. A copy will be sent to you as soon as it is reprinted, and copies will be available for reference at the March 16 meeting. I am writing to say that if you would care to show it to anyone I am asking that you should do so at your discretion and subject to the above remarks.

My address till April 12 (for receipt not despatch of communications) will be Berkeley University California; thereafter till April 20 Washington (British Embassy).[5]

I do hope you will on return make the air-raid problem your main thing for the time.

Nicolson to Vita Sackville-West, 9 March 1938 (Quoted in Nicolson, *Vita and Harold*, pp. 297–298)

I had a depressing day yesterday. We had a private meeting at Chatham House to discuss the present situation. We came to the unhappy conclusion that now that Russia has dropped out we are simply not strong enough to resist Germany. Or rather we did not come to so extreme a conclusion. But we did feel that 80 million fully armed Germans plus the Italians were more than we and France could safely take on. What tremendous things have happened in these five years! We are suddenly faced by the complete collapse of our authority, our Empire and our independence. Poor England [. . .] opinion is at the moment as gloomy as in the days after Austerlitz [*1805*]. Nobody who is well informed believes that there is any chance of negotiations with Germany leading to anything at all. We may get some little scrap out of Italy but it will be a mere crumb of comfort and quite unreliable.

Curtis to Halifax,[6] 10 March 1938 (ms. Curtis 12, fos 55–57)

The information which prompts this letter has come from a source which is not British but is so authoritative that I am passing it on to you [. . .].

[5] In fact Salter hastily returned from the United States after Germany invaded Austria on 12 March 1938. He later recalled: 'I had gone to Berkeley, California for what was intended to be a six weeks series of lectures. When the news came I cancelled all the remaining lectures (I had only given one), much to the annoyance of my hosts & hurried back to Westminster – thinking, wrongly, "this is the moment when we face the facts".' Letter, Salter to Rowse, 4 April 1961, Rowse papers, EUL MS 113/3/1/Corr.S.

[6] 1st Earl of Halifax (1881–1959) Viceroy of India, 1926–1931; Secretary of State for Foreign Affairs, 1938–1940; Ambassador to the USA, 1941–1946.

My informant believes that war, if it happens, will initiate chaos which might last for centuries, and that the next six months are the most dangerous in human history. His reason is that the two or three youngish people who now control Germany feel that their population is effectively organized against panic in air raid. They have 800,000 men and women specially trained to do all that needs to be done when bombs begin to fall on towns [...].

The upshot of my informant's view is that nothing would so diminish the risk of war as the rapid passage of a short bill [...] giving the Home Office the compulsory powers to organize the population against panic in air raids [...]. The point is that passage of such a bill now would be the most effective step to avert such an outbreak, by convincing Berlin that the English people are prepared to face war with all its modern horrors if it is forced on them [...]. The opposition cannot clamour for a strong line against dictators and at the same time vote against measures which alone will avert panic and enable the population to protect itself against air raids, if war results.

You cannot answer this letter as I am just leaving for a three-week voyage in the Mediterranean [...].

Wint to Curtis, 11 March 1938 (ms. Curtis, 12, fos 58–62)

Thank you for your letter. I had a talk with Hodson yesterday, and he is going to think over the whole matter of propaganda and the best procedure. In the meanwhile, I enclose an outline of the kind of pamphlet which I think it might be very useful to get published at this stage. I was in fact urging Hodson to draft something rather on these lines – something very clear, simple, popular. Perhaps you could let me know your comments on such a proposition? Best wishes for your holiday.

Part 1

The public is bewildered by the Eden crisis.

For more than a decade a large section of it has cherished the League policy as a guarantor of peace. The collective system and how it was expected to work.

The ideas of many League supporters are, however, being changed by events. They may have deplored the attitude of the government over Manchuria and Abyssinia. But what, in concrete terms, is the collective system likely to mean today?

Possible course of events with regard to Czechoslovakia. War – which the League system set out to avoid; and a long war, the issue of which would be very uncertain. The military situation has been transformed by the fortification of the Rhineland. Our air defences are still very weak. Ought we thus lightly to jeopardize the Empire?

Even if it were possible, by a British-French-Russian agreement, to secure a temporary preponderance of strength as against Germany, Germany would see in this an encirclement and would probably prepare aggressive action for the first moment of crisis in one of these countries. Thus the collective system can, in present circumstances, assure no *lasting* peace.

If we attempt to make it function, we ought to propose conscription.

And we must think clearly about (a) the probable consequences of a prolonged war, the social and economic dislocation, and the collapse of democracy which it would most likely involve; (b) the kind of peace which we should aim at on the conclusion of the war, i.e. count the *full* cost of the action advocated.

Part 2

What are our objectives?

(1) Peace.
(2) Defence of democracy in the British Empire, covering so large a part of the civilized world.

A survey suggests that, if we limit ourselves to these objectives, the outlook is not so black. Three powers are dangerous to us – Germany, Japan, and Italy. But the latter two lose much of their importance in the event of an improvement in the relations between ourselves and Germany.

A German offensive westwards is not likely in view of the great preponderance in strength, in modern warfare, of the defensive as against the offensive. Italy, in the last analysis, is dangerous to us only in that it may attempt to drag Germany into war, as Austria dragged it in 1914. Thus Italy is a menace only if Germany is desperate. Similarly, Japan's success depends on our being distracted in Europe.

The real danger of embroilment with Germany is localized in central and eastern Europe. It seems clear that Germany is determined, to the extent of sooner or later making war if necessary, to assert its protectorship over all the important irredentist German communities in that area. If we are determined to prevent this, also to the extent of making war if necessary, then war is inevitable.

The element of justice in Germany's claim in eastern Europe is not sufficiently recognized, due to our dislike of Germany's own internal politics. Examination of Germany's claims.

Impossibility of keeping Germany down permanently. If you try to do it, you are certain to have war. And the longer you deny Germany's reasonable claims, the more you excite unreasonable ones.

Fallacy of thinking German collapse imminent. Compare Russia.

The long-period view. A satiated Germany. What satiation means: having gained so much, Germany will fear to hazard what it has obtained by striving to gain still more. This factor would counterbalance Germany's increased strength.

Our best policy would appear to be to facilitate Germany realizing its ambitions in this part of the world, but in their least obnoxious form, i.e. a minimum of actual annexation of territory by Germany, and friendly agreements, economic and political, between Germany and the countries concerned.

It is true that this may mean strengthening fascist ideas in eastern Europe. But none of the eastern countries, except Czechoslovakia, are real democracies, and it would be disproportionate to jeopardize the peace of the whole world – and thus also the very existence of democracy – for the defence of the democratic system of the relatively small Czech population.

This is not a policy of surrender. By obtaining agreement with Germany, we strengthen our hands for the defence of what is vitally important, and put ourselves on a footing to secure more satisfactory relations with Japan and Italy.

We should not be endangering our own democracy – any more than by an understanding with Russia, and much less than by putting it to the test of war.

We should contemplate without disquiet a Russo-German détente, both as a contribution to appeasement, and as relieving tension in the Far East.

The ultimate objective would be a European appeasement which is the indispensable condition for any recreation of the collective system. In ten or twenty years, with Germany a satisfied country anxious for some kind of stabilization, and with a possible development of US policy, the circumstances may be really favourable for the re-establishment of a League system.

The League could be made to function if the discontented powers were too weak to be able effectively to challenge it. It could be made to function if all the great powers were relatively satisfied and desired stability. But in the present circumstances, with Germany dissatisfied and very powerful, a straight League policy involves the gravest danger of war.

Harold Nicolson diaries (Nicolson papers)

Wednesday, 16 March 1938

We had a meeting of the All Souls Group up in Norman Angell's Rooms. Then adjourned for sandwiches and beer in my chambers.

We began by discussing the Spanish situation, and Walter Layton told us that from telephone messages he had received from Barcelona it looked as if the Spanish government could only hold out for another three weeks. The French government have opened the frontier and are pouring in munitions. They are also contemplating seizing Spanish Morocco. Liddell Hart points out that the second German war really began in July 1936 when the Germans and the Italians transported Franco's troops across to Spain. He feels that the great mistake which we made in this country was to regard the Spanish situation from the political angle when it was, in reality, a purely military problem. Strategically, we are in a better position for war today than we should be next August, although our air defences are absolutely farcical. In other words, we have to decide between forcing an issue on the Spanish question, where we have the advantage of sea power and united opinion in this country and the unpopularity of the Spanish venture in Germany and Italy, or allowing the fascists to establish themselves in Spain and close the Straits of Gibraltar. If it happened, of course, our whole future action would be paralysed. He feels that if the present government have a policy at all, it is to put everything off until the Germans are in such a position of supremacy that we shall be unable to fight anyhow.

[. . .] get to the House. The Labour Party force an adjournment of the House for the purpose of discussing Spain. I have to go down to the City in order to address a group of bankers summoned by Falk. I do so, pointing out to them that it is a vital British interest to save something from the Spanish wreck. They accept what I say with grim determination. Then back to the House where the Spanish debate opens at 7.30.

The Prime Minister states with the utmost precision that nothing will induce him to get drawn into the Spanish muddle. I have a feeling that the sense of the House is opposed to this declaration and that the Conservative Party are really seriously alarmed at what is going on.

I am asked by all sides to take part in the debate and to point out the purely strategical aspect. I therefore do so, giving a modified version of Liddell Hart's argument and appealing for unity between the two parties in respect of the precaution [*sic*] of British rights, interests, and security. It is well received by the Opposition and not at all badly received by the Government. When I sit down, the Prime Minister passes along a message through Kingsley Wood [*Secretary of State for Health*] saying 'but what do you want us to do?' I say, 'occupy Minorca'. 'Occupy Minorca', Kingsley Wood hisses to Walter Elliot [*Secretary of State for Scotland*]. 'Occupy Minorca', Walter Elliot whispers to David Margesson [*Government Chief Whip*]. 'Occupy Minorca', David Margesson whispers to Chamberlain. The latter flings back his head with a gesture of angered despair [. . .].

I go back to KBW in a mood of slight anxiety and some depression. Thinking over the day, I find that opinion is shifting as rapidly as it did between August 1 and 3 in 1914. Even Lothian, whom I saw for a minute, said 'I know that we may have to fight'. Many people urged me to try and persuade Eden to return from the Riviera. I shall do nothing of the sort.[7]

Foreign Affairs Group, 16 March 1938 (Liddell Hart papers, LH 5/1)[8]

The meeting took place in the setting of the German coup in Austria, the apparent success of General Franco's offensive in Aragon, and the agitation in London for the government to take a more active line in Spain and Central Europe.

Spain

One of the members reported that military opinion doubted whether, in existing circumstances with the enormous material assistance being received by Franco from Germany and Italy, the Spanish government could hold out for more than three weeks.The serious strategic consequences of this for France and Great Britain were stressed, as

[7] See too entry of 16 March 1938, Harold Nicolson, *Diaries and Letters 1930–1939*, Nigel Nicolson (ed.) (London, 1966), pp. 329–330.

[8] The minutes record the following in attendance: A.L. Rowse, Radcliffe-Brown, Hudson, Layton, Barratt Brown, Allen, Macmillan, Toynbee, Liddell Hart, and Hodson; regrets came from Murray, Woodward, Adams, Salter, and Curtis.

at previous meetings. It was suggested that the 'next great war' had begun in July 1936; that its present phase was the manoeuvring for position by Germany and Italy; and that if they made good their hold in Spain they might have put themselves into a strategic position so advantageous against England and France that they would have virtually won the war. A German success in Spain would be a disaster to us, whatever policy we adopted in central Europe. If we were anxious to intervene over Czechoslovakia, it was essential that our war effort should not be extended and distracted, as it would be with Spain as a base of operations. On the other hand, if we avoided commitments east of the Rhine, our security depended on France and England being in such a position as to make an offensive against them very unattractive; and this depended on the neutrality of Spain.

It was reported that, to meet the crisis, the French frontier had been secretly opened; France had also plans for the occupation of Spanish Morocco; and if the situation grew worse Blum would be under great pressure to put these, or even more far-reaching measures, into effect. It was suggested that, as Empire communications might be affected, the dominions would probably be willing to support the British government in energetic action. But in London important members of the Cabinet remained unaware of the extent to which a Franco victory would threaten our national interests, and were still convinced that on the conclusion of the war Franco would turn out his allies and, while a section of National Government supporters in the House of Commons was very alarmed, only a handful would be ready to take action against the official line.

The measures which the group would like to see adopted in Spain, and the best means of bringing pressure on the government to consider them, were then discussed; and it was decided to send to editors of all principal newspapers a confidential aide-mémoire, explaining the gravity of the situation, and refuting inter alia the idea that Franco could make himself independent of his allies. At the same time it was understood that members would also work privately, in whatever ways offered themselves, to put across their view of the crisis. On the exact nature of the measures which the group desired the government to take there did not seem to be clear agreement; and these were therefore not mentioned in the communication to the press.

Czechoslovakia

The group then passed to a study of the Czechoslovakian problem. It was pointed out that if England and France took drastic steps in Spain, such as would concentrate attention there, Germany might well decide that was the moment for settling with Czechoslovakia.

It was remarked that, while very few Conservative Members of Parliament were in favour of action in Spain, a considerable number was ready for a pledge to Czechoslovakia.

The military position of Czechoslovakia has been worsened, but not catastrophically worsened, by the German occupation of Austria. In war, Czechoslovakia would have interior lines; its army was well equipped and well led; the plan of campaign was sound; and provided that the Czechs did not lose all power in the air, they would probably be able to hold out for a period of months against an army numerically three times as strong as their own.

It was argued that, if England did not give a pledge to Czechoslovakia, Germany would decide that it was safe to go ahead with its plans, counting on France not, in fact, intervening if England stood out. But, when the crisis arose, France *would* intervene, and we should be dragged in with her. Thus it would be the uncertainty of our attitude which would lead to war: as had happened in 1914. Moreover, failure on our part to give a pledge would strengthen the right wing in France, and lead to a further and very dangerous instability in French politics. But these views were not accepted by all the group.

The possibility of giving a pledge as a bluff, with the mental reservation that it need not necessarily be honoured, was then discussed, and it was agreed that this would be a mistake from every point of view. It might lead the Czechs to refuse agreement with Germany, which they would otherwise accept; and our bluff would almost certainly be called.

If Franco gained a complete victory in Spain, the strategic situation of France and England would be such that it would be extremely doubtful whether they could render any aid to Czechoslovakia. In such circumstances the group might need to urge caution upon the government as formerly they had urged action.

If Russia were to give any assistance to Czechoslovakia other than in the air, it would be by forcing a way through Poland and Romania. This would probably bring these countries on to the side of Germany, and it was asked whether this would not tip the balance in Germany's favour.

One view was that, if Germany invaded Czechoslovakia and France and Russia came to its assistance, England might remain neutral, provided that Italy also remained neutral. We might, however, aid France by acting as a channel of supplies, by preventing Germany from blockading France, and by keeping Spain free from German invasion.

The recent interview of Benes in the *Sunday Times*, in which he offered to negotiate with France and Great Britain for an improved status for the *Sudeten Deutsch*, was mentioned, and it was agreed that this was an important offer which should be taken up as quickly as possible. At the same time some members were of opinion that cantonalization was no solution, since it would not satisfy Germany, and would weaken Czechoslovakia. It was asked what would be our attitude if Hitler asked for a plebiscite among the *Sudenten Deutsch*, on the same terms as the Saar plebiscite, to decide on revision of frontiers.

The meeting ended without coming to a decision on Czechoslovakia: except that it was agreed that no statement should be contemplated before it was seen how events would turn in Spain; and what results were to be expected from the Anglo-Italian negotiations. There was some tendency to question whether a Czechoslovakian crisis was imminent. Germany's interests might now well be directed towards agreement with Hungary. And, if Franco was successful in Spain, Germany might prefer to work against Czechoslovakia indirectly, by intrigues in France to cause disunion and paralysis.

A decision about Czechoslovakia may have eluded the group. But some measure of agreement was reached, with another meeting being called for on Wednesday, 23 March, at 8 pm in Norman Angell's Chambers.[9]

Hodson to Liddell Hart, 16 March 1938 (Liddell Hart papers, LH 5/1)

[An aide-mémoire] was drawn up by the Foreign Affairs Group this afternoon, and approved by those who remained at the end of the discussions. It is proposed to send it, *not for publication*,[10] to newspaper editors. It is important to know at once which members of the group would like their names attached to the document for this purpose. (Reply to Miss Hole, 62 High Street, Oxford).

Liddell Hart to Hodson, 17 March 1938 (Liddell Hart papers, LH 5/1)[11]

[...] I hope that the formal letter accompanying this aide-mémoire will emphasize that the Foreign Affairs Group has been carrying out a

[9] Hole to Liddell Hart, 17 March 1938, Liddell Hart papers, LH 5/1.

[10] Rowse had already pre-empted his colleagues in the group with a letter to *The Times*, 16 March 1938. Given Spain's significance for British strategy, Rowse urged the establishment of a 'London–Paris–Madrid axis' to ensure stability in western Europe.

[11] Liddell Hart enclosed a copy of his letter to Hole and the suggested amendments to the aide-mémoire. See Liddell Hart to Hole, 17 March 1938, and Hole to Liddell Hart, 19 March 1938, Liddell Hart papers, LH 5/1.

scientific examination of the foreign situation in general during the last few months, and that these are the conclusions which it has reached as regards western Europe.

Notes on the aide-mémoire of the All Souls Group by Liddell Hart, 17 March 1938 (Liddell Hart papers, LH 5/1)

(1) I would rather not be so definite as to say that the war in Spain 'is rapidly approaching a final decision'. I would rather say that 'a final decision may come with the continued success of General Franco's offensive'.

(2) (Second paragraph). It is going beyond the facts to say that General Franco has no 'appreciable strength' of his own in aircraft, etc. To say 'small strength' would be preferable.

(3) (Page 2, iii). It would be more certain and significant to say: 'could very easily render untenable the anchorage at Gibraltar, and thus nullify its use as a naval base'.

Hodson to Liddell Hart, 18 March 1938 (Liddell Hart papers, LH 5/1)

Thank you for your letter and enclosures. I note your emendations, and I hope that it will be possible to make them. The formal letter accompanying the aide-mémoire will take the following form:

> The attached aide-mémoire is a product of discussions among a group which has been meeting during the past few months to consider problems of foreign policy. It is sent to you *for information and comment, but not for publication*, as a valuable indication of considered opinion, and as an expression of grave anxiety on an urgent issue. The group included the following:

This is not exactly what you suggest but I hope it meets with your acceptance.

Aide-mémoire on Spain (Liddell Hart papers, LH 5/1)[12]

The war in Spain, in which a final decision may come with the continued success of General Franco's offensive, carried out with the aid of German and Italian forces and war supplies, raises an issue of the greatest urgency for British foreign policy and our very security. It is even more urgent than the issue of central Europe.

A victory for the Spanish insurgents, won with this German and Italian aid, would confront Great Britain and France with a Spain under the domination of Germany and Italy. We must not delude ourselves with the idea that, in such an event, a Spanish nationalist government would be able to get rid of its foreign auxiliaries. General Franco has, at present, small strength of his own in aircraft, artillery, and other technical services, apart from the German and Italian forces. He therefore cannot dispense with these foreign forces if he is to maintain his hold on Spain. He is thus bound to accept a dictation from Rome and Berlin over his general policy; and it is not difficult to foresee the ends to which this dictation will be directed.

One of the chief objectives of German and Italian policy is to immobilize the two great west European Powers in order to obtain a free hand in achieving ambitions in other directions (e.g. Czechoslovakia). Spain could be invaluable to Germany and Italy as an instrument for paralysing Great Britain and France. Without needing to violate, in the letter, their pledges to respect the territorial integrity of Spain, they could attain their objects there by securing strategic facilities from a Spanish government which would be in no position to deny them.

A strategic hold on Spain would give Germany and Italy the following formidable advantages against Great Britain and France:

(1) From the east coast of Spain and the Balearic Islands they could harass, and possibly sever, the sea communications between France and French Africa across the western Mediterranean.

[12] The aide-mémoire on Spain reproduced here was contained in Hole to Nicolson, 19 March 1938, Liddell Hart Papers, LH 5/1. The letter listed the signatories as: Lord Allen of Hurtwood, Sir Norman Angell, W. Arnold-Forster, H.V. Hodson, G.F. Hudson, Sir Walter Layton, Captain B.H. Liddell Hart, H. Macmillan MP, Dr Gilbert Murray, Hon. H. Nicolson MP, Professor Radcliffe-Brown, A.L. Rowse, and Professor A. Toynbee. The *News Chronicle*, on 18 March 1938 used the aide-mémoire as the basis for an article from a 'military observer'. For Liddell Hart's additional views at this time, see Angell to Liddell Hart, 18 March 1938, and enclosures, Liddell Hart papers, LH 1/16/4–6, 'Military lessons from Spain', *New Republic*, 91 (4 August 1937), pp. 357–359.

(2) From the Pyrenees frontier they could threaten in the rear a France who already has two land frontiers to defend on the Rhine and on the Alps.
(3) From the south coast of Spain and Spanish Morocco they could threaten, and perhaps close, the western entrance to the Mediterranean, and could very easily render untenable the anchorage at Gibraltar, and thus nullify its use as a naval base.
(4) From the north-west corner of Spain and the Canaries they could menace the alternative route to India, Australia, and Singapore round the Cape, and our communications with West and South Africa, and South America.

For these reasons, the Spanish problem is of much more direct concern than central European problems are to the British Commonwealth as a whole, and especially to the three dominions of Australia, New Zealand, and South Africa. There is therefore every reason to think that decisive action by the United Kingdom government in regard to Spain would secure the support of the other governments of the Commonwealth.

This is not the first time that the command of the Peninsula has played a vital part in deciding the destinies of Great Britain and France. It was so in the War of the Spanish Succession, when we acquired Gibraltar, and again in the Peninsular War. The Peninsula has always been, and still is today, of critical importance for British foreign policy and for the strategic security of the British Empire.

In the Spanish theatre of operations, a camouflaged European war, with ultimate objectives far transcending any purely Spanish issues, has now been going on for more than a year and a half. At the present moment, there is imminent danger of a decision in Spain in favour of Italy and Germany. If events are simply allowed to take their course, these two powers will have obtained an advantage of such magnitude as, in all probability, to prove decisive in any subsequent European conflict.

Unless and until this Italo-German success in Spain is completed, Great Britain and France still have it in their power to save the situation. In the Peninsula, geography and sea power still tell heavily in our favour. If, however, action is not taken immediately, the possibility of acting effectively may be lost once for all.

Before the meeting scheduled for 23 March, the fluid European situation spurred several members of the group to put pen to paper, canvass opinion across a broad political spectrum, or press the government for action.

Memorandum by Alfred Barratt Brown, n.d. (Liddell Hart papers, LH 5/1)

I have kept silence during the recent discussions on international questions because I have been aware that I start out from such entirely different premises that I should unduly interrupt the line of argument.

May I at this stage, however, encouraged by the restrained and restraining memorandum from S[alter], which was circulated at our last meeting, put a few considerations before the group, as briefly as possible, and without obtruding my pacifism.

(1) My friends in the LNU have frequently assured me that when they spoke of 'collective security' they had in mind a system of agreements to combine against an aggressor that would arrest his violence and make impossible a general war.

But increasingly of late they have been advocating under the name of 'collective security' measures which, in the present circumstances of the League, would inevitably involve a European war, and that under conditions in which there could be no guarantee of success.

(2) I appreciate the courage, however quixotic, of those who advocate that we should 'put force behind law', even though the law is called in question and the force is inadequate to sustain it. But an heroic stand of the kind they advocate would seem to demand three conditions:

(a) that the nations taking part in it should be clear of the charge that under the guise of 'public law of Europe' they are supporting their own national interests and a status quo that is unjust;

(b) that they should make sure that they have the full support of those – both men and women – on whom the consequences will fall (and in the case of Great Britain, the people of the dominions as well as our own countrymen and women must be taken into account);

(c) that they should enter on the crusade with their eyes open to the probable consequences of a major war, not only in the destruction of the great cities of Europe and the suffering and panic of their populations, but also in the militarization of the democratic peoples, whether they are victorious or defeated.

I believe that if we have regard to these considerations we shall hesitate to support counsels that are fraught with so much uncertainty if not fatality, and we shall turn instead to devising measures which will, at the same time, avoid war and promote the methods of political and economic appeasement on which we are all agreed.

At least I would ask that we should refrain from urging on our government a policy that might lead to war, while endeavouring to dissuade it from condoning aggression and perpetuating injustices.

Notes on the European situation
G.F. Hudson, 18 March 1938
(Liddell Hart papers, LH 5/1)[13]

At the time of writing this memorandum (Friday, 18 March) it appears that our discussion next week will have to take account of three definite facts in the European situation:

(1) that the British government is still unwilling to do anything to assist the Spanish government, but that France is giving assistance and that for the moment Franco's forces are being held up;
(2) that the British government is still unwilling to commit itself over Czechoslovakia, but that both France and Soviet Russia are determined to go to war in case of a German attack on Czechoslovakia;
(3) that Russia is resolved, in order to fulfil the Czecho-Soviet pact, to force a passage through Poland.

The following memorandum is an attempt to estimate the bearing of these facts, beginning with the third, which appears to create a 'Polish Question' no less important than the problem of Czechoslovakia.

1. The position of Poland

Two statements have been made in Moscow with regard to the position in case of a German war on Czechoslovakia:

(1) Report of the *Daily Telegraph* Moscow correspondent (17 March) of statement by 'a high official' (name not given, but 'no one could speak with greater authority'). To quote from this report: 'He (when reminded that Russia had no common frontier with Czechoslovakia) declared: "A corridor must be created" [. . .]. The Romanian route from Russia to Czechoslovakia forms a poor and primitive line of

[13] A copy of this note was enclosed in Hole to Liddell Hart, 19 March 1938, Liddell Hart papers, LH 5/1. For a pen portrait of Hudson, see A.L. Rowse, *A Cornishman Abroad* (London 1976), pp. 191–193.

communication. The centre of the whole problem is Poland whose ideas on the passage of Red troops through her territory are well known. I can only repeat that – in view of the nature of the problems, both political and military, involved – the "high Soviet official" declares that a "corridor must be created". Or, if Poland today no longer likes the word "corridor", then let us say "a way" must be found.'

(2) Livinov's statement reported today. According to the *Daily Telegraph*: 'M. Litvinov refused to be drawn as to how the Soviet would send aid to Czechoslovakia if the need arose. He had nothing to say today regarding "corridors" to link the two countries together in a military sense. He merely said "you have a proverb, where there's a will there's a way".'

It is clear from these statements that the Russian military plan is to force a passage for the Russian army through Poland. It is clear also from the reports that the invasion would be justified by invoking the Covenant of the League, Article XVI, clause 3, in which the members of the League 'agree [. . .] that they will take the necessary steps to afford passage through their territory to the forces of any of the members of the League which are co-operating to protect the covenants of the League'. To quote again from the above report: 'If Czechoslovakia became the victim of an aggression she would immediately invoke Article XVI, under which Poland and Romania are, like everybody else, pledged to allow the passage of troops across their territories when the aggression has been proved.'

The doctrine thus asserted needs to be examined both from a legal and from a practical political point of view. As regards the legality of the proposed coercion of Poland on the basis of the League Covenant, it seems to me that such a procedure could not be justified. The wording of Article XVI is throughout very ambiguous, but I fail to see how the clause concerned could be held to cover a demand for passage of troops under a mutual assistance pact which, though compatible with the Covenant, is certainly not a part of it. Both the Franco-Soviet and Czecho-Soviet pacts have been so framed as to be compatible with the League Covenant, but, in so far as they provide for immediate action on the judgement of the signatories without a due verdict of the whole League, they cannot be regarded as binding on League members who are not signatories, and it was precisely to avoid the extra obligation that Poland refused to enter Barthou's 'Eastern Locarno', which was to have included both Poland and Russia and to have committed Poland to allow the passage of a Russian army. It is surely clear that in so far as the Czecho-Soviet pact goes beyond the League Covenant, it cannot be binding on Poland merely because of its compatibility with the Covenant.

If, on the other hand, Poland's obligation to allow the passage is claimed on the general principle that no League member can rightly be a neutral in case of an attack on another League member, we are at once (quite apart from the fact that the permanent neutrality of Switzerland was accepted by the League Council in 1920, in spite of the provisions of Article XVI) faced with the problem of 'proving' aggression which has always been a crux in the interpretation of article XVI. If each League member is left to decide separately whether aggression has taken place or not, it is open to Poland to decide differently from France and Russia; if, on the other hand, the decision is referred to the Council, Poland as a Council member could frustrate the required unanimity of states, not parties, to the dispute under Article XV. In taking such a line, Poland's motives would, no doubt, be purely political, but she would be within her legal rights, and in case of a *Sudeten Deutsch* revolt with German 'volunteer' support, the point at which 'aggression' took place might be extremely difficult to determine.

It may seem that in the present state of Europe such local points are of no importance, but in so far as our concern for Czechoslovakia is put on a moral basis, they cannot be ignored. If we are to approve of a Russian invasion of Poland in the name of collective security and the League Covenant, we should consider seriously whether it can be so justified; if, on the other hand, we approve it as a matter of sheer military necessity, then we should not deceive ourselves with sophistries of the kind suggested from Moscow.

As to the practical issue, it seems most probable that Poland, as at present constituted, will resist any Russian attempt to force a passage. According to Mme Tabouis (*Blackmail or War*, pp. 182–183) a definite military convention already exists between Poland and Romania with a view to such resistance. The present ruling elements, both in Poland and Romania, are pro-French but anti-Russian, and the efforts of France since 1934 to obtain their consent to the passage of Russian forces through their territories have merely driven them more and more into the German camp; their supreme aim is to preserve the independence of their countries in a neutral bloc between Germany and Russia, but if they cannot preserve this independence, there can be no doubt of their preference for a German rather than a Russian domination.

2. Russian policy

If it is assumed that Russia, in going to war on behalf of Czechoslovakia, would have no other aim than to preserve the independence and integrity of all the states of east central Europe against German aggression, there is no real ground for the fears of Poland and Romania. But the Warsaw and Bucharest governments do not believe that Russia's intentions are as simple as they are said to be by M. Litvinov, and to persuade them to trust Russia is a task probably beyond the powers of French diplomacy.

If, then, Poland and Romania, despite their dislike of a German ascendancy, are likely to adhere to the Rome–Berlin axis rather than allow Russian troops to pass their frontiers, are we to advocate a policy which endorses the proposal to force a passage through these states? This is a question to which I find it not at all easy to give an answer, for any answer must involve an estimate of the real aims of Russian policy, and ultimately of the character of Stalin and his regime.

In the event of a European war arising out of a German attack on Czechoslovakia, there seem to be four possible results as regards east central Europe:

(1) Germany would be decisively victorious.
(2) Germany would be defeated, and Russian troops would subsequently be withdrawn within the present frontiers of the USSR, restoring complete independence to all the states of east central Europe.
(3) Germany would be defeated and the independence of Czechoslovakia preserved, but Poland and Romania would be absorbed by the Soviet Union, probably through puppet governments set up with the aid of Russian troops.
(4) The war would end with a virtual partition of east central Europe after the Russian and German armies had met in the middle of Poland. By such a settlement a diminished Poland might be left as a buffer state, but Russia would probably acquire Vilna, the Polish Ukraine, and most of Romania, while Germany acquired Bohemia, Polish Silesia, and the Polish Corridor, and Hungary got Slovakia.

I am inclined to think that the fourth of these results would be the most likely. It would be highly satisfactory for both Hitler and Stalin, though for the former it might fall short of anticipations. It is improbable that either Hitler or Stalin would have the will to fight to the finish, for whereas a short, successful war would strengthen both these autocracies, neither of them could afford to take the risks of a prolonged struggle. The temptation to compromise at the expense of third parties would be very strong for both powers after the initial phase of the war, which would consist mainly of manoeuvres for position.

It is only nine years since Russia herself waged a war of aggression by invading Manchuria, and only four since she abandoned (owing to

Hitler's menaces) an anti-French entente with Germany and entered the League of Nations. Russia is undoubtedly alarmed at the prospect of a German-controlled *Mitteleuropa*, and in particular is afraid of an extension of German power to the Black Sea via Hungary and Romania. To prevent such an expansion of Germany and forestall Germany on the lower Danube, Russia must enter into a coalition with states hostile to Germany; there is, however, no good reason to suppose that she would be unduly concerned about the fate of Bohemia, if she had once secured for herself the passes of the eastern Carpathians, the Romanian oil wells and the mouths of the Danube – for, with the conquest of Romania, Russia would be covered against any attack from the south-west and could afford to tolerate a limited German advance. The political record of Stalin does not inspire confidence in the sincerity of his devotion to the principles of the League of Nations, and in so far as we desire to promote real 'collective security' for the states of central Europe this aspect of the problem must be very seriously considered. Do we really aim at preserving the independence of these states or do we merely want to hold Germany in check and keep a balance of great powers by calling in Russian forces? And would it really be worth while for France and England to wage a war in which they would get nothing but hard knocks, if it is likely that the main result of such a war would be a partition settlement in central Europe on the lines indicated above?

Since writing the above notes on the position of Poland I have read the news of the Polish ultimatum to Lithuania. It is not yet clear whether or not this will lead to war, but in any case the crisis is closely related to the Russo-Polish tension. If Russia is to invade Poland in case of a Czecho-German war, the obvious course for Poland is to try and dispose in advance of the implacable enemy on her left flank – for Lithuania would almost certainly throw in her lot with Russia, in the hope of obtaining Vilna, as soon as the Russian army crossed the Polish frontier.

3. The idea of a west European bloc

In the circumstances of the present European situation we have to ask: (1) whether a general European war on a central European issue would be likely to yield any result adequate to be set against the universal devastation it would involve; and (2) whether a retreat of France and England 'behind the Maginot Line' would involve a loss of essential security and leave them at the mercy of the fascist powers. I have suggested a negative answer to the first question and I would give a similar reply to the second on one condition, namely, that Spain is delivered from the Italo-German invasion. I believe that a London–Paris–Madrid axis would be strong enough to maintain itself against the Rome–Berlin axis even if Germany were to extend her rule further in central Europe; such a compact geographical grouping would provide the maximum of security and the minimum of provocation. It would imply a large measure of surrender; it could not be justified as anything but a lesser evil; yet it appears to offer the best chance of avoiding a general European war without fatally compromising the independence of France and Britain.

Allen to Cecil,[14] 19 March 1938 (Quoted in Gilbert, *Plough My Own Furrow*, p. 399)

A declaration in advance made by Russia and Britain that they would go to war to defend Czechoslovakia would be taken by Germany as a modern form of an actual ultimatum, though it would be described as a 'deferred ultimatum'. Once a declaration is made the Germans may consider that the ultimatum has come from our side.[15]

Cecil to Allen, 22 March 1938 (Allen papers, box 15, correspondence, 1937–1938)

Thank you very much for your letter.

I do not think I have ignored the point which you make. The difficulty in my mind is this: the French are, by their treaty, bound to go to the assistance of Czechoslovakia and, as far as I can make out, they intend to carry out their obligation. If that is so, I do not see how we could avoid – from any point of view – going to the assistance of

[14] 1st Viscount Cecil of Chelwood (1864–1958) Parliamentary Under-Secretary for Foreign Affairs, 1915–1918; Assistant Secretary of State, Foreign Affairs, 1918–1919; Lord Privy Seal, 1923; Chancellor of the Duchy of Lancaster, 1924–1927; Nobel Peace Prize, 1937.

[15] This was in response to a letter Cecil had written to Allen on 16 March 1938 thus: 'I personally doubt very much whether Germany would attack Czechoslovakia for instance if she knew that she would have against her France, Russia and ourselves.' Allen papers, box 15, correspondence, 1937–1938. In public, too, Allen continued to campaign in favour of appeasement. Negotiations with the dictators must be free of any preconditions, he argued. Good faith was the result not the precondition of talks. 'Let us neither madden dictators with too rigid emphasis upon law', he stated, 'nor woo them with baits and concessions'. Quoted in Gilbert, *Plough My Own Furrow*, p. 395.

France. It would be insane to allow her to be knocked out and then have to face Germany alone a little later on. It was that policy that brought France to grief in 1870. But if we do believe that we shall have to fight, with France, it seems to me that we have a better chance to avoid having to do so by making our position clear in good time.

Fundamentally I am afraid that you and I do disagree, because you believe that it is advantageous to negotiate with and try to placate the dictators. I am, unfortunately, convinced that a policy of that kind merely increases their prestige without making it materially less probable that they will adopt an aggressive attitude.

However, I personally entirely assent to your last paragraph, though I admit that I have not been able to agree with your recent action, yet I have never privately or publicly attributed it to anything like disloyalty.

Nicolson to Cadogan,[16] 21 March 1938 (FO371/22641, W4440/83/41)

During the last few months a group of people of all shades of opinion who are interested in foreign policy have been meeting for weekends at All Souls. The meetings have been of considerable value to us in that they have done much to clear our minds.

At out last meeting we decided to draw up an aide-mémoire upon the Spanish situation, since we felt that opinion in this country had not realized that Italy and Germany, under a cloak of ideology, were really occupying vital strategical points behind our back.

We therefore drew up the enclosed memorandum (incorrectly called an aide-mémoire) which we have sent to the editors of all the leading papers. We have asked these editors to keep the memorandum for their own information and not to publish it either as an article or as a letter. This would only do harm.

The memorandum has been signed by Allen of Hurtwood, Norman Angell, Arnold-Forster, H.V. Hodson of the Round Table, Walter Layton, Liddell Hart, Harold Macmillan, Gilbert Murray, A.L. Rowse, Arnold Toynbee, and myself.

I think it may be of some interest to you. I am sending another copy to Dunglass, the Prime Minister's PPS.[17]

[16] Sir Alexander Cadogan (1884–1968) Foreign Office, 1914–1918; Head of League of Nations section, 1921–1933; Minister at Peking, 1934–1935; Deputy and then Permanent Under-Secretary of State, 1936–1946.

[17] The list of signatories which Nicolson gave to Cadogan left out Hudson and Radcliffe-Brown. To a fellow MP, Nicolson summed up his efforts thus: 'All I have tried to do is to

Harold Nicolson diaries
(Nicolson papers)

Thursday, 22 March 1938

[...] I have to do an article for *Time and Tide* in answer to Scrutator's last article in the *Sunday Times*. In that article he had taken the view that Czechoslovakia was not a British interest. My line is that this is a dishonest point of view and the only honest point of view is to say that it is a British interest but that we are not strong enough to defend it [...]. I am not going to vote against the government if they will say frankly that we cannot risk a European war in order to defend Czechoslovakia. What we are trying to get the Prime Minister to do is to adopt our All Souls formula – namely pressure on the Czechs, to give greater concessions to the *Sudeten* Germans, coupled with some assurances that if they do that we will protect their frontier. The difficulty is, of course, that Germany has now no need actually to violate Czechoslovakian territory but can squeeze the Czechs into any shape she likes.

In the interim, another member of the group, Lord Allen, drew up a twenty-eight-page memorandum, entitled 'Foreign policy now'. The mandate for the exercise derived from the meeting on 26 February 1938. The document tabled then was now expanded into nine chapters.

'Foreign policy now', n.d.
(Liddell Hart papers, LH 5/1)

Introduction

This paper is the outcome of six week-end discussions on foreign policy by a group of people drawn from different parties not including the extreme political right or left.

Our object was to think out, as precisely as was possible for us as laymen, what kind of foreign policy we should like to see the British

wake people up to the Spanish danger.' Nicolson to Paul Emrys-Evans, 22 March 1938, add.ms. Evans 58248, fo. 50, British Library, London. For Cadogan's reply and Nicolson's angry retort see below, pp. 144–145.

government following now; what should be the long-range objective and direction, and what kind of action should be taken in the present dangerous circumstances.

In considering such a policy, we did not try either to make our proposals conform with what we believed to be the present government's outlook, or to contribute to the propaganda of opposition to this government. We did not discuss questions of political strategy such as the demand for a general election; we did not ask ourselves, as a group, whether, assuming the policy of this paper to be sound, it was reasonable to hope that the present government could be persuaded to adopt and carry it out with the necessary conviction and resource. In short, we confined ourselves to the enormous question indicated in our title – 'Foreign policy now'.

We met with no preconceived agenda and no initial resolve to try to produce a memorandum for private or public circulation. But certain conclusions emerged so clearly from our non-partisan discussions, and these conclusions appear to us to be so relevant to the present crisis, that we finally decided to prepare and publish this paper, in the hope that it may contribute something towards a sound estimate of the actual choice before the nation.

In jointly signing this introduction and commending the following pages, we do not commit ourselves to endorsement of every detail of the proposals; but we are in agreement on the general policy here proposed, believing that, whilst no course is free from risk, this policy indicates the most practical way of ensuring peace, promoting international justice and economic welfare, and safeguarding political liberty and democracy.

[Signatures]

Chapter 1: The present situation

The nation is now faced with much the most dangerous situation that has arisen since the Great War. Indeed, it is probably fair to say that civilized man has never before been confronted with so fearful a man-made disaster as that which hangs over western Europe now. Modern weapons, particularly the bombing aeroplane, have created a now problem of survival for urban mankind.

The danger has been enormously increased since 1931, when Japan invaded Manchuria: since 1933–1934 when the last chances of pulling some agreement out of the wreckage of the Disarmament Conference were thrown away: since 1935–1936, when the League's power to restrain the aggressor in the Ethiopian war was used half-heartedly and too late: and above all since July 1936, when the Italo-German collaboration with the rebel forces in Spain gave to the Spanish struggle the character of an international war of aggression.

Today, beyond doubt, confidence in the League guarantees of collective defence against aggression has crumbled to dust. Today, the League has not the backing which could still make it a potent instrument of collective security, or of peaceful change, or of general disarmament. And so today competition in armaments has become more frantic in pace and far more dangerous in character than ever in history before; and the great open alliance against war, which the League should be, is treated as if it were of no value to our own country or to others. 'Each for himself, and Devil take the hindmost'. The old description of anarchy has become today's description of the policy of most of the governments. Will the Devil take the lot? Or will the governments have the strength and vision to stand together in defending the elements of peaceful order? That question has become fearfully urgent. For in truth, the world war is with us already: in the military and strategic sense, if not in the political sense, it has begun. It began in July 1936, if not in September 1931.

At this moment, war is raging over a vast area in Asia. It is destroying the life of Spain. It has just been used, in effect, to smash the independence of Austria: and it may be used tomorrow to smash the independence of Lithuania. It continues, even now, in Ethiopia. And week by week the aggressor powers are mastering new strategic positions; now on the flank of Czechoslovakia, now on the Atlantic seaboards, now in the Pyrenees, now in the Mediterranean. The strategic position of France and of England and of the British dominions is being changed, apparently worsened, with every new resolute blow by the dictators. Somewhere, somehow, some day, a stand will be made. Where? In what conditions? For what cause, and in what company, would British power be used, if it has to be used, in war? And for what objective should the efforts of British diplomacy be directed now, when the fatal cry of '*Sauve qui peut*' has been raised?

Chapter 2: Rebuild the collective peace system

Our long-range objectives

The nation has to choose, more realistically than ever before, between two directions which British foreign policy might follow.

Should the object of British diplomacy be to 'make anarchy work' for as long as possible without an actual explosion on our own doorstep? Should we go on improvising methods for dealing with each crisis as it arises, guided by no principles other than that suggested by our own interpretation of our own national interest?

Or should the object [be] to create conditions in which a collective peace system can function properly; a system which does genuinely provide, *inter alia*, for collective action to prevent and stop aggression, for the promotion of peaceful change of existing rights, and for general disarmament under international supervision?

Should British power be used simply as an instrument of national policy, either in complete isolation or in co-operation with a few other members of an exclusive alliance directed against certain 'prospective enemies'?

Or should British power be used rather as a contribution to the collective defence of certain standards of peaceful behaviour – standards whose observance is to the interest of every peace-keeping people?

The nation is confronted now with the broad choice between these two kinds of foreign policy, not only because of the challenging action of the German, Italian, and Japanese governments, but also because of the challenging words of the Prime Minister in his speeches of 22 February and 7 March.

Collective security abandoned: Prime Minister's speeches

In his speech of 22 February, Mr Chamberlain apparently rejected the principle of collective security as being both impracticable and undesirable. He said that 'the League as constituted today is unable to provide collective security for anybody'; that 'today you will not find anywhere in the League any conviction that collective security can be provided by the League as now constituted': that the League cannot be expected to use its powers, and that 'the nations which remain in the League must not be saddled with liabilities or risks which they are not prepared to undertake. Nor must other nations expect that the League will provide that security which it was once hoped it would provide.' Mr Chamberlain did not stop short at saying that the League could not now, in its present condition, provide collective security for anybody: he indicated that he was opposed to sanctions altogether. 'I doubt very much whether the League will ever do its best work as long as its members are nominally bound to impose sanctions or to use force in support of obligations.'

Strangely enough, after this emphatic repudiation, Mr Chamberlain said that he was not in favour of deleting a single article from the Covenant, not even Article XVI, which pledges us to certain sanctions in the event of a state resorting to war in breach of the Covenant.

It is evident that Mr Chamberlain's rejection of the principle of collective defence was no mere *obiter dictum*: for his speech on defence on 7 March included a statement of the four purposes for which the new armament programmes are being designed and this statement excluded any reference to our obligations under the Covenant as completely as if it had been made in 1914. 'Our first main effort', he said, 'must have two main objectives: we must protect this country, and we must preserve the trade routes upon which we depend for our food and raw materials. Our third objective is the defence of British territories overseas from attack, whether by sea, or by land or air [. . .]. Our fourth and last objective is co-operation in the defence of the territories of any allies we might have in case of war.'

A change of policy?

We asked ourselves, in our discussions, whether these speeches indicated a major change of policy, or whether they represented only a change of method or a change of emphasis. We were agreed in thinking that they do register a change of profound importance – a change even more important to the life of the nation than the abandonment of free trade in favour of protectionism.

It may be contended, with much force, that the view now expressed openly by Mr Chamberlain does not really mark a new departure since it only puts into words the policy actually pursued by the National Government since the fall of Addis Ababa. Certainly the British government has not, during these last two years, shown by its action any whole-hearted belief in the principle of pooled defence except in the solitary and heartening case of the Nyon Agreement. But hitherto it has been possible, with the help of various ministerial declarations, to claim that the British government did still stand, nominally at any rate, for the entire policy outlined in the Covenant. Here, for instance, are three statements on collective security which were made by members of the government in 1935.

> *Mr Eden, May 1935*: It is clear that our part should be to pursue a foreign policy that is frank, stalwart, and above all firm in support of the League of Nations and of the collective peace system. We shall always be found ranged on the side of the collective peace system against any government or people who seek by a return to pre-war politics to break up the peace which, by that system, we are seeking to create.

> *Sir Samuel Hoare, as Foreign Secretary, 11 September 1935*: In conformity with its precise and explicit obligations the League stands, and my country stands with it, for the collective maintenance of the Covenant in its entirety, and particularly for steady and collective resistance to all acts

> of unprovoked aggression. The attitude of the British nation in the past few weeks has clearly demonstrated the fact that this is no variable and unreliable sentiment but a principle of international conduct to which they and their government hold with a firm, enduring, and universal persistence.
>
> *Mr Chamberlain, 1935*: If the League were to abdicate its functions under the Covenant, then every weak nation would first begin to arm, then to seek alliance with its strongest neighbour and before long the peace of Europe would be at the mercy of the biggest and strongest power in Europe.

It was in accordance with the spirit of these declarations that the leaders of the three parties forming the National Government issued their manifesto to the nation during the Election of November 1935:

> The League of Nations will remain, as heretofore, the keystone of British foreign policy. The prevention of war and the establishment of settled peace in the world must always be the most vital interest of the British people, and the League is the instrument which has been framed, and to which we look, for the attainment of these objects. We shall therefore do all in our power to uphold the Covenant and to maintain and increase the efficiency of the League. In the present unhappy dispute between Italy and Abyssinia, there would be no wavering in the policy we hitherto pursued.

Comparing these declarations with the Prime Minister's recent speeches, we cannot doubt that there has been a radical change of direction in the government's policy. Evidently Mr Chamberlain has completely lost faith in the League as a potential instrument of collective security. 'At the last election it was still possible', he says, 'to hope that the League might afford collective security. I believed it myself. I do not believe it now.'

Is collective defence a desirable objective?

We went on to ask ourselves, in our discussions, whether the building up of a reliable system of collective security is a desirable objective: and whether, assuming this to be desirable, there is any prospect of achieving it through the weakened League of Nations.

Take first the question of desirability. On this fundamental issue our group found itself nearly, though not quite, unanimous.

We agreed, most of us, in holding that the definitive abandonment by the League of its principles of collective defence would almost certainly mean the dissolution of the League, would destroy whatever chance remains of stopping the armaments race before some shattering explosion occurs, and would involve the gravest danger to the security of the scattered and vulnerable British Commonwealth.

We shall not attempt here to set out fully our grounds for this belief. (A fuller statement of the argument than is possible here was given in a book, *The Next Five Years*, which many of us endorsed.) But the main points that emerged from our discussions may here be summarized.

Firstly, we held that sanctions are an indispensable part, though only a part, of the needed barrier against war. Of course, the world community needs also a practical method of determining impartially what changes of existing rights are desirable in the general interest, and a method of ensuring that such changes shall be carried out with the minimum risk of war. The world urgently needs all-round limitation and reduction of armaments, under international supervision. But these and other necessary elements of an acceptable world order are not alternative to collective defence: they are complementary to it. One of the plainest lessons of the post-war years has been that such objectives as general disarmament and peaceful change will not be accepted by the anxious countries except in conjunction with collective security. If the community offers no guarantees of pooled defence against lawless violence, then no government in these anxious countries can induce its people to renounce anything of their power or possessions. Thus, the re-vindication of the League's sanctions is one of the conditions necessary for advance along the road of closer co-operation towards the elimination of the war method and towards the creation of some kind of pacific confederacy of the nations.

In short, in our view, it is not true that the League will do its best work if it has no call upon its members 'to use force in support of moral obligations'. If the League cannot enlist the power of its members for the lawful purpose supporting elementary obligations of peace-keeping, then the power of the nations will not be left unused; it will be used lawlessly as an instrument of self-judged and conflicting national interests.

But these general arguments in favour of the principle of sanctions occupied little time in our discussions. We were more concerned to review what would be the probable effect of a definitive abandonment of sanctions by the League, and what are the present consequences of the failure to carry out the existing obligations.

Beyond dispute, there is now a complete and general lack of confidence that collective security will be effectively provided by the League. (That is not to say that the League could not act effectively anywhere, but only that the will to act collectively appears to be lacking under present conditions. Nor does it amount to saying that confidence could not be restored if a strong lead were given by British and France in co-operation with Russia, and with the goodwill of the United States.) Why has confidence thus crumbled away? Not because an engine, wholly independent of the League's members, has been fairly tested and has provided itself incapable of achieving the purposes of collective defence: but rather because certain members of the League, notably the British and French governments, have in the last few years been unwilling to carry out resolutely and in good time their obligations under the sanctions article of the Covenant. Events have shown that the policy of retreat has not reduced but has greatly increased the risks of a world-wide explosion. If now the British government throws over altogether the policy of collective security, the effect will be to quicken apprehension and to encourage isolationism. It is perhaps no accident that the Prime Minister's speech of 22 February has already been followed by the most menacing words and actions on the part of Germany that have been known since 1918. And it is certainly no accident that the French chamber has since reaffirmed, with the utmost possible emphasis, its continued faith in the principle of collective security, and its continued resolve to sustain France's engagements to Czechoslovakia and to Soviet Russia.

We were continually being reminded, during our discussions, both before and after the Prime Minister's speech, of the dangerous consequences of liquidating the League's open alliance against aggression. It was pointed out that, to the extent to which this open alliance against war is weakened, French policy always turns towards the much more dangerous policy of exclusive alliances directed, in effect, against Germany. It was pointed out that Soviet Russia is now an indispensable contributor to the collective power on the League's side; if Russia had to be counted out, there would be little chance of enlisting on the League's side that preponderant power which is indispensable. Russia joined the League after Japan and Germany had left it, not simply from altruism, but chiefly for the good reason that she looked to it as a contributor to her own security against war in the east and the west. If now the League's guarantee of collective defence were to be abandoned, then, as M. Litvinoff warned the League Council in January last, Russia's attitude towards the League would be reconsidered. Nothing emerged more clearly from our discussions than this: there would be immense danger to the world in any policy which drove Russia back towards isolationism, towards Trotskyism, or towards a military alliance with Nazi Germany. Not least of these dangers would be the danger of the intensification of class warfare in France and elsewhere.

Another point stressed during our discussions was the injurious effect which a repudiation of the principle of collective defence would have upon formed American opinion. It was pointed out that whenever the League Powers have shown themselves willing, in recent years, to take risks in support of the Covenants of Peace, there has been a quick growth of American sympathy for the League: but that, on the contrary, whenever League members have appeared to be using their power simply for defence of their own national interests, leaving the League aside, American opinion has swung back towards isolationism. If, for instance British power in the Far East is used, apparently, only for the defence of a British ambassador or of Hong Kong, and not at all for the defence of China and the fulfilment of the pledges of the Covenant, then America takes the line that such a struggle is no concern of hers. 'Each for himself and Devil take the hindmost' is an infectious doctrine. If Britain says to the anxious countries of central Europe '*Sauve qui peut*', then these countries will, as Mr Chamberlain predicted in 1935 'first begin to arm, then to seek alliances with their strongest neighbour, and before long the peace of Europe would be at the mercy of the biggest and strongest power in Europe'. That is, of course, what is happening in Europe now. If we suppose that the adhesion of the smaller powers, such as the Scandinavian democracies, is of no substantial importance, we are blind both to the value of their economic and material resources and to the moral significance of their collaboration.

As for the British dominions, our discussion reminded us that there is only one basis on which we can expect to harmonize the external policy of all these diverse units, namely, their common interest in the maintenance of such standards of peace and justice as the Covenant embodies. The slogan 'My country right or wrong' is only good enough nowadays for peoples who have been blinded by nationalism: the slogan 'My mother country right or wrong' is certainly not good enough for the peoples which have managed to achieve the Statute of Westminister.

As for Great Britain itself, and the colonial empire, such an alliance against war as the collective peace system might represent is surely a necessity. No empire is so scattered or more vulnerable. If that empire is to be defended in time of war Britannia cannot hope to do the job alone, especially in waters east of Singapore. If Great Britain, with her extraordinary dependence upon export trade and imported food and raw materials, wants to live at peace and be rid of the burden and risks of the armament race, she cannot afford to stand aside from, or to weaken, the collective peace system of the League, which still offers the best hope of peaceful order and a fair deal for the British trader overseas. If Britain is now within easy striking distance of the bombing squadrons of Europe, she certainly cannot afford to allow her potential supporters in Europe to be subjugated one by one. In short, in the world which has been transformed by the invention of the bombing aeroplane, this country must desire the building up of a collective peace system. And such a system cannot exist if this country, with its great power, is not willing to afford to others such mutual assistance against lawless violence as it will need to receive from them.

Is a collective peace system practicable?

Assuming, then, that a collective peace system is desirable, we then discussed the question of whether what remains of the League's obligation of collective defence can be kept alive and can be developed into a reliable system after the injuries and betrayals that the League has suffered. Is this objective still attainable?

We recognized, of course, that the present situation could hardly be more dangerous, and that after so many failures, shameful or excusable, to apply the sanctions of the Covenant, the flight from collective security has gone very far indeed. For the time being, at any rate, the League's guarantees afford no reliable assurance to the anxious countries and no serious deterrent to the aggressive powers. In these circumstances, the rebuilding of a real collective security must inevitably be slow and difficult. Even if the British government, with the vast power now at its command, were fully persuaded of the need, and were now, as part of its task of democratic leadership, explaining to the country the case for 'steady and collective resistance to all acts of unprovoked aggression', there could be no immediate transformation, though the effect would soon become profound.

We recognized also that sanctions can never achieve their purpose of preventing and stopping aggression unless there exists, actually and manifestly, a preponderance of power on the League's side. The preponderance must be sufficiently evident to discourage a would-be aggressor from gambling, and to encourage the League's supporters to take the risk of participation in the sanctions. No government is likely to be able to enlist the support of its people for economic or military sanctions if the enterprise appears from the outset to be doomed to failure. It will always be difficult to induce a nation to renounce its trade with an aggressor if it believes that the only effect of such renunciation would be to transfer the trade to someone else.

With Germany, Italy, and Japan outside the League and in opposition to its principles, and with the United States outside and incalculable, although sympathetic, there are only three powers within the League which possess great armed strength individually. What estimate should be made now of the armed strength of Russia, after the execution of so many of the military chiefs for alleged or actual treason? We found it impossible, in our discussions, to give an adequate answer to this momentous question. What is certain is that, on paper at any rate, the Russian power on land and in the air is colossal. It is clear too – only too clear – that without that power the League's authority would be dependent upon a dangerously slight superiority of strength or no superiority at all. Thus, for many reasons, it is of the first importance that Britain as well as France should maintain close co-operation with the Soviet government.

It would be a great mistake to write off as unimportant the military contribution of some of the smaller powers, notably Czechoslovakia. And we should be blind if we ignored the importance of the economic power and the control of raw materials possessed by such countries as Canada and Sweden.

It should not be forgotten, in these days when defeatism is widespread, that the League still has fifty-six members, representing between them four-fifths of the population of the globe and controlling the great bulk of the raw materials indispensable for any prolonged war. It may be objected that the danger that we now have to face is not so much the danger of a prolonged war but the danger of a sudden, fearfully destructive, quickly decisive blow. That is true to some extent; but, as we were repeatedly reminded during our discussions, there is reason to think that the strength of the defence is now very great in relation to the strength of the offensive. These developments tends to favour the success of a collective defence.

The power is there on the League's side. What of the will to use it? And what of the confidence that it will be used resolutely and in good time?

The nations which may be called upon to bear the major risks and burdens of collective defence will certainly refuse to commit themselves in advance unless they feel that the risks are sufficiently limited and foreseeable. Rightly or wrongly, the authors of the Covenant did not try to make the new-born League into a world government with executive power and armed forces under its own direct authority. There is not now an organically international force, and the conditions for creating such a force appear to be lacking at present. In these circumstances, the League has to rely upon the contingents which its members may be willing to contribute 'to protect the covenants of the League'. And no nation will commit itself to risks which might prove mortal, in contingencies which are quite unpredictable.

We did not try in our discussions to define appropriate limitations of the obligation to co-operate in sanctions. We recognized that the limitations imposed by geography and by armed strength must be admitted and must be given a very wide interpretation under present conditions. And we recognized that Article XVI of the Covenant, the sanctions article, is by no means a well-drafted text.

The point was made, in particular, that the two kinds of obligation which are included in the first paragraph of Article XVI should be clearly differentiated. By the first part of this paragraph League members are obliged to cut off their own commercial relations with a Covenant-breaking state – a measure which would involve only 'municipal' action at home. But the paragraph goes on to impose an obligation to cut off commerce between the Covenant-breaker and states outside the League – a measure which might involve the use of naval force, and might result in a serious danger of clash with the nine-member state. Clearly, this latter provision, desirable as it may be in theory, is quite different in character from the other and involves much more formidable risks.

Lastly we recognized that, if the sanctions are to achieve their primary purpose of preventing war and of creating that confidence in which policies of appeasement and disarmament can succeed, they must be made as predictable as possible. In this connection, we tried to answer responsibly this searching question. 'If you were Foreign Secretary, would you seek Cabinet authority and national backing for a declaration, more explicit than Mr Eden's speech at Leamington in November 1936, that this country would at once go to the aid of Czechoslovakia in the event of her being the victim of aggression?' Our answer to that question is given in the following chapter.

To sum up: our discussion led us to agreement, broadly speaking, that the development of a working collective peace system is a supremely desirable objective; and that this objective could in all probability still be realized, granted resolute and persistent British leadership. But certainly it cannot be attained quickly or without steady effort and firm conviction.

League policy now

We should like to see the British government reaffirm that the main and persistent object of British policy is to help in rebuilding a collective peace system such as will afford to all nations, including Britain, reliable collective defence against aggression, and effective means of promoting peaceful change of existing rights and general disarmament. The government should declare that it is prepared to join in using every opportunity, whenever conditions offer a reasonable prospect of success (as at Nyon) to enlist preponderant power behind law, either by economic or military collective action.

All suggestions for emasculating the Covenant, e.g. by eliminating Article XVI, should be resisted. But every effort should be made to demonstrate the sincerity of the claim that the sanctions are not retained simply as a means of crystallizing a questionable status quo.

The government should reaffirm its earlier declaration in favour of the signing of a new protocol whereby the League Covenant and the statutes of the ILO would be re-subscribed without being associated with the Treaties of Peace.

The government should use its influence to secure the maximum amount of practical co-operation by non-members of the League with the League, on the basis of the common interest of all peoples in the maintenance of law and order and in the expansion of mutually advantageous services. Powers who are not members of the League might, when suitable occasion offers, be invited to discuss whether they would be prepared to regard any war or threat of war as a matter of concern to themselves as signatories of the Kellogg pact; whether in such a case they would be prepared to confer with the members of the League without thereby accepting any commitment to take action; whether they would also be prepared to undertake that, in the event of their endorsing the League's judgement about an aggression, they would do nothing to prejudice the League's war-stopping sanctions; and whether they would themselves consider, in such a case, withholding aid from the aggressor country.

The government, especially now when it has embarked upon an immense armament programme, should be at pains to prove by its action that British power would be used not simply to safeguard British interests but as a contribution to the collective power required for the promotion of justice and the protection of law. Unless Britain makes this clear to the United States and other countries, she may find herself without sympathy, without moral support, and without that economic and military aid which she may find indispensable in a day of trouble.

Chapter 3: The layman's role

In the previous chapter we discussed the direction, the long-range objective, of Britain's foreign policy. We turn now to some of the immediate problems.

Our discussion of these problems was prefaced and governed by as thorough a review as we could make of the probable risks of action, and of inaction, in each case. In making this review, we were deeply conscious that a group of people in our unofficial position lacking such exact, up-to-date knowledge of the armaments and defences of this and other countries, can only make an approximate estimate of these risks. Is London, for instance, dangerously lacking, at present, in such defences against air attack as could be provided? If so, how soon will this be repaired? Is the nation's storage of food in peacetime sufficient to enable this island to tide over a serious interruption of imports in wartime? Has the military power of Russia been seriously weakened by the sweeping 'purges' of the military and naval personnel? Such questions as these need answering with the help of such secret information as only the technical advisers of the Cabinet possess. We recognize fully that, whenever we recommend in the following pages that some line of policy should be chosen, the counsel we venture to offer must always be liable to qualification in the light of some facts which only the government has access to. We are entitled, as laymen, to say that in our view some particular course appears to be less dangerous than another; but allowance must always be made for the incompleteness of our information, within a certain limited but very important sphere. But to say this is not to say that such an attempt to assess the relative merits of this and that foreign policy is necessarily a waste of time unless it is undertaken by those who have access to the information of the Committee of Imperial Defence. Far from it.

The task must be undertaken unofficially as well as officially if the democratic system is to work effectively. And the layman may have a special contribution to bring: he may be more sensitive than the government's technical advisers to the movements of public opinion – movements which must be taken into account in choosing a foreign policy; he may be in some ways better placed for choosing between the ultimate risks of action and of inaction than those whose whole attention has to be devoted wholly to the technical problems of the fighting services. We make no apology, therefore, for expressing strong opinions as to the choice of policies which do involve risks of war; our proposals must, as we have emphasized, be subject to the reserve imposed by the fact that we are not in an official position: but such proposals, from unofficial and therefore incompletely informed sources, are a most necessary contribution to the answer given by a democratic nation to the supreme question – 'For what purpose shall this nation's power and influence be used?'

Chapter 4: Spain

We have assumed, throughout this paper, that there is some interest or principle which the bulk of the people of this country would be willing to fight for. At some point, rightly or wrongly, the British will say 'Halt', if that interest or principle is challenged: they will risk their lives, and use the colossal killing-machine which they have paid for, in order to enforce that 'Halt'.

What should Britain defend? We have argued in an earlier chapter that British power should be used not simply in defence of British interests, in the narrow interpretation of that phrase, but as a contribution to the defence of 'the Constitution' – the world's generally accepted standards of peace-keeping.

Where should this defence be made? We have suggested that peace-breaking anywhere must be regarded as a matter of deep concern to this country; but that the extent to which this country could make an effective contribution to the collective defence against violence must always be conditioned by circumstances – by geographical situation, by military and economic strength, and especially by the amount of support for collective action which would be certainly and promptly available.

At this moment, the question – 'Where can Britain's power and influence be used most effectively, for defence against the far-reaching aggressions of Japan, Italy and Germany?' is the most urgent in politics. In a strategic sense, the 'world war' is going on now, and the aggressive powers have been rapidly capturing the strategic positions which will give them a stranglehold. Where, when, and how should British power be used, if it is ever to be used in support of the Covenant or in defence of Czechoslovakia, or of France, or of the British Commonwealth, or of the British Isles?

The answer which emerged from our discussions was – '*In Spain, now*, in collaboration with France and other loyal members of the League.'

It is in Spain, rather than in Czechoslovakia, that British power – which is still in the main naval power – can be brought to bear most effectively.

It is in Spain, in Catalonia now, [*footnote in original: 'This is written on March 19th, 1938'*] that the danger of a new victory for aggression is most imminent.

It is in Spain that the most obvious and far-reaching danger to British and French interests would arise if aggression were to triumph. If the Italian and German invaders enable Franco to subdue the whole of Spain, only the blindest optimist can suppose that there will be no danger that German aeroplanes will find convenient bases on the south side of the Pyrenees; or that Italian aeroplane and submarines will have no opportunity of commanding the route from French Africa to France; or that German submarines will have no station on the trade routes to the Cape and the East; or that Gibraltar and the Straits will not be menaced. From an Imperialist standpoint, at any rate, these are very important interests: and the dangers that would result from domination of the Mediterranean and Atlantic seaways by the German and Italian dictators are the concern of every democrat.

The disastrous experiment called 'non-intervention' has been in reality a competition in interventions on the rebel side and the government side, the intervention for the rebels being resolute and on great scale, the intervention on behalf of the lawful government of Spain being half-hearted and on a far lesser scale.

The claim has been made that 'non-intervention', though far from complete, has kept us out of war, and should be continued lest we should burn our fingers. But this 'non-intervention' policy is even now burning much more than our fingers.

The claim is made that at long last, after many lies and evasions and delays, the negotiations for withdrawal of the so-called 'volunteers' may be about to result (in connection with an Anglo-Italian agreement) in some actual withdrawals of Italian forces in Spain. We deal below with the difficulty of ensuring that these withdrawals shall really be of such a character as to leave Spain to the Spaniards. But even if no such difficulties existed, the fact is that the withdrawals may now, in all probability, come too late to weaken General Franco's blows against Barcelona and Madrid. The aggression will have succeeded before, not after, foreign aggressors have made any substantial reduction of their forces. Why, indeed, should any other outcome be expected, under present conditions? Have not Mussolini and Hitler alike declared their determination not to tolerate 'Bolshevism' – i.e. the Spanish government – in Spain?

We consider that 'non-intervention' is an experiment which has been tried out, and that, whatever its merits, the will to work it honestly has been found lacking. We consider that it is doing deadly injury now to the government of Spain, and to the interests of France and Britain and the democratic peoples generally. We hope that this failure will be frankly recognized forthwith, and that the Spanish government will have restored to it its right to obtain arms and supplies from abroad. We hope that the purchase and transport of such supplies from Great Britain will be facilitated. And we consider, on such information as we possess, that the British government should inform the French government that it will contribute naval force to whatever action France may think fit to take, as a fellow member of the League, to prevent the victory of the Rome–Berlin Axis in Spain.

This is, in our view, the lesser risk.

Chapter 5: Italy

For good or ill, official conversations with Italy have now been begun. What kind of outcome should be regarded as satisfactory?

Circumstances in which the negotiations began

Firstly we recalled in our discussion the extraordinary circumstances in which these negotiations were undertaken.

The Cabinet decided on 20 February to reject Mr Eden's counsel, knowing that his resignation would result; and it did so at a moment when Herr Hitler had just made a strong public attack on the Foreign Secretary, and when the official Italian press was conducting a campaign against him and announcing that negotiations would be impossible 'until British policy ceases to be directed by Mr Eden'. We asked ourselves why the Cabinet did this, and did it at a moment so extremely unpropitious. We could only infer that the Italian communication to the British government on 18 February had really been of so pressing and menacing a character as to make an immediate decision necessary; and that the Cabinet at its long special meetings during the following weekend, decided that the manifest risks of throwing over their Foreign Minister under these conditions were less than the risks of accepting his considered advice.

The Cabinet decided to open official conversations with Italy forthwith, despite the Italian attitude, and despite Mr Eden's insistence that, 'progress should first have been made with the fulfilment of engagements already entered into before seeking to negotiate other agreements covering the same issues'. Mr Eden, with his close experience of the Italian government's prolonged evasions and repeated breaches of faith, has warned the nation that negotiations thus undertaken will not, in his opinion, 'contribute to European appeasement', but exactly the opposite: the conception and method of these negotiations will, he contends, undermine instead of strengthening 'the foundations upon which international confidence rests'.

Why did the Cabinet decide to ignore so grave a warning? We could only conclude that the Cabinet thought it less dangerous to brush aside Italy's broken pledges and to negotiate new ones than to press for the fulfilment of the existing pledges, and that it hoped, with a new Foreign Secretary, to be in a better position to negotiate a modus vivendi that will be both honourable and prudent.

Few, if any, of those who took part in our discussions felt the slightest confidence that conversations thus undertaken would lead to an agreement of substantial value. How is it possible, we asked ourselves, to find a sufficient community of purpose between these two governments, when the dictator in Italy glories in his use of 'war as an instrument of national policy' and is at this moment employing it in Europe and Africa, whilst the British government is impelled by every motive of honour and self-interest to treat this as the supreme crime against humanity? Is it not only too likely that Signor Mussolini, having just won so signal a diplomatic triumph, will feel emboldened to crack his whip again and to put his terms very high, believing that Mr Chamberlain has staked his political fortunes upon pulling off as agreement? It is not probable, too, that Mussolini will be the less disposed to make a real withdrawal of his forces from Spain, after having accepted without protest Hitler's seizure of Austria? There was a time when Mussolini would tell the Senate that Italy 'could never tolerate so open a violation of the treaties' as the Austro-German *Anschluss*, and the German annexation of Austria 'would frustrate the Italian victory'. Today it is evident from Mussolini's complaisance in face of the annexation that the Italo-German agreement of November 1936 did indeed promise a free hand to the German aggressor in Austria in return for a free hand and material support for the Italo-German aggression in Spain. Mussolini will insist upon his quid pro quo.

However, the negotiations have begun. That being so, we can only hope that they will 'contribute to European appeasement' and we can only be glad that they are in the hands of men who do believe that negotiations so begun have a fair chance of such success.

Tests of success

But we must all ask ourselves, without partisanship, what kind of Anglo-Italian agreement should be recognized as a success; what kind of contribution should be looked for from the British side and the Italian.

Obviously, the agreement ought first to reduce the immediate tension and ill-will caused by deliberate acts of provocation and menace (such as the hostile Italian campaign of propaganda in the Near East). It ought to involve comparable contributions from both parties, not simply some revocable promises from one side in return for irrevocable deeds from the other side. It ought not to buy 'appeasement' for one country at the expense of the rights and securities of another people; it would be inexcusable to treat the interests of other countries as a matter for Anglo-Italian bargains. Above all, the agreement must include nothing that does violence to the principles and obligations of our Covenant, nothing which would prejudice the chance of building up a strong open alliance against war and injustice such as the League ought to become.

The blindest of all errors would be to attempt to buy a brief respite for ourselves by encouraging the allied dictators to direct their next explosion eastwards, southwards, anywhere rather than westwards, in return for such concessions on our part as would sustain their aggressive power. To make such an agreement would be to connive at the destruction of our prospective allies in the cause of peaceful order, and in doing so to destroy our own defences by the most dangerous kind of 'unilateral disarmament'.

With these criteria of 'success' in mind, we reviewed some of the contributions which might be sought by Britain and Italy respectively.

What Italy might offer

(a) *Cessation of hostile propaganda* The easiest concession that Signor Mussolini could offer would be a promise to stop hostile propaganda from the Bari broadcasting station, and other forms of anti-British agitation in the Near East and elsewhere. It should be unnecessary to pay a price for cessation of the deliberate poisoning of the air; but cessation (if it lasted) would at least be something gained.

(b) *Withdrawals from Spain* Secondly, Signor Mussolini might be prepared to make a reality at last of the long discussed withdrawal of certain Italian forces from Spain. Here again, it ought not to be necessary to pay a price for the withdrawal of an invasion which ought never to have been committed. But a genuine withdrawal, on such a scale as to leave Spain free from Italian interference, coupled with the withdrawal of other foreign forces, and involving a genuine cessation of war supplies, would at least achieve the purpose for which the experiment called 'non-intervention' was undertaken.

It must be recognized, however, that the prospects of securing such a genuine withdrawal are far from bright. When Herr Hitler declared some months ago that he would not tolerate 'Bolshevism' in Spain – Bolshevism representing in this context the legitimate government of Spain – he was saying in effect that he would support Mussolini's adventure in Spain; and when he suddenly committed his act of war against Austria without a protest on the part of Mussolini, it was apparent that the two dictators had, in fact, as has long been supposed, made a bargain on this subject: a free hand for the invader in Austria, in return for a free hand and support with war materials for the invasion in Spain. In these circumstances it seems unlikely that Mussolini will agree to any such reduction of his forces in Spain as would seriously weaken General Franco's attack.

Fears were expressed during our discussions lest a compromise might be arrived at on such terms as would leave Mussolini free to maintain material and technical aid to Franco's blockade, and that the granting of belligerent rights would thus be made under such conditions as to facilitate the establishment of a more or less 'effective' blockade. It was also feared that, if Italian troops were withdrawn, they might simply be replaced with other troops from Italian Libya, who might be represented as 'Moors' in Franco's service. Plainly, if an agreement of this kind about withdrawal is to be concluded, it will have to be safeguarded very carefully.

The view was expressed, in our discussions, that any such agreement, based on the assumption that the Spanish government and the Spanish rebels should be treated on equal terms, was a dangerous departure from international law, and that it had been a mistake from the outset to deny to the Spanish government the protection against foreign invasion to which it was entitled under the Covenant. In any case, we thought it probable that the withdrawal would come too late to afford sensible relief to the Spanish government.

(c) *Reduction of Italian forces in Libya* A third concession that Italy might offer would be the withdrawal of some of her forces from Libya. These forces were greatly augmented for the purpose of threatening Egypt and thereby serving as an instrument of political pressure against the British government. If they have served their turn in helping to buy an important political agreement, Mussolini may be glad to economize by bringing them home. But here again something would be gained by the abandonment (at least for the time being) of such a threat.

(d) *Other concessions* which we discussed included an agreement about fortification of the Italian island of Pentellaria (which we thought very unlikely) and agreements concerning Italian plans in the Balearic Islands and Ceuta, or other places on the Mediterranean route.

(e) *Arms limitation* We considered the possibility that Italy might accept (and gain) an agreement on naval armaments which would check the Franco-Italian naval competition. We thought it unlikely that Mussolini would now accept any agreement that would not allow for numerical parity with France, and very unlikely that France would accept such parity unless as part of a far-reaching settlement, which would include issues concerning northern Africa and for which some special British guarantee in the Mediterranean would probably be sought.

(f) *Italy and a pact* Lastly, we considered whether it would be desirable and possible to induce Italy to join some kind of pact, some system providing for consultation and certain reciprocal advantages between two, three, or four powers.

We agreed that it was out of the question for Britain to seek a bilateral pact with Italy, whilst the Rome–Berlin axis remains intact. One obvious objection would be that Britain would in effect be joining the Rome–Berlin Group and the anti-comintern front, leaving France outside.

Would it be desirable to try to split the Rome–Berlin axis, by getting Italy to reform the 'Stresa front' with Britain and France? We agreed that it was most improbable, after what has happened, that such an attempt would succeed: and that, even if it were possible to induce one of the partners of the Rome–Berlin axis to double-cross the other, this would contribute nothing towards strengthening 'the foundation upon which international confidence rests'.

Would it be possible or desirable to create – or recreate – some kind of four-power pact between Britain, France, Italy, and Germany? Obviously, it would be an immense step towards the establishment of European peace if these four powers, which together with Russia are the most powerful in Europe, were to reach such an agreement as would settle their present differences and provide for the settlement of their future differences *without injury to the interests of other states*. But we held emphatically that peace and justice in Europe are the concern of many other powers besides these four, and that any pact which would in effect supplant the League, or would lead to attempts by the four powers to decide the fortunes of other nations without their full collaboration would be disastrous. In particular, we held that it would be a fatal error to make a pact which, whilst including the two aggressive powers, would exclude Russia: fatal because it would morally endanger the League, because it would stimulate Russian isolationism, because it would intensify that 'ideological conflict' which the anti-comintern pact seeks to foster and which Mr Eden has laboured to prevent. If Hitler could thus decisively separate Britain from Russia, he would have won his most dangerous victory.

What Britain might offer

Next, we asked ourselves what should Great Britain be prepared to offer to Italy?

(a) *Belligerent rights for Franco* The government is already committed in principle to according belligerent rights to General Franco under certain conditions. Those conditions include the withdrawal of a certain number of 'volunteers', so that the struggle may be left to the Spaniards themselves. Any such withdrawal, if it is to be reckoned effective for the purposes of this agreement, must involve both German and Italian forces, must apply to the sea and air as well as the land, and must certainly cover armaments as well as men. It must be remembered that both Hitler and Mussolini have announced their determination that Franco shall win: so there is good reason to expect that the evasions and delays which have continued for so long will be prolonged by the Italian authorities if this seems likely to aid General Franco.

But it may well be the case that Franco now needs something else much more than he needs the support of Italian arms. Probably his chief need now is for German war material, and above all for the means of making an effective blockade of the coast of governmental Spain. If belligerent rights are to be conceded to Franco as part of an Anglo-Italian agreement they ought to be strictly confined within the limits of international law; and there shall be no question of the British government helping Franco to make his blockade effective by means of pressure from the British Admiralty upon British shipping. In particular, the stipulation concerning withdrawal of Italian and German forces should include precautions against the retention of war materials and technicians for service in the blockade.

But in truth the whole of this bargain is based upon rotten foundations. It involves from the outset a violation of those principles which the Covenant was meant to sustain.

(b) *Financial help* A direct government loan from Britain to Italy may possibly be asked for, since the Italian budgetary position is becoming extremely grave. After the assurances that have been recently given by government spokesmen, we assume that there is no chance of such a loan being conceded.

It does, however, seem possible that financial assistance may be offered in the form of export credits, and that an attempt may be made to commend this to the British public on the ground that it would promote Italian purchases of British goods and so help to revive British trade in districts where it is now slackening. Credits to Italy would not now be extended by British firms on a large scale without government backing. If now the government were to offer the backing of the export credits scheme, and if the Italians were to fail to pay the British manufacturers, then the British taxpayer would be under an obligation to do so.

We consider that any such financial assistance to Italy under present conditions would be in effect an indirect contribution to Italy's armament programme. It would be a self-deception to pretend that such assistance could somehow be earmarked for purely commercial purposes and would do nothing to assist the regime in developing its war policy. Both on League principles and on grounds of British interest, the grant of export credits should be rejected.

(c) *Abyssinia* The British government will no doubt be urged to grant *de jure* recognition of Italian sovereignty over the whole of Ethiopia.

This would be open to two grave objections. Firstly, it would be a breach of our explicit engagements. We are still pledged by Article X of the Covenant to 'respect and preserve the territorial integrity and existing political independence' of the Ethiopia which was admitted into League membership. We have joined in affirming that 'no infringement of the territorial integrity, and no change in the political independence of any member of the League, brought about in disregard of this Article ought to be recognized as valid and effectual by the members of the League of Nations'. In 1933 we joined with the League Assembly in formally declaring that 'it is incumbent upon the members of the League not to recognize any situation, treaty, or agreement which may be brought about by means contrary to the Covenant of the League or to the Pact of Paris'. The United States government attaches great importance to this principle and officially approves the League's declaration. Secondly, if we were to violate this assurance, we should be damaging British repute throughout a Commonwealth of 470 million people, only 70 million of whom are white. And we should be putting ourselves into the position of saying to the Emperor Haile Selassie that we deny his right henceforth to send delegates to Geneva, and to plead the cause of his country if an occasion arises for doing so. Such an occasion may well arise before long. Italy's conquest is very far from complete: the difficulties, economic and military, are such as to impose an exhausting strain upon the invader.

It is useless, however, merely to stand as diehards in defence of juridical formula, regardless of explosive forces which threaten to destroy everything which that formula was meant to safeguard. A great part of Ethiopia has undoubtedly been conquered, for the time being at any rate, by a ruthless aggressor. We considered in our discussions, whether it would not be advisable, on balance, for the British government to work for a compromise whereby Italian sovereignty would be recognized over that part of Ethiopia which is effectively under Italian control, Ethiopian sovereignty in the rest of the country being restored and specially guaranteed. We have much doubt as to whether such a compromise could possibly be negotiated at present, or whether, if negotiated, it could be made to work. But if it were of such a character that the Emperor would be prepared to accept it on behalf of his people it might be better than nothing.

What we do feel no doubt about is that the British government ought not simply to recognize the King of Italy as legitimate ruler over the whole of the still half-conquered Ethiopia in order to purchase some concession from Italy in Spain or elsewhere.

'I have always taken the view', the Prime Minister said on 21 February, 'that the question of the formal recognition of the Italian position in Abyssinia was one that could only be morally justified if it was found to be a factor, and an essential factor, in a general appeasement'. We do not see how such moral justification could be claimed if the 'general appeasement' referred to were not to include the people most directly concerned, namely the Ethiopians themselves.

(d) *Suez Canal* Italy may ask for a share in the military control of the Suez Canal zone, a control which is at present in the hands of Britain and Egypt subject to the provisions of the Suez Canal Convention. We recognize that the present provision, whether at Suez or Gibraltar, is impossible to defend on broad grounds of international equity: the control of the narrow seas ought not to be in the hands of any one power, however pacific and disinterested. President Wilson recognized this long ago in the second of his Fourteen Points, where he laid down the principle that the seas should only be closed, if closed at all, by 'international action for the enforcement of international covenants'. There is a strong case for Italy's contention that Britain ought not to be in the position to close the gates of the Mediterranean, whether at the eastern end or the western, for the coercion of her own private enemies in time of war. But that does not mean that the international objections to the present situation could be removed by making Italy alone a partner in this British control. Italy has her rights, as we have, in the use of the international waterway of the Suez Canal; but other countries have no less right. The proper solution would be the creation of an international regime with adequate force at its disposal, so as to ensure that the narrow seas shall not be controlled by any one nation, or two nations, as 'instruments of national policy' but shall only be closed by international action and in defence of the international laws of peace-keeping.

(e) *Colonies* Other concessions which Italy might ask for may include cession of territory on the borders of Kenya, and perhaps some kind of condominium in Aden and Port Said.

(f) *Naval parity* Reference has already been made to the question of naval parity for Italy with France. This, of course, could only form part of a wider negotiation.

It will have been noted that, if the respective contributions of the two powers are of the kind we anticipate, Mussolini would be offering nothing comparable in permanence to the concessions which Britain would be asked to make. We should have taken steps which could not be retraced: Mussolini would merely have suspended operations which he could renew whenever it suited him to do so.

How then can we hope to buy Mussolini's loyal co-operation in the pursuit of a common objective, unless our own objectives are radically changed? Either we do or we do not support the League's open alliance against the war method: we cannot be on both sides of that barricade. Either we mean to use our power to strengthen the collective defences against those who preach and practise aggression: or else we mean to strengthen the hands of those who oppose the collective peace system.

The conclusion we drew from our discussion was that it seemed very unlikely that an agreement could be concluded on such terms as to be acceptable to public opinion in this country; and that it was useless to look for an agreement which could secure as a continuing instrument for the achievement of major objectives desired by both governments alike. The chief aim of one of these two governments is to prevent and stop war, and to remove the causes of war by peaceful means. The other government openly opposes and derides this objective. 'This harmful doctrine of peace is hostile to fascism.' So long as this fundamental opposition remains, the two governments can never find themselves 'on the same side of the barricade'. The best that can be hoped for, in the present Anglo-Italian negotiations, is an alleviation of immediate causes of friction between the two countries; but an alleviation achieved by such means as will do nothing to strengthen Italy's aggressive power, and nothing to weaken what remains of the collective peace system.

Chapter 6:. Germany and Czechoslovakia

Official conversations with Germany were just beginning when Hitler struck his blow against Austria. The blow struck immediately after the Berchtesgaden discussion with Dr Schussnigg, in flagrant violation of Germany's pledges and assurances. It has been justified to the German people by a flood of lies and exaggerations remarkable even in the records of totalitarian propaganda.

In these circumstances, the prospects of fruitful negotiations with the German government appear for the present to have been destroyed. It is not with this Germany that we can hope to negotiate the all-round settlement that would serve the cause for which the League stands. And it is only in connection with such a settlement that we should be justified in making concessions ourselves which would strengthen Germany's power, or in urging others to make concession of this character. If, for instance, Germany were a trustworthy partner in the building up of a peaceful Europe, there would be much to be said for encouraging preferential economic arrangements such as would give her an economic position in central and south-eastern Europe superior to that which we claim for ourselves. But who can regard Germany as such a partner?

If Germany did not turn her back upon international co-operation and reject any consultation which would bring her into partnership with the Russians, every problem concerning Germany's colonial claim, concerning the reduction of trade barriers, or involving the development of civil aviation on international lines, etc. would become immeasurably easier to solve. But the barrier is there. The fact that this barrier was created partly through the errors of the peace treaties and the tragic errors of French and British policy in the post-war years is generally recognized now: but this does not make the barrier itself less formidable.

Most of our discussion took place before the Austrian invasion. Some of the proposals which we were then inclined to regard favourably we should now dismiss. But it is worth recording the substance of the discussion.

Moral liabilities

We noted, firstly, that again and again during the post-war years Franco-British policy in relation to Germany had been paralysed or weakened by the feeling that there was something morally amiss with the case that we were defending on the basis of the Versailles Treaty. The reparations system itself broke down eventually not only because of economic difficulties and German resistance but also, in some degree, because of a feeling on the part of the claimants that their claim was morally shaky. So too with the one-sided disarmament clauses: when the disarmament conference failed to do business with Bruning or with the Hitler of 1933 on the basis of equality of treatment, there was a widespread feeling that the moral basis for opposition to German rearmament had crumbled away. The same applied to the unilateral provisions about demilitarization on the Rhine. It certainly applied to the *Anschluss*, which was prohibited unless a unanimous Council of the League gave its consent. (In our discussions, before the German Putsch, we expressed the opinion that the *Anschluss* should not be opposed, through of course this would not by itself solve Austria's problem or ease the economic difficulties of the Danubian states.) In all these matters, and in some others, an element of doubt has prevented a resolute defence of the treaty clauses; there has not been sufficient magnanimity and resolution to bringing about a revision of the unequal *status quo* whilst the going was good; and so the treaty has been destroyed piecemeal in the worst of all possible ways.

We asked ourselves whether there were not still one or two legacies of Versailles to which similar considerations still apply. We thought it would be desirable that an official statement should be made on some appropriate occasion to the effect that historical responsibility for the war is, in the British view, not a matter on which it is suitable for combatants on one side to impose their judgement upon the combatants of the other side: and that [it] is therefore desirable for the relevant clause to be eliminated from the treaties of peace. The same should apply to any reflections that were passed upon Germany's pre-war colonial administration.

There is at least one major problem outstanding concerning which this sense of the strength of the German case still exercises a potent effect: namely the colonial claim. (Perhaps the German claims in the Polish corridor, in Memel, and in Silesia, deserve to be classed in the same category; but these issues are at present, comparatively speaking, dormant.)

We deal below with proposals concerning the colonial problem and concerning general economic policy. Before reviewing these questions, we may indicate the substance of our discussion about the quid pro quo to be offered in Anglo-German negotiations.

What Germany might offer

We thought it possible that Germany might offer the following items as contributions towards an Anglo-German agreement:

(a) *The French frontier* Hitler might offer to reaffirm his previous pledges not to cross the French frontier.

(b) *Czechoslovakia* Hitler might promise not to annexe Czechoslovakia, provided that a relatively small alteration of frontier were made in northern Bohemia and provided that some far-reaching cantonal scheme were accepted.

(c) *Colonies* Hitler might perhaps offer not to press the whole of his colonial claim, provided that satisfaction were given for the present by the return of, say, Tanganyika, Togoland, and Cameroon. He would insist upon the return of these colonies to German sovereignty, free from any restrictions such as those imposed by the mandate system.

(d) *A four-power pact* Hitler might be willing, we thought, to join a four-power pact with Italy, France, and Britain, whilst being unwilling to join a five-power pact including Russia.

What Britain might offer

We were inclined to think that Great Britain might, as part of an agreement, express willingness to advise Czechoslovakia to adopt some kind of cantonal system. We recognized the case for admitting Germany's special economic interests in central and eastern Europe. We outlined the proposals on economic policy which are set out in the next chapter.

As regards colonies, we thought it important that Great Britain should offer forthwith – not as part of the negotiations with

Germany – to extend the principles of the mandate system to all her non-self-governing colonial territories, at least in equatorial Africa to begin with. This would have the advantage of removing the distinction between those African colonies (such as Tanganyika) which have been subject to the international safeguard and restrictions of the mandate system, and those which have been free from such safeguards and restrictions or subject only to the restrictions of the Congo Basin Convention (concerning equality of trading opportunity, etc). We should then be in a much better position for negotiating with Germany about colonies, with a view to her acceptance of such principles. We recognized that it would be very desirable to improve the mandate system and to strengthen the Mandates Commission and its powers.

Our discussion brought out the point that in the negotiations with Germany about colonies, Great Britain ought never to forget that the problem is primarily a problem properly concerning the better government of the native peoples (and the relatively few white settlers) rather than a problem concerning the better division of a colonial cake.

Lastly, we thought that, if and when a real peace settlement with Germany and the rest of Europe becomes possible, something might be done to reassure Germany herself against the use by another power of Czechoslovakia as a spearhead for attack against Germany. This might be achieved, it was suggested, by some scheme of guaranteed neutralization of Czechoslovakia (though we recognized that this was a highly contentious proposal), parallel with a comprehensive rebuilding and strengthening of the League's system of collective defence. In that event, but only in that event, it would be practicable to terminate the Franco-Soviet pact and the Soviet-Czech pact and the Franco-Czech pact.

But all these proposals appear academic at present in the light of Hitler's aggression against Austria.

Czechoslovakia

There remains the burning question of Czechoslovakia. We discussed this again and again, with the help of all the technical information we could gather. Should the British government make a declaration similar to those made by France and Russia, to the effect that, if Czechoslovakia were to be the victim of flagrant aggression, we should immediately go to her assistance?

We did not reach agreement. Some of us felt that the risks of such a commitment were now too great; the difficulties in the way of bringing preponderant powers to bear in support of Czechoslovakia appeared too formidable. Others considered that now, when France and Russia have given their explicit pledges, it would be virtually impossible for Britain to stand out if war did come: and that it would be better to make a declaration now, unequivocably, on the same lines as the French, so that it may serve if possible as a *preventive* of war. Those of us who held this view thought that the British government should promise a contribution of air power and economic power, backed by naval action, in the event of Czechoslovakia being the victim of flagrant aggression or being the victim of such interference as amounts, in the League's judgement, to aggression. It would have to be made clear that this guarantee, designed as it is for the *prevention* of war, could operate only if Great Britain were assured of the full support of France and Russia.

A necessary corollary of such a guarantee would be discussion with the French and Russian authorities as to the form which the co-operation of the powers should take in the event of war.

We recognized, of course, that any such guarantee is open to grave objections and involves very grave risks. Unless the issue is very clearly explained to this nation, millions of Englishmen would be in great doubt as to whether the guarantee should have been given.

Perhaps the gravest of all the dangers of such a policy is the danger that it may stimulate the 'encirclement' complex in Germany. And in fact it would be an encirclement, a '*cordon sanitaire*' around a power which is using, and threatens to use, war as an instrument of a ruthless national policy, and which refuses, apparently, to join any working alliance for the defence of peaceful order. To have to admit the complete failure of efforts to win German collaboration with France and the other powers outside the Rome–Berlin axis would mean that one of the main objectives of British diplomacy is unattainable at present. But there is one thing more dangerous and evil than the division of the world into two camps with the powers of the triangle on the one side and the loyal members of the League on the other: namely, the piecemeal destruction of those who stand, however imperfectly, for peaceful order and government by persuasion. The lesson of the Austrian *Putsch* is that we must hang together or we shall be hanged separately.

Chapter 7: China and Japan

We were agreed in our discussion that the failure to take collective action to restrain the Japanese aggressions involved grave injury to China, very serious further discrediting of British pledges of collective defence, and immense dangers to British and other foreign interests in the Pacific and eastern Asia. Beyond doubt, the nations which have condoned Japan's aggression have the power, if they have the will, to prevent that aggression from succeeding. The British Empire and the United States between them buy more than half of Japan's exports and supply more than half of her imports, including much more than half of her imported supplies of materials essential for war purposes. If Japan successfully carries through a long campaign, it will be because the British Empire and the Americans have enabled her to do so. We regard this policy as being morally unsound and politically injurious. We believe that the risks and evils involved in continuing to aid the aggressor were certainly greater than the risks involved in joint economic action to restrain him.

We recognized, in our discussion, that co-operation with the United States is indispensable, if this restraint is to be effective and if the risk of Japan hitting back with armed force (in addition to the economic pressure which she is now employing) are to be reduced within sufficiently narrow limits. But we recognized also that it was most unlikely last autumn, and still more unlikely now, that America would move first; we thought it probable that, after previous experiences and disillusionment in the Manchurian and Ethiopian crises, the United States government would not feel able to act at all unless the first public move came from the British side.

We recognized also that, if British power in the Far East is used only for defence of British interests, and not at all as a contribution to the defence of China and the collective peace system, the growth of American sympathy and collaboration is impossible. This point is extremely important in any calculation of British policy in China. It is, of course, most important also to secure the full collaboration of Soviet Russia. In this respect the situation now is much more manageable than it was in 1931.

With these considerations in mind, we concluded that the British government would do well to intimate plainly but privately to the American government that this country will go as far as America in any kind of joint action to restrain Japan and to aid China. The British should make known to the Americans that they think it desirable that economic pressure should be brought to bear upon Japan, and that this is practicable without excessive risk, provided that co-operation with America is forthcoming. This pressure should take the form of prohibition of financial facilities, refusal of exports from Japan, and withholding of all war supplies, including oil. We thought it very important that British policy in the Far East should not be paralysed by the belief that Hong Kong is in effect a hostage in Japan's hands which Britain cannot afford to abandon, but which could not without very great risk be defended from so distant a base as Singapore.

We were of opinion that the evacuation of British women and children from Hong Kong should be put in hand; and that it would probably be inexpedient to attempt to defend Hong Kong by a fleet action in Chinese waters in the event of Japanese attack. If abandonment did prove necessary, it need only be temporary, if the long-range economic pressure on Japan succeeded.

Chapter 8: 'Rearmament'

The whole of this paper has been based on the principle that, in existing circumstances, British foreign policy must contrive a display of real strength and an evidence of sincere willingness to meet legitimate grievances and claims.

We need not here emphasize the disastrous burdens and deadly risks of the present armament race, or recall the errors which led to the breakdown of the disarmament conference. We will only say here that we are forced to the conclusion that an increase of British armaments on a great scale is needed now, as a contribution to that 'collective defence' which we have defined. We urge that the British government should make a public declaration that Britain would be prepared to cease rearming, providing other countries would do the same, and provided that an arms agreement was accepted which recognized the principle of parity for comparable powers in Europe (so that no one country should be able alone to dominate the continent). It must, however, be recognized that 'parity', useful though it may be for psychological reasons in a world of competing sovereign states, is not a 'yardstick' which can be applied with scientific precision so as to give equality of strength to nations diversely situated.

We were deeply impressed by such evidence as we were able to gather as to the apparent lag in the defensive parts of the British armament programme. We concluded that a great effort should be made forthwith to improve London's air defences and especially to increase the storage of food (especially fats) and other essential commodities which this island has to import.

We briefly discussed the question – what effective sanctions can be devised to ensure the fulfilment of a disarmament agreement? The suggestion was made that, in the event of some country having been found (under the system of supervision which will be required) to have exceeded its agreed limits of armament, the other parties to the agreement should consult each other with a view to readjusting their own programmes, so as to ensure that the violator of the agreement will be unable to achieve the relative superiority which it seeks.

We were reminded again and again in our discussions that 'rearmament' is not simply a matter of adding guns and planes to the national armoury. To reduce the nation's vulnerability, to increase its power of passive endurance, may be just as important. We did not forget the importance of 'moral rearmament' – that kind of strengthening of a nation's will which may result from the timely concession of claims about which the nation is (or should be) morally uneasy. In particular, we want to emphasize the decisive importance in any realistic calculation of this nation's defences, of maintaining that great 'open alliance against war' which the League of Nations can still be. To liquidate that alliance by abandoning our fair share in the responsibilities of collective defence, would be a 'unilateral disarmament' more sweeping and more perilous than the scrapping of many ships and guns. The nation's rearmament programme cannot be made technically sufficient or morally acceptable if it is the instrument of a policy which is wholly national and self-regarding. To throw over the principle of collective security, whilst pressing on with the rearmament which was demanded in the name of collective security would be to subject national unity to the severest strain at a most dangerous time.

Chapter 9: Economic policy

Today, in a war-threatened world, some nations are pouring their energies into costly efforts to make themselves self-sufficient; and all nations have found themselves impelled by new fears, or by new economic pressures, to tighten their economic controls.

Our discussion was based on the assumption that a loosening of these economic controls was supremely desirable. We consider that those nations which desire a less controlled economic system should negotiate between themselves such agreements as will extend their economic interdependence and relax their economic controls. These nations would thus become more closely bound to each other, and their economic prosperity, and ultimately their strength and resources, would be increased.

Such an economic bloc should be open to adhesion by any nation, whatever its political complexion. But adhesion would, *ipso facto*, involve a freer economic policy on the part of the signatory: and this would evidently run counter to the totalitarian and militaristic principles upon which certain states have organized their national life.

While no direct or exclusive advances should be made to Germany or Italy, it should be made clear that the participation of these countries in the bloc, on the terms described, would be welcomed. It is especially desirable that the agreements should not seem to be directed against any power or powers.

The negotiation of the agreement should be linked with the League of Nations, through its economic section, and should not be conducted outside the Geneva framework. This would have the effect of linking membership of the League with tangible economic benefits, which would be an advantage in countering the attraction of the Rome–Berlin axis for the east European states.

Germany and Italy might be unwilling to enter into negotiations directly sponsored by the League. This difficulty might, however, be reduced by giving the economic section of the League an independent status, on the lines of the ILO.

The government should offer to join with other League powers in economic facilities to the central, eastern and south-eastern countries of Europe, and in any other practicable plan for improving their economic position. Plans for this purpose should be worked out by the Bank of International Settlements, in conjunction with the League of Nations: and should be conditional on their tending to an improvement of the general political situation. In the event of an all-round settlement becoming possible, there should not be excluded from consideration the possibility of preferential economic arrangements, such as would give Germany an economic position in central and south-east Europe superior to that which we ourselves claim.

The view was expressed in our discussion that under present conditions, the calling of such an economic conference as was proposed in the Van Zeeland Report would not serve a useful purpose for the present.

We agreed that it is most desirable that the negotiations for a trade treaty with the United States should be expedited; and that any surrender to vested interests by the British government, such as would reduce the importance of the treaty, would make a deplorable impression in America. We attached great importance also to the amplification of the existing tripartite agreement about currencies between Britain, America, and France. And we considered that a private intimation might with advantage be conveyed by the British government to the American, indicating that this country is ready to start negotiations about the British debt to the United States whenever the American government thinks the occasion appropriate.

We have referred in the chapter on Germany to the importance of extending the principle of equality of trading opportunity to all non-self-governing colonies, at least in equatorial Africa to begin with. We urged this, not as a concession to any one country, but as a step which should be taken on its own merits, now.

We suggest that the British government should propose the setting up of an international commission to make recommendations on the subject of migration.

Foreign Affairs Group, Meeting of 23 March 1938[18] (Liddell Hart papers, LH 5/1)

The meeting took place one day before the Prime Minister's statement on foreign policy, and the group had constantly in mind that pending this statement any comments on the foreign situation must be of a very provisional nature.

Views were exchanged on the developments during the previous week. Tension over the Austrian crisis had greatly relaxed, but there remained behind a new attitude towards Germany and a sharper awareness of the dangerous situation. It was stated that there had also been a distinct change of sentiment in government circles about Spain, the strategic importance of which to the British Empire was now more fully realized. Though the view was still taken in some quarters that Franco would ultimately be dependent on us, owing to his financial difficulties, others were now becoming impressed by the pro-German record over many years of the Spanish military caste. Moreover, they doubted whether Franco would be able to eject his allies, even if he should wish to do so; and there was even talk of eventual military action against Franco in case he proved recalcitrant. At this stage the government was, however, not prepared to take any steps, or to give France any assurances in the event of her intervening and finding herself in difficulties with Italy or Germany – since, among other reasons, it feared that if France received such assurances she would go too far. The Foreign Office view was that it was now too late to stop Franco; and intervention at this stage would only have the effect of spoiling our negotiations with Italy. It was possible that France might intervene even without our support.

The government attitude towards Italy had become more cautious. Mussolini desired agreement before Hitler's visit on 9 May; this caused a serious difficulty since the government, in recognizing Italian sovereignty over Abyssinia, wished to proceed through the League, and the Council was not due to meet until after the Hitler visit.

[18] Neither the minutes nor any other source indicate the names of those present.

The group then passed to a discussion of policy on (a) the Spanish, (b) the Czechoslovakia problems, the discussion being based on a memorandum submitted by one of the members. As regards Spain, there was some support for a policy expressed in the following formula:

> We hope that the purchase and transport of supplies from Great Britain will be facilitated to counterbalance the war material poured in by Germany and Italy. And we consider that the British government should give a clear intimation to France that they will stand by her if in doing no more than Italy and Germany openly boast of continuing to do, she is threatened by these powers.

With regard to Czechoslovakia, it was argued that if France, owing to her pledge, were involved in war we should be bound to come in and for reasons of air strategy would probably be in from the start. Therefore as we could not stay out in any case, the best course would be for us to join in a pledge to Czechoslovakia, in the hope that this would itself prevent the outbreak of war; and the question was discussed whether a clearer indication to Germany in 1914 of our intention to intervene would not have prevented war. The essence of the situation was that we were France's prisoner: we were bound to protect her in war, whatever her policy. We might, however, put pressure on France to modify her pledge to Czechoslovakia according to the new military situation created by the fortification of the Rhineland, and according to Czechoslovakia's attitude to the redress of minority grievances.

The question of such redress was discussed, and different views were put forward about the intentions of the Czechoslovakian government.

It was questioned whether it was to be expected that Germany's next move would be against Czechoslovakia, or whether Germany would not aim rather at encircling and strangling Czechoslovakia by bringing into being a pro-German government in Hungary.

There was some discussion, similar to that at the previous meeting, whether action by France in Spain would precipitate German action against Czechoslovakia; and also whether, if Spain were once lost, France and Great Britain would be able to give any aid to Czechoslovakia.

One member suggested as the main lines of our policy that we might guarantee the neutrality of the Low Countries and of Switzerland, and also the French Alpine frontier. The effect of this would be to bring us into war if Germany attacked France through the Low Countries or Switzerland, or if Italy joined Germany in war against France. (Such an agreement would in fact be similar to the first Anglo-Japanese alliance – we should come to the aid of our ally if attacked by *more than one* enemy.) In the event of a war between Germany and France in which our guarantees did not become operative, we should be neutral: but in such a case France would have a very limited frontier to defend, and would probably not be endangered. We should preserve our force during such a war, and would at a suitable stage mediate. If such a policy were adopted there would be no need for us to give a pledge to Czechoslovakia: and the main argument for our doing so – that we are tied to France – would have fallen to the ground.

The meeting concluded with a further discussion as to the wisdom of seeking to prepare a manifesto to which all members would agree; and one view put forward was that the chief function of the group should be discussion and the exchange of news and views.

Rowse to the *Manchester Guardian*, 24 March 1938

[...]. In the letter you published on February 25, on Mr Eden's resignation, I envisaged in certain circumstances a joining together of all sections of opinion that were agreed upon collective security as the proper basis of our policy, to form an alternative government to the demoralized and disastrous 'National' government. In your leader you commented on such a widely based government, based upon the Liberal and Labour parties, and perhaps including Mr Churchill, Mr Eden, and some of the younger Conservatives, as possible only in an earthquake. I agreed; but if you look at the condition of Europe now, a few weeks afterwards, it looks as if the earthquake is not so far away as you thought.

On 24 March Christina Hole sent out letters notifying the group that the next meeting was scheduled for 8.15, Thursday, 31 March in Angell's Chambers in the Temple.[19]

Angell to the *Manchester Guardian*, 25 March 1938

The nation's supreme desire is to avoid a repetition of 1914, of the error which caused us to stumble and blunder into Armageddon.

What was that error? [...]. The war might, many are of the opinion it would, have been avoided if the Western powers, which finally felt

[19] Hole to Liddell Hart, 24 March 1938, Liddell Hart papers, LH 5/1.

compelled on behalf of their own security to enter the field against Germany, had been able to say sufficiently long beforehand that they would do so [. . .].

The confusions of 1914 [. . .] are sometimes explained by the fact that the British government could not be more definite because 'the public would not stand for it', that the danger had to be on top of the public before they would make their decisions. Is that to be the explanation of the next war also?

Allen to the *Manchester Guardian*, 30 March 1938

May I beseech the peace movement to exercise some measure of restraint[20] in its demand that the government should commit itself to declarations that might lead to war? I know only too well that Professor Tawney and Sir Norman Angell favour this policy of clarification of commitment because they believe it might *prevent* war, whereas absence of clarity might in the end lead to war [. . .]. I cannot but feel that they – and others like them – may do grievous injury to the cause of peace and to the rule of law by their attempt to arouse public opinion to compel the government to enter upon further specific commitments that may in the broken circumstances of the present lead to, rather than prevent, war.

God knows, we have every reason to distrust the judgement – perhaps even the bona fides – of the present government. But even that does not justify us in demanding a policy so fraught with possible danger without a knowledge far greater than any of us 'in Opposition' possess or have a right to publish even if we did possess it.

[. . .]. I plead for a constructive peace policy which shall frankly recognize the unhappy conflict between the principle of law and the principle of growth that has been allowed to come about.

[. . .]. Can we not therefore all unite in more insistent demands than we have ever made for a generous policy in order to develop new methods of government in colonial areas and to resume the flow of migration; for some contribution – nay, even sacrifice – in efforts towards economic co-operation; for an attempt to assist in disentangling the social, political and economic problems of eastern and south-eastern Europe; and for a deliberate initiative to rebuild the League itself despite every difficulty?

[20] In a letter to *The Times*, 19 March 1938, Allen had used similar language, pleading for 'some measure of restraint in the agitation that is being directed at the Prime Minister as to the making of declarations in the present grave international situation'.

Harold Nicolson diaries (Nicolson papers)

Tuesday, 29 March 1938

[. . .]. I am convinced that Germany and Italy are trying to chloroform us while they occupy strategic points to our disadvantage; that I consider eastern Europe is now lost with the seizure of Austria; and that we should make our naval strength felt in Spain [. . .]. [Liddell Hart] really thinks we are done unless we can prevent the Germans and Italians getting strategic control of Spain.

CHAPTER 3

'REALISTS AND MORALISTS', APRIL–MAY 1938

Harold Nicolson diaries (Nicolson papers)

Thursday, 31 March 1938

The House adjourns early and I go to Norman Angell's rooms where the All Souls group are meeting. We are somewhat inconclusive but our main line is that a purely negative policy gets us nowhere and that there must be some more constructive drive.

Foreign Affairs Group, Meeting of 31 March 1938[1] (Liddell Hart papers, LH 5/1)

Government statement on foreign policy

It was reported that in its first draft the statement had been completely isolationist, and had virtually repudiated the League and entirely repudiated responsibility over Czechoslovakia. The references to the League and Czechoslovakia had, however, been modified to meet the mood of the left-wing conservatives and younger ministers.

Spain

The government was quite determined not to intervene in favour of the republic. It was true there was a group in the Cabinet which now looked at the Spanish war in terms of British interests, and was

[1] Neither the minutes nor any other source indicate the names of those present.

disturbed at the strategic situation which was developing. There was even talk of very strong action against Franco, including force, if he should prove unreasonable upon the conclusion of the war; such action would then meet with less opposition within the Conservative Party, since it would be action *against Spain in defence of British interests, not action in support of the Spanish republic.* There was also still a widespread belief that Franco would desire to rid himself of his allies, and might therefore welcome our help in turning them out.

Italy

The Prime Minister remained convinced that in the last resort Mussolini would be with us, and not against us, in the event of war.

General attitude of the government

The guiding principle of its policy was to avoid war in the immediate future. To avoid an immediate crisis it was therefore willing to take grave political risks, and was also willing to contemplate important new political orientations. Its main fear was of a war breaking out as the result of drift.

House of Commons

The 'revolt' was now over, and the Conservative Party was solidly behind the government. The left-wing conservatives were, however, watching very anxiously the Anglo-Italian negotiations, and Chamberlain's prestige would be much reduced if the agreement was not a far-reaching one. The country also appeared to support the Chamberlain policy.

Discussion by the group

This was on the basis of the facts reported above. It was asked whether, now that the government had decided on its policy, it was not a grave mistake of the opposition to badger them. The aggressive line taken by the opposition would lead the government to underline its policy of avoiding conflict: and debates might therefore convey to foreign countries an exaggerated idea of the extent to which Great Britain would stand aloof. The consequences of such a misunderstanding might be disastrous.

It was expected that the dictators, knowing that we were at this stage so anxious to avoid war, would in the next period try to exploit their position to the full. This was, however, to some extent balanced out by the fact that the dictators themselves were also unready for war. Germany would probably aim at pushing on its expansion in central Europe but would aim at avoiding a head-on collision over Czechoslovakia. Our policy in these circumstances should be very flexible, but we should be alert to utilize whatever diplomatic and economic instruments were available to us in order to prevent a landslide.

There was some tendency to criticize the government for neglecting the imponderables of the situation. In all countries there was growing fear of and resentment against the dictators. If we advertised more clearly that we stand for law, individualism, etc. we should be able to mobilize behind us a great force of good will and thus increase our prestige.

A concrete instance of our failure to utilize the imponderables was our attitude to the League. The government ought to say that we had certain obligations which we would carry out wherever possible. Instead it said that we had obligations which we would carry out when our interests were at stake (it stated that we would not fulfil our League obligations even when it was possible for us to do so). Similarly the government gave the impression that it was neutral as between the League outlook and the Hitler–Mussolini outlook, and regarded both attitudes as of equal moral value. This followed from the fear of dividing Europe into two camps, but the fear was an exaggerated one.

There was further discussion upon the aims of Italy. One of the members pointed out that there had for some time been current the idea of a bloc of three Latin states, Italy, France, and Spain, all under fascist governments, with Italy as the leading partner. A Franco victory in Spain would give a strong impetus to fascism in France. Mussolini's inclinations did not appear to be towards the German alliance, and he was not alarmed by Bolshevism. His real fear was of democratic liberalism, since this was the force which might eventually unseat him in Italy. A fascist revolution in France would thus be very welcome to him, as reducing the danger from this source, and also as facilitating a new international alignment by which a check might be put upon Germany's expansion, and also Great Britain might be eased out of the Mediterranean. Against this, it was pointed out that an alliance *with France against Germany* held out to Mussolini little prospect of loot; whereas from an alliance *with Germany against France* he might look to obtain the French north-African colonies. The most probable view was that Mussolini's present aim was to become the pivot of the two axes. An agreement with Great Britain would enable him to raise his price as against Hitler.

Should recognition of Ethiopia form part of the Anglo-Italian agreement? One member stressed the importance of the doctrine of non-recognition; to abandon it would be the gravest possible blow to the League system and would worsen our relations with America. This view was, however, not accepted by the rest of the group, and it was suggested that the country as a whole would regard a strong stand on non-recognition as disproportionate. It was of the greatest importance that persons working for peace should not be made to appear as cranks.

Italy would probably agree to withdraw volunteers after Franco's victory, and, in view of our great naval superiority, we should probably be able to enforce the agreement. Nevertheless, there would probably continue a close contact between the Spanish national government and the general staffs of the dictatorship powers, including material assistance and the continued presence in Spain of technicians. Their relation would resemble that between Germany and the Young Turks after 1912, and would be extremely dangerous to us.

The internal situation in France was then discussed. Blum, it was reported, was weary of office and wished to withdraw. The position of Herriot was touched on, and it was suggested that he was not a man of sufficiently tough fibre to dominate the situation in an emergency. A Franco victory in Spain would probably create an emergency of the first order. On the one hand, it would encourage the right wing in France to take more active steps; on the other, the left would have a sense of betrayal and might react with great violence. The French left was of a very different order from the German social democrats, and there would be a strong possibility of civil war.

Hitler was perhaps counting on this. France would be either immobilized, or, if the right came to power, would perhaps enter a fascist bloc; and it would be possible to drive a wedge between England and France.

In spite of these alarming prospects, the group tended to feel that the situation in Spain had developed too far for any effective countermeasures now to be taken; and therefore turned to a long-range view of the situation.

With the western powers neutralized, the dictators might be able to fulfil, without war, their ambitions in eastern Europe and the Mediterranean. There would be an enormous shift of power, and Great Britain would gradually find itself isolated and without friends on the Continent. Eventually, when we had been manoeuvred into a position of great weakness, we might be presented with very heavy demands by Germany and Italy. Reason would possible dictate their acceptance, since our strategic position would be very weak; and if – as was possible – the demands were for the surrender to the dictators of our rights in Africa, we might consider that we had paid a price for peace which was not excessive. But popular opinion would probably insist on war. In other words, though the man in the street would not fight to prevent the dictators enveloping us, he would react violently as soon as our territory was actually seized. If the government of the day was in such circumstances disposed to surrender, the result might very well be a fascist revolution in England, based on the slogan of defence of the Empire. It was agreed, however, that such forecasts were extremely speculative.

The group then discussed what kind of lead it was desirable to give to the country. If the strategic situation was such as to rule out the straight League policy, it was important not to disguise the fact from the public. In any case it was very doubtful whether, after recent experiences, the public could still be induced to risk war in the defence of international law. At the same time, the public should not be allowed to become demoralized; a very dangerous situation would develop if it lost faith in all its ideals. The public must once again become conscious of what England stood for, and the question was to determine what was the best rallying-point. Some suggested that the appeal should be directed to the defence of democracy – this would meet with response from the American public also, which had been lukewarm to the appeal for the defence of law. Another suggestion was to base ourselves upon the defence of humane standards of government.

Pursuit of such ideals would, of course, not be by methods necessarily involving war. In this connection there was a case for allowing the coercive functions of the League to fall into the background, and for developing its technical functions. The technical services of the League had been starved, and the group agreed that it would welcome a strong lead by the British government to encourage their extension. This would be the best method of keeping alive the League ideal. At the same time, the government should make quite clear that in its relations with the countries which stood for law it would follow a full League policy: e.g. it would submit to third-party judgements, etc. (Only it must be recognized that, in relation to governments not accepting the rule of law, we were not in a position strong enough to attempt to impose law by force.)

The group also agreed that it would welcome an initiative by the government offering to make sacrifices in the cause of general appeasement, thus demonstrating that we did not merely stand for the status quo.

It was decided to attempt to draw up a statement somewhat on the above lines; and the meeting concluded with a discussion of future activity, including the making of contact with groups in other countries, and considered the possible addition of new members.

Hole to Liddell Hart, 1 April 1938 (Liddell Hart papers, LH 5/1)

The next meeting of the Foreign Affairs Group has been provisionally for Sunday, April 10 at 12 noon at All Souls College, Oxford. Definite confirmation of this will be sent to you immediately after Sir Arthur Salter's return to England on Monday next [*i.e. 4 April*]. [*As it transpired, the meeting was rescheduled on 15 April for 24 April at 12 noon at All Souls*].

Angell to Layton, 2 April 1938 (Layton papers, 1)

[. . .] Italy cannot for years, if at all, achieve an effective occupation of the greater part of Abyssinia [. . .]. As this bears upon the negotiations with Italy I thought you would be interested.

Cadogan to Nicolson, 2 April 1938 (FO371/22641, W4440/83/41)

I should have acknowledged before now the receipt of your letter of March 21 enclosing a memorandum (incorrectly called an 'aide-mémoire'!) on Spain. I have read it with great interest, and infer from it that you are in favour of immediate and open intervention by His Majesty's Government on the side of the Spanish government. As you know, that would be directly contrary to the policy of the government, and I see no prospect of that policy being changed.

Nicolson to Cadogan, 4 April 1938 (FO371/22642, W4471/83/41)

Many thanks for your letter about our aide-mémoire of the All Souls Group. The implication of that aide mémoire was not that we should intervene on the side of the Spanish government, but that, if there exists the real danger of some agreement between Franco and the dictator states similar to that concluded between Wangenheim and Enver, we should be prepared, in conjunction with the French, to take certain 'gages' such as occupying Minorca and Ceuta. The All Souls Group consist of such upright gentlemen that to suggest any such thing in writing would have been agony to their souls, but I quite see that any such action is not within the scope of present policy.[2]

Woodward to Allen, 6 April 1938 (Allen papers, box 15, correspondence, 1937–1938)

It amused me at the last meeting in Oxford to hear Arnold-Forster saying things which made my hair stand on end, and at the same time assuming that everyone in the room agreed with him [. . .]. I would say that if the government's policy fails, this failure, which will be a most sinister thing for Europe, ought not to be used as an instrument of party tactics. I'm afraid that if I stated these views at our meeting, Rowse, at least, would go up in smoke, but I rather think that a less unbalanced and fanatical person – Murray for example – would be inclined to agree.

Murray to Allen, 9 April 1938 (ms. Murray 232, fo. 106)

[. . .] I very largely agree with it [*Allen's letter to the* Manchester Guardian, *30 March 1938*]. My feeling is not so much that I differ from the government as that I can't trust them.

Hole to Liddell Hart, 15 April 1938 (Liddell Hart papers, LH 5/1)

In view of the conclusion of the Anglo-Italian agreement,[3] and the discussions which may be expected as soon as parliament meets on

[2] See also minutes by Frank Roberts and George Mounsey, 21 April 1938, FO371/22642, W4471/83/41.

[3] The group eventually met on 24 April but with Liddell Hart and Nicolson abroad. For Nicolson's report on the conclusion of his tour of Bulgaria, Romania, and Yugoslavia, see Nicolson to Vansittart, 2 May 1938, FO371/22342, R4737/94/67. On the same day he wrote to Angell: 'On the one hand I do not approve of Chamberlain's policy in all its aspects, yet on the other I cannot place any faith in the Opposition'; Nicolson to Angell, 2 May 1938, Sir Norman Angell papers, Ball State University, Muncie, IN. See also Halifax to Nicolson, 21 May 1938, FO371/22342, R5045/94/67.

April 26th, it is felt to be very desirable that there should be an early exchange of views between members of the group. It is therefore hoped that members will make a special effort to be present at this meeting.

Allen to Wint, 19 April 1938
(Allen papers, box 15, correspondence, 1937–1938)

I have at last got my good secretary home again and just write to book myself in for all meals next Sunday. I have written the Warden to see whether he will put me up for the night.

I entirely share your view that the time is coming when perhaps some statement should be issued by those of us who are willing to join, possibly under the auspices of the Next-Five-Years Group. That group has always been an elastic body through which different signatories at different times can sign different statements, and I feel that you are right in thinking that the present is a moment when it could usefully function and indeed continue to do so with more vigour than ever. I think perhaps we had better wait until after the discussion on Sunday and then we will have a talk about it with Salter.

I was immensely impressed with the document you sent me arising out of your talk with G.F. Hudson. Might I suggest that you discuss with Salter whether this might not be circulated as one of the Sunday documents. It represents a most important contribution.

Now that we are all back again I hope we can take up our work with increasing vigour.

Almost from the first meeting of the All Souls Group, disquiet had been expressed about Britain's vulnerability to air attack. That ongoing concern led Salter and Curtis,[4] *with the assistance of such public figures as L.S. Amery,*[5] *Sir*

[4] Curtis soon dropped out of the project and instead sent Salter a donation. In reply Salter wrote: 'It is *your* driving fire + *other* people's money that is really wanted'; quoted in Deborah Lavin, *From Empire to International Commonwealth: A Biography of Lionel Curtis* (London, 1995), p. 281.

[5] L.S. Amery (1873–1955) statesman and writer; Fellow of All Souls, 1897–1955; MP, 1911–1945; Parliamentary Under-Secretary, Colonial Office, 1919–1921; First Lord of the Admiralty, 1922–1924; Colonial Secretary, 1924–1929; Dominions Secretary, 1925–1929; Secretary of State for India, 1940–1945.

John Anderson,[6] *R.H. Brand,*[7] *Lord Nuffield,*[8] *Ernest Simon,*[9] *and Sir Ralph Wedgewood*[10] *to spearhead – as a parallel pressure group – the formation of an Air Raid Defence League. Its objectives seemed to gain support following the appointment of Anderson on 1 November 1938 as Lord Privy Seal responsible for supervising the ARP department of the Home Office and co-ordinating all civil defence measures.*[11] *The official launch on 7 February 1939 was followed by a nation-wide campaign of meetings, press publicity and the issue of relevant pamphlets.*

Curtis to Nuffield, 21 April 1938 (ms. Curtis 12, fos 89–90)

With reference to our conversation in the train yesterday, may I say that Sir Arthur Salter, who represents the University in Parliament, has just been to call on me and has given me an appalling account of our general unpreparedness against air raids. I attach great weight to what he says because he was the man, during the war, who convinced the Cabinet that we should be down and out pretty quickly if the Admiralty went on refusing to institute the convoy system. At his instance, the Cabinet ordered the institution of the convoy system which saved the whole situation. He is a highly trained civil servant who knows what he is talking about. One of his points is that in Germany and in Czechoslovakia the munition factories have now been made largely immune from air attack and are to a great extent, strange as it may seem, actually underground, whereas our munition factories are for the most part hopelessly exposed to attack.

[6] John Anderson, 1st Viscount Anderson (1882–1958) Permanent Under-Secretary, Home Office, 1922–1932; Governor of Bengal, 1932–1937; Lord Privy Seal, 1938–1939; Home Secretary, 1939–1940; Lord President of the Council, 1940–1943; Chancellor of the Exchequer, 1943–1945.

[7] Robert Henry Brand, 1st Baron Brand (1878–1963) banker and public servant; with Lazard Brothers, bankers, 1909–1960; senior British member, British American Combined Food Board, 1941–1944.

[8] William Morris, Viscount Nuffield (1877–1963) industrialist and philanthropist; founded Morris Motors Ltd., 1919, and Nuffield College, 1937.

[9] Ernest Simon, 1st Baron Simon of Wythenshawe (1879–1960) industrialist and public servant; Liberal MP, 1923–1924, 1929–1931; Chairman, BBC, 1947–1952.

[10] Sir Ralph Wedgewood (1874–1956) railway administrator; Chief General Manager, London and North Eastern Railway, 1923–1939.

[11] See Salter, *Memoirs of a Public Servant*, pp. 259–261; *idem, Slave of the Lamp*, pp. 132–137; and John W. Wheeler-Bennett, *John Anderson: Viscount Waverley* (London, 1962), pp. 210–219.

He has just learnt confidentially from Sir John Anderson that in 1930, when Anderson was permanent head of the Home Office, he was Chairman of a sub-committee appointed by the Committee of Imperial Defence, to report on precautions against air raids. Full recommendations were then made by his sub-committee and nothing whatever was done on them until the last few months.

Sir John Anderson, as you know, has been elected to Parliament to represent the University of Edinburgh, and owing to his great success as Governor of Bengal is in a very strong position. It so happens that he is coming to stay with me at all Souls on the 7 May. Sir Arthur Salter also lives in All Souls and is very anxious to see you about the matter, so I am writing to ask whether, in view of its great importance, you could make it possible to meet Sir Arthur Salter and Sir John Anderson and myself alone at breakfast at 9 am at All Souls on Sunday the 8 May? Sir Arthur Salter would then be prepared to give you a succinct account of the whole position so far as he has been able to ascertain it, and he is probably better informed than anyone else outside government circles and than most people in them. He would then like to discuss what people like you, he, Anderson, and myself can do to get matters put right. In this connection I enclose for your information in the strictest confidence a copy of a letter I wrote to Halifax a month ago, which I will ask you to return in the enclosed addressed envelope when read.

You might also look at the enclosed letter from a Mrs Bell to Macadam, the Secretary of Chatham House, which suggests possible lines upon which action might be taken.[12] Please return this also.

I was much obliged to you for the lift you were good enough to give me yesterday to Chatham House.

Curtis to Macadam, 22 April 1938 (ms. Curtis 12, fo. 95)

[...] Salter came to see me yesterday. He is concentrating on the air defence problem and his account of the position in all its aspects based on really first rate knowledge is hair-raising. As I have got John Anderson to stay with me for the weekend of the 7 May, I have written asking Nuffield to meet him, Salter and me on the 8th to discuss the whole situation.

[12] The enclosures mentioned are not available.

Foreign Affairs Group, Meeting of 24 April 1938[13] (Liddell Hart papers, LH 5/1)

Appeasement

The case for a policy of appeasement and conciliation was stated. Until recently we had stood for a policy of collective security and resistance to aggression. But now it was necessary to take into account other considerations – considerations of relative strength and vulnerability. A straight League policy involved grave danger of war; those who advocated it were certainly out of touch with the government, and probably out of touch with a majority of the public. In these circumstances, to press for a strict application of the Covenant would be to render the idea of the League intolerable to the public. When on the conclusion of the war the Covenant had been first discussed in the Cabinet, it was never understood that we should be obliged to take warlike action in its defence except in circumstances of a completed League (that is, unless the USA was an active member).

We should recognize that the League as at present constituted was not able to fulfil the functions which we had expected of it. We had come to the end of the 'Versailles period', and were faced with a war danger due to the emergence of insurgent states. League action offered no chance of reconciling these states with the rest of Europe. Germany and Italy would have nothing to do with Geneva, and there was in consequence no hope of appeasement through the League.

At present the capital task of diplomacy was not resistance to aggression whenever and wherever it might occur, but the preservation of peace – and of traditions of civilized government, liberalism, mercy. During the nineteenth century the general trend had been towards an improved international morality; nevertheless, to those living in that period the trend had been partially disguised by the occurrence at frequent intervals of disappointing and shocking events. Similarly, today we were experiencing a setback, and must probably expect to witness in the coming years even more tragic events than in the last period. Nevertheless, if we could preserve European peace, the trend, at the end of a sufficient period of time when the neurotic element in the dictatorship states might have had time to dissipate itself, might again be found to have been upwards. The incidental casualties in Europe were the price which must be paid for the maintenance of peace, upon which all further progress depended.

[13] There is no indication in the minutes of who participated in this meeting.

Translated into concrete terms, this meant that the primary effort of British policy should be directed not to resistance to aggression, but to appeasement and the finding of a modus vivendi with the aggressor states. Without this there was probably, in the long run, no way of avoiding European war. Large sections of the German public were in a sacrificial mood. Though Germany was not antagonistic to the British Empire as such, it bitterly resented any inclination by us to stop the expansion of its influence towards the Balkans and Asia Minor; and was also determined to obtain colonial possessions. We were obliged to accept this mood as a fact; it was no use attempting to demonstrate that it was unreasonable, and to resist all concession to it was probably to precipitate war. We had to choose a middle policy between resistance and retreat. An accommodation would certainly not be easy to find. The only constructive course was to try to get agreement between Italy, France, Germany, and England – the four powers which had built up European civilization; and in this connection to discuss the concessions which we could reasonably make to Germany.

Germany's ambitions could probably be divided into two categories: those to which it attached such importance that it was ready to go to war to realize them; those which it sought to achieve by diplomatic means. In the first category should perhaps be put the incorporation of all important irredentist communities within the *Reich*, and (eventually) the acquisition of colonies. Unyielding resistance to these ambitions would, sooner or later, probably mean war. Their satisfaction in some measure would need therefore to be part of any successful programme of conciliation.

If such were to be our policy, it was very dangerous to specify exact circumstances in which we should go to war; the Prime Minister's statement on March 24 went, in this respect, quite far enough in indicating our interest in central Europe. We ought to bring pressure upon France to press Czechoslovakia to go very far in meeting German demands, at least as far as accepting a cantonal system; and we ought probably to be prepared to countenance the total disappearance of Czechoslovakia. We should welcome the Anglo-Italian agreement, and the recreation, if it should prove possible, of the Stresa front; and should then aim at expanding this into the four-power pact. Whether this would require the cancellation of the Franco-Russian pact was uncertain; on the whole it was desirable to leave this pact at least formally in existence.

To adopt a policy of this kind was not to admit that the creation of the League had been a mistake, nor was it to abandon the League ideal. The League would remain in being, and its technique of co-operation between states might prove vital to the success of an appeasement programme. But League action would no longer be based upon force, upon Articles X and XVI. A League was needed which was capable of taking action; it was paradoxical but true to say that at present League action was impeded by its obligation to take action. With the League working on this reformed basis, it might be possible eventually to attract into its membership the USA, and in order to secure this a most drastic revision of the Covenant would be justified.

Other matters discussed

Czechoslovakia

If a crisis occurred, our action would probably depend on the action taken by France; and it was possible that France would not proceed beyond mobilization until it saw what action Russia intended to take. It was suggested that, in view of our weakness in the air, we ought not to go to war unless Russia had clearly shown that it intended to fight with its full power – Russia's air strength would then largely neutralize our weakness.

Our policy had so far left Hitler guessing about our intentions. His own intentions were equally obscure. Possibly he would try to encircle Czechoslovakia, keep the country in a ferment and strangle it economically: possibly he would attempt an *attaque brusquée*. There was some danger that the extremist Nazis, elated by success, might have got out of hand and would precipitate a crisis. The need of a 'constructive' policy was urged. A guarantee by us to maintain the status quo would be futile and dangerous. At worst it would precipitate war; at best, Germany would regard it as an obstacle which it must find a way of circumventing – and our chance of general agreement with Germany would be worsened.

Spain

The war might still last three or four months. Even if France desired to increase its aid to the government, it was too short of munitions to risk putting large quantities (which might be promptly captured) into Spain. Moreover, French munition factories had been concentrated in the Pyrenees, to be as remote as possible from the German air bases, and the government therefore feared complications upon the frontier. Any overt move against Franco would run the risk not only of opposition from abroad but also from officers in the French army who favoured his cause.

The Germans had consolidated their position in Spain more successfully than the Italians. There were fewer Germans, but they were experts holding key positions, and Franco would find it impossible to dislodge them. The Italians on the other hand were principally infantrymen who would probably be withdrawn.

Efforts at bringing about a truce seemed unlikely to succeed, since Franco demanded the unconditional surrender of the government.

Anglo-Italian agreement

There was agreement that its importance did not depend so much upon its contents as upon the interests and intentions of Italy. There were reasons for thinking that Mussolini, in order not to become a vassal of Hitler, would desire to draw closer to France and England. Furthermore, the agreement had let loose a flood of pro-British feeling in Italy, which would probably influence Mussolini's actions. But it was a mistake to think that the Stresa front had been recreated. With the Germans on the Brenner, Mussolini could not provoke Hitler. His policy would probably be to keep a foot in both camps.

Colonies

If war broke out on the question of colonies, we should have the minimum of sympathy and aid from the rest of the world. The wisest course was perhaps to prevent tension becoming acute by the grant of something which, in prestige and economic value, was satisfactory to Germany. Colonies would not in fact relieve her economic difficulties: the best arrangement would therefore perhaps be the transfer of *some* colonial territory as a prestige matter, accompanied by economic measures designed to improve her economic position.

Air weakness

Details of this were given, and it was agreed that we had not devoted enough money or ability to the programme of air defence and offence. Far too great a proportion of the defence appropriation had been spent on the navy which, if we lost command of the air, might never come into action before we were forced to sue for peace. The vulnerability of London to air attack was perhaps the greatest immediate danger to peace; but it was a danger which could be reduced. It was fantastic that the fate of our civilization should depend on three or four thousand aeroplanes; and it was agreed that the whole scale of our programme should be transformed. The experience of Barcelona showed the devastating effect on morale of continuous bombardment. The main obstacle to the creation of efficient air defences was that responsibility rested with the fighting services – which of all their duties always took least interest in civilian defence – and with the Home Office, which had no experience of large-scale creative undertakings.

British public opinion

For the first time since the war there was a real and bitter difference among the public upon our foreign policy; and the split was widening. Large sections of the public had been indoctrinated with collective security, and started with the assumption that war was the only efficient instrument of international policy – that the only way of preventing injustice was by a threat of war. Thus there was great suspicion of the Chamberlain policy of appeasement, and a real divergence between this section of the public and the government. This might become a serious matter and considerably weaken the government in its foreign policy – and the disunity in English thought would, in foreign eyes, contrast badly with the apparent unanimity of the dictatorship states. There was some difference of view as to whether there was a similar clash of opinion between Great Britain and the dominions.

Public opinion would be gravely disturbed and the chances of the appeasement programme therefore affected, if a great massacre followed the capture of Barcelona.

United States

The American public was showing an increasing dislike of the dictatorships and their methods, and felt a corresponding sympathy for France and Great Britain. But as the crisis had intensified these emotions were complicated by: (a) an increased desire for isolation, and escape from the troubles of Europe; and (b) a disposition, psychologically very understandable, to seize on an opportunity of complaint against Great Britain and France.

The growing naval strength of the USA was having some effect on opinion, but the result to be expected was a stiff policy in the Far East rather than in Europe. Yet even economic action against Japan was not likely until Japan had clearly lost its power to retaliate.

The Irish agreement would have an excellent effect on American opinion.

So far as the USA could co-operate with the Western democracies without any risk of being entangled in war, it would willingly do so. Thus there was room for economic agreements. But it was still very shy of any political action.

Anti-isolation propaganda in the USA was being conducted on wrong lines. It should be frankly admitted that, if war came, America might well avoid being drawn in. The points which should be made were (1) that, if war came, the *economic* consequences to America might be catastrophic; (2) that the USA was so strong and so invulnerable that, if it chose to pursue an active foreign policy, it could, *without real risk to itself*, tip the balance against war breaking out.

As regards debts, there was still bitterness in certain circles. A proposal by us to reopen the question would, however, embarrass the administration: we should privately make clear that we were willing to open discussions whenever the administration so wished.

Far East

Our international position had in one respect greatly improved: as a result of the slow progress by the Japanese an attack upon Hong Kong was now unlikely.

Failure by Japan would have important effects upon Russian and Germany policy. Germany, finding Japan no longer of use, might be expected to view more favourably an understanding with Russia; Russia, freed from the Japanese danger, might either feel able to co-operate more actively with the democratic powers in the West, or, on the contrary, might feel that their friendship was no longer essential and might therefore turn to an isolationist, or even to a pro-German policy.

Activities of the group

It was desirable that, pending negotiations, there should be private and unofficial contact with Germany, and this some of the members of the group were peculiarly fitted to maintain. It was suggested that the line to be taken with Germans was (a) to warn them, by the example of 1914, of basing their policy on the illusion of British decadence; (b) to point out that, if they were willing to co-operate with the other European powers they could probably fulfil peacefully most of their ambitions – e.g. those in central and eastern Europe and with regard to colonies; but that their present methods threatened an explosion.

It was suggested also that in view of the bewilderment of British public opinion, and of the serious consequences which the growing sense of drift and bitterness might have for our democracy, a statement on policy by the group would be timely. It was therefore decided to make another attempt at drafting a statement which at least some members would be willing to sign.

Curtis to Brand, 25 April 1938 (ms. Curtis 12, fos 101–103)

I have now discussed with Salter how the best use can be made of the opportunity offered by the fact that Nuffield has agreed to discuss the question of air-raid protection with John Anderson and ourselves at 10.30 am in All Souls on Sunday 8 May. We have now definitely decided that it will help if you, Nel[?], and Swinton are there. You, through your firm, know a lot about the mutual jealousies of the industries, the difficulties of labour, etc. Nel's experience during the war in overcoming the difficulties created by the shortage of skilled labour is simply invaluable; Swinton, too, from his war experience knows a lot about the interdepartmental difficulties in Whitehall, apart from his first-rate qualifications as a technician.

I think it is pretty clear that far too large a share of our financial and industrial resources have been secured by the navy at the expense of air defence and, as Swinton says, without adequate air defence a war might be over and lost before the navy could even come into action. One important factor in this position is the excellent work of the Navy League for several generations. The Air Ministry is the youngest and much the weakest of the three defence services, and what we need is an Air Defence League to educate public opinion to the fact that the advent of air power demands drastic modification of the traditional idea that the navy can always be depended on to keep the Empire safe. We shall not effect much by meeting and talking in All Souls unless we can bring into being some organization from which continuous pressure can be brought to bear on public opinion and the government. Such an organization to do anything must have adequate clerical staff at its command. Given an adequate office and clerical staff I foresee that such a League could get access to all the technical advise it needs.

Hitherto when it has been necessary to start anything new, e.g. Chatham House, I have always had old Abe [*Sir Abe Bailey*][14] to put up something for the necessary clerical expenses; but Abe is not available now, but that is the first fence to be got over. In starting an Air Defence League there is one great advantage to which we can avail ourselves at the outset if the matter is properly handled. You can rope in men from all parties, not excluding the conscientious pacifists. You have the widest appeal you can possibly make if we can lay hands on enough money at the outset to avail ourselves of this advantage and make

[14] Sir Abe Bailey (1864–1940) South African financier and statesman; benefactor of Chatham House.

a proper start. An Air Defence League, should, like the League of Nations Union, be able to get a very large membership with a small subscription, that is to get into a really sound financial position. If we have the luck to get two men like John Anderson and Nuffield together on the 8th we must make the best of our opportunity by talking in a more businesslike way than we sometimes do at the Moot [*a session of the Round Table movement*]. So, if you do not mind, I propose to act as a sort of conductor to the orchestra and try to ration out the time available to the various people present. We will start off by getting Salter to give a careful survey of the whole air position so far as he has been able to ascertain it.

By the way, you should get and read King-Hall's newsletter of 21 April. I have sent my copy to Nuffield but your secretary could get a copy from 27 Cresswell Place, London SW 10.

This, I take it, means that you will be sleeping at All Souls on the night of Saturday 7 May and I will have your room ready for you. That night is the annual dinner of the Ralegh Club at which John Anderson is speaking. Would you care to come to it?

Hole to Liddell Hart, 27 April 1938 (Liddell Hart papers, LH 5/1)

The next meeting of the Foreign Affairs Group will be at 12 noon on Sunday, May 15 at All Souls.

Allen to members of the Foreign Affairs Group, n.d. (Liddell Hart papers, LH 5/1)

I was asked, at the conclusion of the meeting of the Foreign Affairs Group at All Souls last Sunday, to add a special whip to the notice of the next meeting which you will be receiving from Miss Hole.

It was agreed at our meeting on April 24 that there was an urgent need for some clarifying statement of policy dealing with the new situation that has arisen in foreign affairs. If there was any chance of such a statement being sponsored by those of us who have been meeting for discussion during recent months, it would undoubtedly have considerable value both as a means of influencing the government and helping a very bewildered public opinion. I was therefore asked to press those who have attended previous meetings to make a special effort to be present on Sunday May 15 if they possibly can.

Brand to Curtis, 28 April 1938 (ms. Curtis 12, fo. 104)

Thanks for your letter of the 25th April. I hope I will be able to be at All Souls on Sunday, 8 May, at 10.30. I may very likely sleep at Eydon. I can't tell yet.

Are you quite certain there is not an Air Defence League? I have had two papers lately – one I think for training young pilots, but I thought the other was something in the form of an Air Defence League. There is certainly a body called the Air League,[15] but whether this does exactly what you have in mind, I do not know.

'The Anglo-Italian agreement' Memorandum by Arnold-Forster,[16] May [*sic*] 1938 (add. ms. Cecil 51140, fos 97–105)

The Anglo-Italian agreement has the immediate advantage of relieving the surface tension between Britain and Italy, but it does so at a disastrous price. On a broad view, it is neither honourable nor prudent.

Not honourable: for the British government traffics in the rights of others which are not ours to sell.

Not prudent: for the agreement weakens and humiliates the League instead of helping to create conditions in which the collective peace system can work properly.

Not even astute as an imperialist deal; for it buys from Mussolini revocable and lightly regarded promises, and sells to him irrevocable and injurious deeds. [*The rest of the memorandum detailed 'What Britain buys' and 'What Britain sells'*].

[15] Founded in 1909 as the Aerial League of the British Empire, it was renamed in 1920 to the Air League of the British Empire. This League was largely concerned with more general aims such as air technology, trade, communications, and defence.

[16] Will Arnold-Forster, 'For what should national power be used?', in Geneva Institute of International Relations, *War Is Not Inevitable, Problems of Peace*, thirteenth series (London, 1938), pp. 225–256, offered a more detailed analysis of his views on the subject of 'a collective peace system'.

Nicolson to Angell, 2 May 1938 (Angell papers)

[. . .] I find my present position one of conflicting loyalties. On the one hand I do not approve of Chamberlain's policy in all its aspects, yet on the other I cannot place any faith in the Opposition. These are the moments when one longs to be an independent.

Wint to Allen, 4 May 1938 (Allen papers, box 15, correspondence, 1937–1938)

At the last meeting Salter outlined the sort of thing which needs to be said (by unofficial visitors) to the Germans – (a) warning them, by the example of 1914, not to base too much on our 'decadence'; (b) suggesting that, if they would only proceed in a co-operative manner, they would probably attain all their main ambitions in east Europe and in colonies; but that their present methods are likely to cause an explosion.

I can imagine few people who could do this better than Salter himself. He has a sufficiently pugnacious manner to impress the Germans; and is sufficiently near the centre to be taken as representative.

I urged him to consider going to Germany immediately after the end of term, and suggested dropping a note to Bernstorff[?] – with whom I expect you are in touch – to sound him on such a project. Salter is, however, not enthusiastic.

If you think there is anything in such a scheme, I wonder if you would perhaps talk it over with him.

Salter to Allen, 4 May 1938 (Allen papers, box 15, correspondence, 1937–1938)

Just a line to say I've not been able to get a talk yet with [. . .] (who's been in Glasgow), but am having tea with him on Monday (when I shall raise the question of seeing PM).

Am also trying, with interruptions and great difficulty, *to draft something*. I shall soon decide whether to publish when I see how it comes out – but anyhow it won't be finished this week.

Allen to Curtis, 10 May 1938 (ms. Curtis 12, fo. 113b)

You will be receiving tomorrow my desperate attempt to draft very hurriedly a line of argument to stimulate discussion in our group on Sunday. I have had to put it together under very adverse circumstances, and I am distressed to see how very bad some of the literary style is. But perhaps it is better to have this document than nothing. The argument sometimes suffers from my attempt to meet points of view which are not entirely my own. I hope everyone in the group will feel free to reject the document out of hand if it should seem to them on the wrong lines.

I find I owe you an apology for never having sent you a draft wording in connection with air-raid precautions. I have been terribly hard pressed and it has slipped my memory. If I can get a moment or two I will have a shot at it before Sunday.

Allen to members of the Foreign Affairs Group, 10 May 1938 (Allen papers, box 17, manuscripts, speeches, etc)[17]

To those who have taken part in the discussion of foreign affairs at All Souls College

On a number of occasions during our discussions it has been suggested that we might be able to help both the government and the public if all of us or some of us jointly published some statement.

The enclosed document is an attempt to outline not the final text of any such publication, but the line of argument that might be considered. It is deliberately drafted with an eye to its temper and practical character – in other words with the object of unlocking the sympathetic attention of less erudite and less converted persons than ourselves.

It is not meant to be the document we should in fact publish, for any publication would need to be written with literary skill. It would also need to be very much shortened, to have its overlapping arguments simplified, its many gaps filled and its order clarified.

[17] A copy of this document is also available in the Liddell Hart papers, LH 5/1.

All I have tried to do is to put before you subject matter for discussion, knowing that the document is faulty and highly controversial. It omits a number of important topics and is dubious in quality at many points. For all this I offer my apologies. I have had no time to do more than dictate these notes in rough fashion, but since no one else seems willing to be draftsman I hope the enclosed may be of some value. It will at least serve to arouse discussion; and then perhaps we may find some one or more of our number who, having heard our arguments together, would bring into being the right kind of document.

A peace policy for the immediate present

Let us explain at the very outset why we join in presenting this statement. It is an attempt to outline a British foreign policy desirable in itself, immediately practicable in the broken circumstances of the present, and capable of rebuilding a system of international collaboration.

Never, we imagine, has public opinion taken a more sustained interest in foreign affairs, and yet felt so completely in the dark as to what can be or ought to be done. This state of mind is not without its dangers. A combination of eager interest and grave bewilderment may constitute a threat to democracy. It can lead either to panic or to irritated frustration. Panic may cause certain sections of the public to resort to the false security offered by political leaders who care little for peace or democracy. Frustration may cause other sections of the public to follow advice that may appear brave and idealistic and yet be unwise or unavailing.

A transitional policy

We believe that public opinion – as also the most devoted advocates of peace amongst us – may have to face the possibility that the nations have reached the end of a definite and heroic stage in 'post-war' foreign policy and international experiment. We may now have to enter a second stage, during which circumstances compel us reluctantly to vary, for a time at any rate, our methods of attempting to safeguard the peace of the world and to rebuild the machinery of international co-operation. In other words, we are compelled to frame and to pursue an essentially transitional policy. In doing so we must take into account the point of view of the government that is likely to be in office in our country during the next few critical years.

It seems to us of no service to the cause of peace at such a time to lay all our emphasis upon the mistakes of the past that have led up to the present disaster. It may be – indeed it most certainly is – true that the dangers of today need not have arisen if America had joined the League, and if our own and other governments had acted differently from the date when the Treaty of Versailles was framed until the present, when tragedies are being enacted in China, North Africa, Spain, and central Europe. It is argued that the Treaty of Versailles was the best that could be hoped for, having regard to the state of public opinion at that time, and taking into account the evidence of war guilt then available. Some of us deny this, and remind the public that we protested against the Treaty of Versailles when it was in the making, and advocated a wiser, more just, and more courageous policy throughout the post-war years; when Germany was showing discontent with her inferior status; when lawful procedure was abandoned in Manchuria and Abyssinia; when the opportunities offered by the Disarmament Conference were allowed to slip; when governments failed to use the League of Nations either to promote a more equal justice or to mobilize its power to forestall and, if necessary, resist unlawful procedure. All this may be true, and it may equally be true that some of us declared it to be so at the time and not after each event – in fact at each stage throughout the whole period of this developing disaster. But we who submit this outline of policy see little value in this retrospective diagnosis – still less in acrimonious denunciation of those upon whom now rests the responsibility of determining policy. By this we do not mean that criticism should be stilled, or that we should release the government from the keenest vigilance. Indeed, the whole purpose of this memorandum is to offer what we can in the way of warning as well as to outline a constructive policy.

National unity in foreign affairs

But we do see considerable danger in allowing foreign policy, of all political topics, to become the issue that divides the nation into bitterly hostile opposing camps. That, in our judgement, would be the worst thing that could happen in a sphere of political policy which deals with such a subject as peace and war, and involves the relationship of this country to other nations. We believe that the art of government through democracy requires, especially in the realm of international policy, an advocacy which is constructive and helpful even when it is critical. Moreover, we are alive to a new and grave consideration which has come into play, and which cannot be treated casually. Just because the structure of the League of Nations has been weakened, we are left – until such time as it can be restored – with an international situation in which there is an alarming revival of power politics. Consequently it is now difficult for the government of the day to take the public fully into its confidence. This, indeed, is not the least of the major disasters which have followed failure to sustain the League of Nations; for among the great advantages of the League was the fact not only that it set up a common rule of behaviour through which the nations could shake themselves free from the intrigues of power politics, but the fact that it enabled international relationships to be discussed and policy framed openly before the public opinion of the world. Unfortunately, we are now passing through a most perilous stage of history, in which on the one hand the citizens of every country are keenly interested in the shaping of foreign policy, whilst on the other hand even democratic governments are less able to take that public into their confidence because of the presence of potential enemies.

We are also conscious of the emergence of a dangerous mood in the domestic discussion of foreign affairs. Whether this difficulty could be met by extending our constitutional procedure by the setting up of a Foreign Affairs Committee in Parliament we do not know. But we see a need for improving the machinery whereby the government of the day can share the knowledge which it alone possesses, with an opposition which will exercise pressure without risk to the efficient and wise shaping of policy.

Depleted membership of the League

There are further difficulties confronting us. However much we still believe in the inherent rightness and practical soundness of the principles and methods of the League and its Covenant, we are doubtful whether it is now possible to serve the cause of peace by insisting rigidly upon the application of those methods or the use of that machinery as though no disaster had occurred, or as though the circumstances of the present had not become what they are. We cannot overlook the fact that the effective membership of the League of Nations is seriously depleted. That has led to a grave consequence, for it means that the essential prerequisite of a system of collective resistance to aggression no longer exists. The value of collective action as a means to security lay in the fact that the membership of the League was so nearly complete that it was possible to restrain the potential aggressor by conveying to him, in advance of his aggression, the knowledge that he would without doubt be confronted by preponderant power. The collective system, in so far as it possessed overwhelming power, was in a position to *prevent* war. Indeed, it was this capacity to *deter* aggression which was the chief advantage of the collective system as compared with the ad hoc alliances of the previous age of power politics. It may still be true that those nations which remain loyal to their obligations to obey the rule of lawful procedure possess in the aggregate superior power, and would, if put to the test, be able to defeat aggression. But an element of uncertainty and therefore of unpredictability has now been introduced, and this makes the effectiveness of the League in its weakened state much less than was previously the case.

Armed strength of the League

Not only has the League membership been depleted, but there is now also an element of doubt as to the relative strength of the armament of the powers loyal to the League, as compared with the nations who are in revolt against the status quo and who remain outside the League. It may be true that the armaments of what are called the League powers, and especially their margin of economic reserves, still remain sufficient to enable them to be victorious. But it is not certain that this superiority in armed power is so overwhelming as to enable them to deter aggressors without a conflict. This is more especially so when those aggressors, by the very nature of their regimes (violent in character and doubtful in permanency) may be more disposed to take risks than the countries still constituting the League of Nations.

Russia

There is one final consideration on this subject of power that we feel cannot be ignored. It is most unfortunate that Russia – one of the most potentially powerful members of the League – should have obstructed the League during its first fifteen years of life, and should also have been the exponent of revolutionary tactics across the frontiers of the countries with whom it is now – all too belatedly – co-operating at the League table. It may be that Russia has now rejected these tactics and this objective. But on this we are still left in grave doubt. Russia, if she so desired, could most certainly make it clear that she had abandoned her previous revolutionary methods. She could do this by closing down what is called the 'Comintern'; and it is much to be desired that she would make this decision. But until she has made this unmistakably clear, some element of unreliability as to her power and bona fides must surround her as a member of the League family.

Grievances and the law

Apart from the question of the power of the League states to deter aggression by overwhelming armaments and a wide membership, there is another difficulty. This arises from the sense of grievance which has been steadily increasing amongst certain nations since the date of the Treaty of Versailles. In other words the moral foundations of the law are called in question. There is no doubt that some, at any rate, of the complaints against the peace settlement are unjustified, whilst others are exaggerated. Nonetheless, mistakes were made at Versailles and, what is still more unfortunate, steps were not taken in the years that followed to remedy those grievances and to remove unreasonable discriminations by the spontaneous initiative of the victorious powers who could have employed the League as an instrument of treaty revision. Two consequences have followed which have now assumed serious proportions. In the first place, public opinion in the nations loyal to the League feels conscience-stricken about certain inequalities and discriminations in the law it is called upon to protect by collective action. In the second place, the aggrieved nations have whipped up their peoples into an almost neurotic state of indignation, with the result that, beginning themselves as the victims of injustice, they now harbour unjust ambitions against others.

It was indeed unfortunate that this first experiment in international collaboration should have found its starting point in peace treaties which were in many respects unwise and even unjust. It was also a misfortune that the United States of America declined to join the League and that the vanquished Germany, with her new Weimar Republic, was excluded from membership instead of at once being welcomed into the family of nations.

Nevertheless, none of these disadvantages need have proved fatal to the basic conception of the League or to its practice if only the statesmen, who had the power to direct world policy at that time, had forthwith acted up to the principles of the League, and immediately set themselves to put its articles into practice. Everything was then favourable to such an initiative. Notwithstanding many obvious difficulties and the disadvantage of war memories, the public opinion of the world could easily have been led to respond – and to respond enthusiastically – to a policy which proceeded without delay to remedy grievances and remove inequalities of status before the law. In the atmosphere of goodwill and confidence which would thus have been created, a start could soon have been made in the reduction and limitation of national armaments.

It was failure to take quick steps towards justice and conciliation, when they could have been carried through from 1920 onwards, and failure to use the asset of a peace-loving public opinion both in the victorious and vanquished nations, that started the process of disintegration, and bit by bit created those evil tempers, new fears, and tangled situations which now embarrass the League. It was not the League nor its constitution which were to blame. It was a failure in human judgement.

We have felt it necessary to record these opinions because some of us think it important to refute the idea, now so widely held, that our present troubles prove the League to have been condemned to failure from the very start by its method and its constitution. The majority of those who sign this document do not believe the facts justify this opinion. We are, however, unanimous in believing that if a transitional policy could now be found, the broken situation could be restored and the work of rebuilding the League be set in motion.

On the other hand, we frankly admit that once the opportunity had slipped for using the League as a means of enabling growth and change to continue by consent, a whole set of new problems arose which have caused the League to become confronted with a situation in which its successful use is impeded.

Conflict between law and growth

Just because the statesmen in power in the post-war years failed to push on rapidly with the use of the League as an instrument of change, the principle of law has inevitably come into conflict with the principle of growth. Once that conflict was allowed to emerge, law became synonymous with the selfish protection of the status quo and the maintenance of its advantages by those nations which at the time of the peace settlement were the most fortunate under the law. The only way in which to exalt the new principle of law would have been for those states, when they bound a steel band of law round the status quo, to have offered proposals for sharing their good fortune by modifying their own ascendancy in a world where historical good luck had given them first place in the family of nations. Since they were not prepared without delay to initiate such changes in the law under which they were the beneficiaries, the whole idea of law fell into disrepute, and since growth did not seem likely to continue by peaceful procedure, it has been resumed by violence. It was, in other words, fantastic to let it appear that, although the world had been changing through century after century, and different nations had been expanding and diminishing throughout history, the powers that had 'arrived' in 1919 could clamp down something they called law and impede the continuance of that growth. What was needed was an immediate initiative so that growth could continue in a legitimate way in the Far East, in Africa, and in central Europe. That initiative was not taken. It is now too late to content ourselves with insisting upon the rigid use of doctrinal policies of law, which were sound in the past, but are inadequate for the present. What we need, therefore, is a transitional policy; not a complete rejection of the League idea, its method, and its constitution, but a programme of action, which is competent both to meet immediate needs and to set us again on the task of successful rebuilding. It is this policy we propose to outline.

Rigid application of law

What then is our first conclusion? We believe it a mistake to let it seem that we lay our principal emphasis upon the League as an instrument to resist aggression. No doubt we must continue to take active steps to devise ways and means of preventing, so far as we can, changes being made by force. These steps we shall outline in due course, for we cannot ignore the fact that certain nations are transforming legitimate grievances into illegitimate ambitions. Nonetheless, we hold that it is no longer of any avail to go out to meet this situation in a narrow mood of legalism. Our opportunity to approach grievances strictly from the standpoint of law has passed. We now need something more than a rigid application of the law, for this rigidity might only lead to some disastrous explosion. We must therefore embark on an effort towards appeasement, even perhaps accepting certain breaches in morality such as that which occurred in Austria, as we make this new attempt to rebuild a system of international collaboration.

This procedure of expediency was the method employed in the days before 1914 and before the coming of the League of Nations. During the nineteenth century casualties in morality did occur, and yet all the time the level of humane conduct in the world was slowly rising. Had the League been used swiftly and courageously from the start, that process could have been expedited and further breaches in morality have been prevented. But we have missed that opportunity, and now we must beware lest, in our zeal and our distress, it should be the League itself and its high moral code which, by too rigid an application, should evoke an explosion more terrible in its consequences than even those casualties in morality which we may have alternatively to accept.

Czechoslovakia

The problem of Czechoslovakia illustrates this. Here is a geographical area distraught with the ambitions of several competing nationalities. It may be worth quoting in this respect a letter to the *Manchester Guardian* from a political thinker of such integrity as Mr J.A. Hobson:

> Czechoslovakia has never been a nation in any intelligible sense: the pretence that it was is one of the worst follies of the post-war treaty. It has possessed

no political or economic unity and self-sufficiency. Is it not natural that the Sudeten Germans, in majority occupation of the most developed industrial areas, should resent a pseudo-national economy which has brought them ruin and unemployment, and should wish to be attached to the German Reich? There are, of course, political and other difficulties. But, if the rights of non-German minorities in the German areas can be safeguarded, is there any ground for denying the claims put forward by Henlein and (presumably) Herr Hitler? Czechoslovakia as a state would not be injured by the withdrawal of a permanently dissatisfied German minority, and though Germany might gain in numbers, territory and industry, is that a proper ground for any further interference on our part? It is to be hoped that we have not pledged ourselves to France (with or without Russia) to any such policy.

If there is such a large element of doubt on this subject of Czechoslovakia, is it right to continue to insist that British youth shall be killed and Europe involved in a ghastly catastrophe to sustain the existing integrity of that country? It is not sufficient to reply that what we are asked to die for is lawful procedure. The chance of upholding that procedure has been seriously diminished by delays which have given rise to evil tempers and because of the depleted power of the League membership. It may be that death and war will in the end become inevitable, but at least let us see what new hope of peace would come if we accepted radical changes in this area of German nationalistic ambition.

Czechoslovakia is not entirely dissimilar from Ireland, where finally division of sovereignty has had to be conceded. It is surely worth considering how far a chance decision to rivet the rule of law on the world at the end of a world war and at a time when that Irish problem was unresolved, would have ended so bitter a controversy. Certainly not, unless from the very moment that the rule of law was thus established, the attempt to revise the law by energetic and peaceful means had been set in motion. Indeed, we must now reflect upon how far it is for the good of the world that we should plunge the world into war to uphold law in eastern Europe where that law has been left unrevised by peaceful means for twenty bitter years.

It is, moreover, a fact that the conception of law is less mature amongst some nations than amongst others – even in Europe. Our first attempt to sustain the rule of law under such circumstances would always have been difficult, and yet the risks involved would have been worth taking had we still the assistance of a League overwhelmingly powerful in armaments and membership. But to insist rigidly upon doing so, as things are today, may be to wreck civilization in the West where it has been achieved, in order to make a doubtfully successful attempt to sustain law where the conception of law is not yet founded.

Will the neurosis of dictatorship pass?

The process of change through power politics has now been resumed by new insurgent nations in Europe and Asia – and under the auspices of regimes and of personalities which have revived primitive emotions of cruelty and ambition. Indeed, it is this revival of cruelty which is almost more alarming than breaches of the law. It is surely the first essential in wisdom to take into account the considerable prospect that all this may pass. This recrudescence of old-time power politics, expressed in personal dictatorship, is not likely to take permanent root in twentieth-century civilization. But everything depends upon whether we are prudent and avoid provoking some grave disaster in the meantime. Democracy is more likely to prove durable and to resume its hold over public imagination than any of the varieties of dictatorship, which have never emerged except for ad hoc reasons such as humiliation in war or the complete breakdown of a nation's social fabric. Indeed, we hold that nothing is more fatal to peace or to the prospect of rebuilding a new League system than to deny the possibility that this neurosis may be temporary; for otherwise we interpret each disastrous event with such emphasis as the certain preliminary to a sequence of further evils that we *insist* upon their culmination in war. To prophesy the inevitability of war in the future is to precipitate it in the present.

The need for strength

The second essential in wisdom is that those nations which still adhere to democracy and desire to create a workmanlike international system should themselves be strong in a world that insists upon being armed. Britain should therefore declare that her rearmament will be expedited in every possible way, especially in defensive armaments which lag behind her other equipment, in the storage of food and other necessary commodities, and above all in the means to sustain the nation if attacked from the air. She should, however, declare that she is prepared to cease rearming at any point of time, provided other countries will do the same, and provided that an arms agreement is accepted, which recognizes parity for comparable powers in Europe, so that no one country should be able to dominate the Continent.

Here, let us say that we do not deny that an armaments race has its inherent danger for the nations concerned. And yet we do believe that in these days of aggressive dictatorship, when democracy is challenged and war exalted, the nations which disavow war and who cherish democracy must, for their part, be strongly armed. The danger from an arms race will, however, be lessened to the extent that rearmament is accompanied by those offers of justice and in favour of rebuilding a peace-keeping system to which we shall later refer.

Britain’s attitude to collective security

As part of her determination to be strong, Britain should again underline her fidelity to League principles and methods. She should make clear that her determination is to make the main and consistent object of her policy the rebuilding of a system to uphold the method of lawful international procedure. She should state her intention to support every effort to provide all nations, including herself, with a means of common defence, which indeed is the only sure means of defence left to us. She should declare that she is prepared to join in making use of every opportunity where conditions make it possible, as they did at Nyon, to get a preponderance of force behind law, either by economic or military collective action.

But in reaffirming her intention to remain loyal to the League as an instrument of collective defence she must, under present circumstances and because of the many reasons we have already mentioned, make clear that a mere formal declaration of intention to fulfil her obligations under the League system is now insufficient. This empty formula places a barrier between the public and the League idea. There are areas where collective action can be successfully employed and areas where that is more doubtful. Consequently, Britain is now compelled to make clear that she is no longer able to think of League obligations as automatic and applicable everywhere. She must now take account of the circumstances under which each act of aggression may arise, and the capacity of the League powers to deal with it on each occasion.

What Britain must, however, never do is to say that she will only act according to the degree to which her own national interests may be involved. That is fatal not only morally, but it may also be disastrous in practice to herself and her Empire, should she at any time need the help of collective defence. What Britain should say is that she remains loyal to the League method, but that, things being what they are, she must be free to consult with other League powers on each occasion to ascertain whether those powers are capable of successfully intervening by joint action, but that she herself is willing to take her part if the capacity to act is proved. Above all she must insist that this consultation should take place before and not only at the time of aggression.

That this is unfortunate we do not deny; but it results from the many reasons we have stated above. It is now a choice of evils – the evil of stretching automatic obligations to an extent which is impracticable and might lead to world catastrophe, and the evil of a less rigid method which may perhaps sometimes involve the acceptance of casualties in lawful procedure, but which will narrow the limits of any misfortune during the period when we are rebuilding not only the road to appeasement but the foundations of the League system itself.

It follows that during this transitional period grave dangers will exist. We must therefore not only help to recreate the system of collective defence through the League of Nations, but further strengthen the capacity for immediate action by close contact with France, economic relationships with America, and consultation with all the nations still loyal to the principles and methods of lawful international practice.

Security through appeasement

But Britain's main contribution to resisting aggression, re-establishing the will to peace and laying the new foundations of an international system must be the offer to negotiate new peace settlements in so far as they may be found possible. A completely new start must here be made. Little hope can be found in continuing old discussions from the starting point of the stage reached by old confusions. Britain must break through the present tangles of anger, fear and resentment. She must hold out the hand of reconciliation even to the lawbreaker. To do this we shall have to accept as a fait accompli events which we regret and which have come about by illegitimate methods. We shall also have to realize that Britain, as the centre of a great Commonwealth covering one quarter of the earth's surface, is peculiarly vulnerable to the criticism of these new insurgent nations. We may ourselves have learnt by now that many of the arguments used to prove the need for empires and territorial expansion are without intellectual or technical justification – whether the object in view be access to raw materials, movements of surplus population, or trade interests. But to present a blank negative to those nations which seek some measure of equality in prestige with ourselves is to diminish our power to extend the area of democracy and peaceful procedure in the world.

(Here should follow our previous proposals on migration, colonies, mandates, the development of tropical Africa and other economic proposals, etc. These proposals would of course need to be amplified and considerably revised.)

Passing to the more strictly political aspects of these efforts to negotiate new peace settlements, it is desirable to refer to two nations in particular.

Italy

We are prepared to support the new Anglo-Italian agreement. If we accept as our main objective this making of a new start in reconstructing the peace of Europe, then it is more important for us to consider how we may collaborate with Italy in the future than to continue our condemnation of her past misdeeds. There should, however, be no shadow of doubt about the implementing of those clauses in the agreement which provide for the complete evacuation of Spain and for the honouring of Italy's undertaking to respect in every detail the political and territorial integrity and independence of that country.

Bitterly though we regret it, we feel compelled, for the sake of the major interest of European peace which we seek to promote by this and other agreements, to recognize Italian sovereignty in Abyssinia. Failure to carry through to success the effort of the nations through the League on behalf of Abyssinia was a fact we deplore. But we must now choose between two evils – the reluctant acceptance of an illegitimate conquest or letting Europe drift from one unsettled state of danger to the next. Had the League not been weakened and had it been used with more determination, we believe this tragedy could have been avoided. Now we feel compelled to recognize the consequences of one disaster rather than drift into a more fatal stage of intrigue and catastrophe, depriving us of any hope of rebuilding peaceful collaboration in Europe and of preventing aggression elsewhere.

We should also remember, when considering the Anglo-Italian agreement, that the relationship of European nations to each other is fluid and in no sense final. Every country is in a mood of apprehension and uncertainty. Therefore Britain, when working for appeasement, and when attempting to lay the foundations for a new start, must take into account how each peace settlement may exercise an influence, not only over the policy of the actual signatories thereto, but over the relationship of those signatories to other nations as well.

In deciding to go forward with a policy of appeasement, some new starting point must indeed be found. That means accepting past events even though we may still deplore them. If we insist upon first undoing the injustice of every situation inherited from the recent past, then no new starting point can be found. As Mr J.A. Spender has put it:

> All international dealings would be brought to a standstill if we pronounced these sentences upon one another and considered them binding [. . .]. When certain principles lead to impossible or extremely undesirable conclusions it is time to consider whether there is not something wrong with the principles [. . .]. Because the method of sanctions has not succeeded, the world cannot be cut off from alternative ways of promoting law and order among

> nations [...]. The Italian agreement is the one obvious way open to us of redressing the balance disturbed by the forcible annexation of Austria, and to that extent relieving the anxieties of other nations threatened by a similar aggression. Perhaps even more important, it breaks the spell under which Europe was rapidly being divided into two camps sundered by unappeasable feuds.

Germany

Here we need first of all to refer to our previous arguments recording the history of the post-war years, so as to remind ourselves of how the present difficulties in central Europe arose, and of Britain's share in allowing the present situation to develop. It is true we cannot tell how far new personalities, new racial and emotional ambitions may have passed beyond control. Stern resistance to aggression may become inevitable. But we can at least show, in the process of peace negotiations, our regret for the past, our desire for an equal settlement in the future, and our hope for friendly collaboration. We must not offer brides: we must offer to negotiate a new peace settlement.

We owe Germany at the very outset the removal of certain moral discriminations which have played an important part in causing her insurgent mood. The new settlement should therefore include a declaration in favour of the signing of a protocol resubscribing the League Covenant and the ILO statutes so that these may become dissociated from the post-war treaties of peace. A statement should also be made to the effect that historical responsibility for the war is, in the British view, not a matter on which it is suitable for the combatants on one side to impose their judgement on the combatants on the other; and that it is therefore desirable for that clause to be eliminated from the treaties of peace, as also any reflections on German colonial administration.

We should then go on to make clear to Germany our willingness to negotiate a colonial readjustment. Britain should offer to extend the Congo Basin regime and should suggest that other countries should do the same. This regime having been established, and the distinction between class 1 and class 2 colonies having been thus abolished, we should invite Germany to accept a similar principle for the status of colonial areas. The question of the return of colonies under full sovereignty cannot be ruled out. We should, however, insist that decisions on this subject must be incorporated in a new all-round settlement. It is no doubt the fact that many changes in the status quo have been unfair or unwise in many peace treaties. This was as true of the Treaty of Brest Litovsk as it was of the Treaty of Versailles. But it is impossible, in the present temper of Europe, to start upon a process of piecemeal readjustment of each separate grievance that any nation may feel against any existing treaty. Evil decisions in the past are no doubt resented, but there is little hope for any new peace settlement unless it is frankly admitted that all claims and counterclaims must be considered together. That is precisely the method employed in the comprehensive agreement with Italy. It must also apply to an agreement with Germany.

At this point, there will naturally arise other German claims such as those concerned in her relationship with Czechoslovakia. Here Britain's good offices can be usefully employed. To this subject we have already referred, and we have reminded ourselves of how Britain was compelled, when dealing with Ireland, to go so far as to concede the granting in that area of groupings under different sovereign governments. The ascertainment of the degree of autonomy, or even partition, that may be necessary must be left to the governments which undertake the negotiations; it cannot and should not be the subject of an unofficial programme. We can only here state that, in our judgement, the prospect of successfully coping with Germany's other claims in south-east Europe will be notably increased if her special claims in Czechoslovakia are as fully met as possible. Britain's commitments meantime in this particular area have been wisely stated by the Prime Minister in his recent speech, and we ourselves have made reference to our view of the manner in which obligations under the League Covenant should be interpreted. We believe it to be unwise to press for further clarification during the present diplomatic exchanges; for in doing so we might foster either intransigence on the one side or aggression on the other.

Britain should also state that she is prepared for Germany to have a preferential economic status in central and south-eastern Europe superior to that which we claim for ourselves; and that this country would join in calling upon Russia to discontinue the activities of the 'Comintern'.

If any such effort to negotiate an agreement with Germany, as we have successfully done with Italy, should fail, no new injury to peace will have been inflicted – on the contrary. If we have offered a settlement based on equality of status, and then find that it is rejected, we shall have mobilized the moral support of the world, not excluding public opinion in America and even within Germany herself. Moreover, the powers in eastern and south-eastern Europe, in Scandinavia, in the Mediterranean Basin, and in western Europe will then be in a far stronger position to consider the extent to which they can join in resistance to ambitions which have become menacing and illegitimate in character.

Rebuilding a system of international collaboration

This leads us to the consideration of the manner in which international co-operation should in future be promoted, and international security be re-established so that all nations may feel able to rely upon the pledged word. Here we shall need first transitional methods, and then more permanent policies represented by action through a League of Nations system.

Let us begin with the transitional.

It may be wise – circumstances being what they have now become – to agree to a four-power pact between Britain, France, Italy, and Germany to ensure the keeping of the peace in western Europe. This would take that place of the old Locarno agreement. We should naturally welcome a similar pact in the east of Europe, but even if that should prove for the present impossible, there seems to be no reason why such a failure should hinder agreement in the west with the restraining influence that a western agreement would undoubtedly exercise.

Pending the completion of wider negotiations for bringing Germany and Italy back into a system of international collaboration, France would continue to adhere to her agreements with east European countries and to her close *entente* with Britain, the present League system being retained, and our obligations defined as we have stated them earlier in these pages. In the event, however, of a new peace settlement being successfully negotiated with Germany, so that she would thereby have found an honourable adjustment of her claims with regard to extra-territorial minorities, her economic position in south-east Europe and her colonial development, then the road would be open to the discussion of the closing down of the Russian Comintern and the future of the League of Nations with Germany once again a member. On the assumption that success were achieved in respect of these two vitally important matters, then the Franco-Soviet pact should surely be abandoned.

We therefore come to the all-important subject of the future of the League of Nations itself. We have stated in a previous section of this 'outline of policy' that most of us believe the League of Nations and its Covenant to have been capable of achieving the promotion of peaceful change and the organization of security. No disaster that has occurred in recent years leads us to alter that judgement. To restore the League of Nations seems to us imperative. There is no alternative method for ensuring the safety of Britain or the peace of the world. The League system must be rebuilt. But we are now of the opinion that, in view of present circumstances, there is no longer any prospect of the nations outside the League returning to it, so long as its present constitution remains. And we consider it absolutely essential to extend the League's membership in order to bring to success the various peace settlements we have outlined, and in order to provide that means of co-operation which will lead to security. These peace settlements and this extended League membership are in fact the essential accompaniments to an arms limitation agreement and to the restarting of the habit of international collaboration.

What we all desire is the possibility of international *action* to promote justice and restrain aggression. It was intended, when the League was framed, that action in respect to both these two objects should be achieved by the nations accepting automatic obligations. But that method of promoting action we believe to be longer practicable – things being what they now are. Indeed, we have come to the conclusion that it is the very existence of automatic obligations which has become one of the principal obstructions to the action we all desire. If, however, we could envisage a League, based upon the favourable foundation of new peace settlements, and including America, and if possible Germany, Italy, and Japan, then we should enter a period during which the continuing habit of international collaboration would make action possible. The frequent presence of so many nations at the League table, and their consequent participation in its manifold peaceful activities, would lead on to the prospect of action against aggression far more surely than will the maintenance of automatic obligations in a depleted League. The method of realizing this proposal need not – in fact should not – be here discussed. Very wise and sympathetic diplomacy, and not public agitation, would be required to ascertain the point of view of the countries concerned, especially that of America. But we believe that those who are the most zealous adherents of the present League system and the present Covenant would be well advised to give this proposal their most sympathetic consideration. Meantime, and until this new decision has been reached, the most energetic steps should be taken to develop the League with its existing Covenant as an instrument of social justice and economic welfare, and to establish close economic relationships with the USA.

(Here should be included our previous discussion of the development of the economic section of the League, either in its present form or with an independent constitution, and here too should be amplified proposals for assisting economically the smaller eastern European countries and for making use of the Van Zeeland Report. Here too should be included reference to the importance of

Anglo-French-American economic co-operation, and the development of the League in all international social services.)

Arms limitation

Finally a word on the need for an arms limitation agreement as desirable not only in order to ease financial burdens but as the most reliable method of guaranteeing any new settlements arrived at. Nothing will more certainly restore confidence in the pledged word and lower the tension of fear in Europe than a cessation of the present armaments race and the knowledge that nations have abandoned their attempts to out-match each other in armed strength. Such an arms limitation agreement would itself be evidence of the admission of equality of status between all the great powers, for it would need to provide equality for comparable powers according to their geographical and other needs, but making it impossible for any one nation to dominate Europe. It would require to be supervised internationally, a principle widely accepted by many powers, including Nazi Germany herself, during the disarmament discussions. The agreement should also be accompanied by a declaration by all signatories that, in the event of a breach of the pledged word leading to any nation exceeding its allotted quota, the other countries would increase their quotas so that any breach might be countered.

And here it seems desirable to emphasize the importance of that oft-used phrase, an 'all-round settlement'. We hope the Italian agreement will prove the value of outlining a peace settlement whose ultimate ratification depends upon the fulfilment of certain agreed conditions. We believe that the peace settlement with Germany touching upon minorities and economic and colonial questions, when worked out in detail, would need for the sake of all-round appeasement to depend upon every nation (including Germany herself) accepting the main principles of an arms limitation agreement and declaring its intention to negotiate the form and character of that agreement. The peace settlement with Germany should similarly include a declaration of willingness to enter into negotiations for the purpose of rebuilding a League system, even though the details thereof must of necessity be left for further discussion.

This outline of an immediate peace policy accepts as facts, however deplorable, the new circumstances of the present situation. It provides for strength and security during the transitional period, draws a veil over the past, and strikes out boldly towards appeasement, hoping thereby to heal the wounds inflicted by the post-war years, and to make possible the rebuilding of a system of international co-operation.

Procedure for advancing the above proposals

It is clear that to carry out this policy will require both private consultation between the nations concerned and public statements. The British government is already actively engaged in private efforts to ascertain the facts necessary to enable a settlement to be considered. At the same time a clarification of general principles in policy, together with an indication of the procedure Britain favours for putting them into operation, are just as urgently needed as is the outline of some, at any rate, of the details of the policy itself. Such declarations are required for the sake of checking the disintegration in world confidence, preventing the drift to an unwanted war, arousing the support of the British electorate, informing opinion in the United States of America, and keeping within the orbit of the League system those many nations which are finding it difficult to know with whom they should associate their foreign policy.

We attach the utmost importance to private diplomatic exchanges; without this prefatory work no good purpose would be served by the calling of another world conference. At the same time we see little hope of restoring the confidence of public opinion, or arousing sympathetic attention amongst all the nations that are concerned – both great and small – if nothing beyond private discussion takes place. The publicity of the League was one of its most fruitful assets.

Suitable and consecutive opportunities should therefore be found either by the British Prime Minister or Foreign Secretary to reaffirm the basic ideas underlying British policy as indicated in this programme, and to outline the main objectives and guiding principles which would govern this initiative towards a new peace settlement and the rebuilding of a peace-keeping system. Mr Chamberlain's recent speech was a valuable example.

The public is unable to grasp the main outlines of a policy for restoring peace if it is only conscious of a series of crises being dealt with separately from moment to moment as each dangerous incident arises. The public needs – as also does the situation itself – some more comprehensive outline of procedure, which could serve as a kind of map of peace policy into which each incident or problem could be fitted.

Democracy and humane standards of conduct

We conclude this outline of an immediate peace policy by a reference to one other subject. We do not believe that the British outlook on international affairs should be exclusively concerned with emphasizing Britain's desire to uphold law between nations – important though that is. Our nation should go further, and declare more openly to the world than she has yet done that we as a people attach great importance to humane conduct and to maintaining liberty for the individual; that we deplore the revival of so much cruelty in the twentieth century at a time when it might have been hoped that such practices had been left far behind in the pages of history. We should make clear that to us British people the spectacle of racial persecution is revolting, and that the principles of humane conduct, liberty, and democratic forms of government have become every bit as necessary to genuine international friendship as the upholding of law itself.

If we made this clear, the government would be able to rally the support of the British public and at the same time stir the conscience of the world. To do so would touch the heart and intelligence of America, of the smaller democratic states, and even of large sections of opinion in the dictatorship states. To do so is also important, for if in the last analysis a resort to force becomes necessary, the British citizen will respond with more determination to protect merciful conduct than to sustain law.

It is, of course, true that Britain has no desire to press the world still more rigidly into ideological camps, dividing the nations into groups according to their internal systems of government. Still less has she any desire to join in the new and dangerous technique of carrying on revolutionary propaganda across frontiers, with the object of forcibly interfering directly or indirectly in the domestic affairs of states which are, or ought to be, co-operating as sovereign powers round the League table. Nonetheless, it is a fact that this division of the nations has already occurred; and since that is so, Britain must not disguise where her sympathies naturally tend in international relationships. She should prove clearly that she is anxious to make her contribution to those changes and adjustments in the status quo which demand attention; that she will make sacrifices to this end; and that those changes should be brought about by lawful procedure and not by violence. But equally she should demonstrate that she is resolute in her belief that the heritage of mercy, liberty, and democracy, built up over so many centuries, shall be sustained by herself, and that she will join with other like-minded nations in an effort to restore it. Indeed, occasions should be found to express Britain's indignation at the revival of cruelties and racial persecution in so many countries both on the Left and on the Right. It is true that her own record is by no means a clean one. She needs to admit this frankly. But she must not keep silent when the world is challenged by so much cruelty. If Sir Henry Campbell-Bannerman, *as a Prime Minister*, could cry, 'The Duma is dead; long live the Duma!', then surely British Prime Ministers should not keep silent now. It would indeed be a strange consequence of the coming of the League of Nations, if it should impose a new convention of silence upon member states in the presence of evil practices in any part of the world. The League should surely confer the prerogative of criticism amongst neighbours.

Conclusion

Thus, we have tried to outline the principles, the objects and the procedure which we believe might lead first to a cessation of tension between the nations, next to a new peace settlement, and finally to the rebuilding of a peace-keeping system.

We believe it essential that both the government and the peace movement should come to see that, however sound may have been the ideas and constitution of the League of Nations as originally formed, and however much they may see the importance of reconstructing that or some similar system, yet the prime necessity of the moment is a transitional policy designed to get us all out of the dangers and entanglements which, for the present, cumber international relationships. During the immediate phase of hysteria and anger it may be that the future of civilization requires that we should exalt the principles of democracy and humane conduct even more than the principle of law.

We have ruled out the practicability of a resort to arms in every quarter of Europe to resist every breach of lawful procedure in the immediate present. It is politically and technically out of the question, and might even be unwise. The alternative policy requires the exercise of prudence for a period of time during which we restore British armed strength, and promote military co-operation with democratic France and economic co-operation with democratic America. During that same period of time, we shall also have made vigorous efforts towards appeasement and have ascertained the conditions under which action through a League of Nations system can be ensured. It may be that before these years have passed changes will have occurred either within the dictator states or between them. If all these hopes should prove vain, we and other democratic nations will at least have gathered strength and restored a better moral foundation for a conflict if it should in the end be forced upon us.

We believe this transitional policy may for the moment prove of more value than a rigid emphasis upon absolute principles, however much we may still believe in them. If, however, the need of the present is a transitional policy of this kind, where strength and conciliation are combined, then it becomes all the more important that the details and procedure of that policy should be outlined, and the temper of its advocacy jealously guarded.

If such a programme could be outlined, it might lower the tension which now threatens peace; give hope of justice where justice is called for; afford the principle of law a more honourable foundation; and revive the hopes and relieve the anxieties of the great mass of ordinary men and women in every nation, who want peace but who do not see how to achieve it.

Curtis to Allen, 11 May 1938
(ms. Curtis 12, fo. 220)

I have your draft and am reading it with deep interest.

We had a meeting in Salter's room on Sunday with Sir John Anderson, R.H. Brand, General Swinton, Lord Nuffield, and Amery. The serious nature of the situation was unfolded and certain steps agreed on for action; but not enough time was left really for us to discuss the organization of the Air Defence League. In doing anything effective in this direction one of my difficulties is that I am now starting for the Sydney conference on foreign affairs in July. I have to go to Edinburgh tomorrow to help to start a Scottish branch of Chatham House; but look forward to seeing you on Sunday.

Toynbee to Allen, 11 May 1938
(copy in Liddell Hart papers, LH 1/698)

I am very sorry that I shall not be able to be present at the meeting of the group on Sunday. I have to get up to Scotland at the end of this week on business connected with Chatham House and I cannot manage to get down to Oxford as well.

Meanwhile, I have been studying the very valuable paper which you have just circulated to us. You are doing the group a great service in helping us in this way to clear up our view and I am sure you know that I respect it; but now that it is put out clearly in this memorandum, I find, with great regret, that as I have rather feared all along, I am not able to associate myself with it. The decisive reason is that I do not feel your 'transitional policy' to be right. Besides that, I do not believe that, if it were applied, it would, in fact, bring about a reconciliation between the great powers. Of course all forecasts of the future are likely to be wrong, especially when things are in the present extraordinarily fluid state. But I will add, quite frankly, that I should still be opposed to the policy, on the ground that it was morally wrong, even if I thought it was likely to keep the peace between the great powers for the next twenty years.

In particular, I am utterly opposed to HMG's policy towards Italy now, after publication of the agreement, just as much as I was at the moment of Eden's resignation.

I read it as nothing but an attempt to buy Italy's neutrality, or if possible her support, in a coming struggle for power between this country and Germany, by paying Italy at other people's expense and not out of our own pockets. I feel that when HMG decided to try to buy Mussolini they ought at least to have paid him in British assets, e.g. in sterling or in British fortresses in the Mediterranean, and not at the expense of the Abyssinians and of the government side in Spain. As to the practical results of the Anglo-Italian agreement, I do not think we shall know where Italy really stands unless and until another Anglo-German war breaks out. As I see it, all that the government have brought about is that we shall now enter another great war dishonoured and divided instead of united in the support of a great cause – unless, of course, when it comes to the point, we abdicate altogether and give up the bulk of our great possessions, which is the price of abdication.

I think that the establishment of law in international relations is by far the most important public cause in the world today, and I do not agree with your antithesis on sheet 26 of the memorandum. As I see it, 'humane conduct and democratic forms of government', so far from being an alternative to the upholding of law, can only exist in so far as law is upheld. Law and liberty and humanism stand or fall together. I believe that if we drop the attempt to maintain law now, the opportunity will be lost forever, and that there will be no possibility of picking up the broken fragments after a period of transition. I do not think that a transitional policy is practical politics. I think this difference of view partly arises from a different interpretation of modern history.

As I see it, the terrible issue which now confronts us is not mainly the result of post-war events, e.g. injustices in the peace settlement or neuroses in certain unhappy countries. I think that the view of modern history that you suggest in passing on pages 10–12 is much too optimistic. At least in things that turn out to be matters of life and death for our civilization now, I do not think that the level of human conduct in the world was slowly rising during the nineteenth century, and I see no reason at all why the present recrudescence of power politics expressed in personal dictatorships is not likely to take permanent root in twentieth-century civilization. I see many reasons in the present social trend to support Mussolini's contention that the future lies with him.

I think we are now confronted with the consequence of a moral and intellectual error which we have been allowing to grow up during the past 400 years – the ideologies of sovereignty and great powers. We have gone on indulging in this until we have let ourselves be overtaken by an enhancement of our powers of organization and technique which has made the modern international anarchy at last become wholly unendurable. I believe that this anarchy cannot continue, and that it is bound to be ended either by the establishment of law in international relations or alternatively by some single great power conquering the world. It may, I fear, be true that we have thrown away our last chance of establishing law and that the other alternative is now inescapable. If this is really the present position, then Great Britain has a choice between two courses. Either we can abdicate at the price of renouncing our great possessions, or we can take part in the coming struggle in the hope that, if we throw our weight into the scales against the European dictatorships, then the world dominion which will be the prize of the struggle will fall, not to Germany and her confederates, but to North America. As we cannot be, and do not want to be, the world conquerors ourselves, there would be much to be said for abdicating and accepting the political impotence and economic poverty which abdication would necessarily carry with it. But I doubt whether this is practical politics. I am afraid my conclusion is gloomy, but I have no belief at all in the possibility of 'getting by' as the Americans say, in the next act of the tragedy.

I look forward to seeing the results of Sunday's meeting in Wint's admirable minutes.[18]

Angell to the *Manchester Guardian*, 11 May 1938

[. . .] Neither Britain nor the Council [*of the League of Nations*] can, without gross disregard of elementary justice, now take a decision without some impartial investigation of the facts, for they are seriously

[18] For further analyses of Toynbee's views on British foreign policy at this time, see William H. McNeill, *Arnold J. Toynbee: A Life* (London, 1989), pp. 169–178; Christopher Brewer, 'Arnold Toynbee and Chatham House', and Andrew J. Crozier, 'Chatham House and appeasement', in Andrea Bosco and Cornelia Navari (eds), *Chatham House and British Foreign Policy, 1919–1945: The Royal Institute of International Affairs During the Inter-War Period* (London, 1994), pp. 137–161, 205–259.

in dispute. If they are as outlined in a recent publication by the Ethiopian legation, then Abyssinia is not conquered by Italy nor anywhere near to being so [. . .]. If this is true, and there is a great body of evidence available, the claim of the British government to be merely recognizing a complete and accomplished conquest is based upon misapprehension or distortion. The case calls for an investigation somewhat on the lines of the Lytton commission on the Sino-Japanese conflict.[19]

No minutes of the meeting of 15 May appear to have survived.[20] As usual Nicolson wrote in his diary.

Harold Nicolson diaries (Nicolson papers)

Sunday, 15 May 1938

Down to Oxford [. . .]. Drive to All Souls. We have a discussion on a paper prepared by Allen. There is really a split between the realists and the moralists. Gilbert Murray and I do not approve of expedients. Allen says that peace should be bought at any price or almost any price. In fact he approves of the government policy. We go on discussing till 7.00 and thereafter dine in Hall.

Toynbee to Allen, 16 May 1938 (Allen papers, box 15, correspondence, 1937–1938)

One point that puzzles me in your attitude is why you support the present policy of the Chamberlain government. The government are, as far as I can judge, mainly concerned to prevent Germany getting the upper hand over this country and, with that aim in view, they are quite methodically trying to weaken Germany and strengthen Great Britain by purchasing Italy with bribes in Spanish and Abyssinian

[19] In a letter to the *Manchester Guardian*, 6 May 1938, Angell and other signatories had appealed to the British government thus: 'If we really faced facts we should not "recognize" the Italian conquest of Abyssinia. For it is not a fact.'

[20] The evidence from the resulting correspondence indicates the attendance among others of Nicolson, Murray, Allen, Salter, Liddell Hart, and Curtis.

coin. But this is not the policy of peace; it is a policy of using war as an instrument of national policy.

Hole to Liddell Hart, 16 May 1938 (Liddell Hart papers, LH 5/1)

The next meeting of the Foreign Affairs Group will be held on Sunday and Monday, 5 and 6 June, at All Souls College, Oxford, beginning at 12 noon on Sunday. I would particularly draw your attention to the fact that this is Whit Sunday and Monday.[21]

Allen to Toynbee, 17 May 1938 (Allen papers, box 15, correspondence, 1937–1938)

I am so grateful to you for troubling to write to me again, and I thought perhaps you would like to know what happened at the meeting in Oxford. We had a very full day's discussion, and I think (I repeat the word 'think') that, in so far as the majority of those present had any definite views, they were on the whole favourable to the line of argument set out in my document. On the other hand they were immensely critical of many of the points, and there was a minority very sharply opposed to it. Whether we shall ever get to the point of an agreed document or even to the point of a document sponsored by some of us, I cannot say.

We decided to ask H.D. Henderson to take in hand the revision of my document or its rewriting, having regard to the nature of our discussion, and we agreed to meet again to go over the result at Whitsuntide. Unluckily, this morning Henderson says he finds, after all, that he will not be able to do the job, and I do not quite know what will happen until I have had a talk with Salter this week. It may be that the document has been of value in so far as it has provoked discussion, but that we shall not be able to get any further, and that even those who have sympathy for the main line of argument will feel unable to sign anything [. . .].

In arguing about the present situation, I am putting completely on one side my pacifist opinions, and am assuming that force must be put behind law in a world which remains armed. With that premise,

[21] A handwritten annotation on this letter states that the meeting was cancelled.

my point is that to uphold under every conceivable circumstance the rule at a time when there is such a huge margin of doubt as to the capacity of aerial force to maintain the law is terribly serious [. . .]. I am prepared to back international law by force and to uphold it, but unless the force is overwhelming I think one then has to choose between two evils – the evil of a catastrophe in trying to uphold law, and the evil of allowing temporary casualties in morality. It is for that reason that I am willing to take risks with morality during the transitional period in the hope – perhaps a vain one – that events will play into our hands.

However, I must not worry you any more with these arguments. I only wish you could have been with us at Oxford to hear our discussions fully and to have taken a conspicuous part yourself.

Curtis to Macadam, 18 May 1938 (ms. Curtis 12, fos 126–128)

[. . .] I have been in close touch with Sir Arthur Salter since he and I returned to this country and organized, this is very confidential, a conference last Sunday week between him, Sir John Anderson, Nuffield, Brand, General Swinton, and Amery. At this conference we came up against the difficulty that there is an existing Air League and also a right-wing organization for organizing national defence under Lord Wellington, run by people like Lord Lloyd and Amery. Our view is that no fresh organization is worth creating unless all parties from the extreme Right to the extreme Left can be brought into it to insist on the organization of the civil population for defence against an air raid if war breaks out. This is a cause in which extreme pacifists could be enlisted. We also tried to think of some born organizer who could give his or her whole time to creating the necessary organization, but failed to hit on any one. Philip Cambry, we found, was already employed by Wellington's organization.

I have since had to explain to Salter my own personal position. When we both left England in March I was then prepared to make the organization of some air-defence league a first claim on my time; but since that, as you know, it has been decided that I must leave in July for Australia to represent Chatham House at the forthcoming conference on foreign affairs [. . .]. This Sydney conference is in some ways the culmination of what has been my main work in life for the last thirty years. As it is now decided that I leave for Australia in July, and will be absent for six months, I cannot now offer to make the emergency organization of an air-defence league a first claim on my time. Salter views this decision with deep disappointment but I cannot alter it [...].

Allen to Spender,[22] 20 May 1938 (add. ms. Spender 46394, IX, fos 103–106)

I am writing to you as a result of a talk which I had with Sir Arthur Salter yesterday. I am afraid my letter will be a little long, but I hope you will have patience to read it through. The object which Salter and I have in mind is to persuade you to do a notable service in the present dangerous and bewildering discussion of international affairs.

During the last five months there has been gathering at All Souls College, in Arthur Salter's rooms, weekend after weekend, of a very representative and distinguished group of international thinkers. Let me give some of their names: Arthur Salter himself, Arnold Toynbee, Harold Nicolson, Lionel Curtis, Liddell Hart of *The Times*, Hodson of 'The Round Table', H.A.L. Fisher,[23] Gilbert Murray, Norman Angell, Walter Layton, and others. Perhaps, as I am writing to you, I ought to explain that they have put me in the chair during the discussions.

Our object was to detach ourselves from the many institutions to which we all belong and to interchange opinions very frankly on international affairs. There are, of course, considerable disagreements still between us, and it may be that, in the end, two or three of the group will fall out if any outline of policy were published. But we have felt that the need for such a statement was becoming almost imperative, for the sake of public opinion, to help the rank-and-file of all the peace organizations, to restrain some expressions of the Opposition, and to assist or bring pressure to bear upon the government. Some reliable group of thinkers must state the case for a new international policy under the broken circumstances of the present. We feel that unless this is done the country will fall apart into bitter divisions, international thought will suffer, and effective peace policies become the subject of destructive controversy.

[22] J. Alfred Spender (1862–1942) journalist, author, and official biographer of Sir Henry Campbell-Bannerman and H.H. Asquith; Editor of the *Westminster Gazette*, 1896–1922; numerous other books include *The Government of Mankind* (London, 1938); *New Lamps and Ancient Lights* (London, 1940); *Between Two Wars* (London, 1943); *Last Essays* (London, 1944); memoirs in *Life, Journalism and Politics*, 2 vols (London, 1927).

[23] This is the only mention, in all the available records, of Fisher's name as a participant in the discussions.

As a result of all our talks a certain number of memoranda were prepared. One or two of these I enclose. The first was a statement chiefly on Czechoslovakia by Sir Arthur Salter, and finally it fell to me to make a desperate attempt to draft the skeletal outline of thought which might conceivably be ultimately incorporated in a public statement of between seven and ten thousand words.

We have just had a meeting to consider that memorandum which I had the audacity to inflict upon the group. It aroused keen discussion, but Salter and I felt that it did represent, on the whole, the line of thought to which a good many of us would be glad to commit ourselves. On the other hand, the document was criticized for its manner of presentation in some respects, and it was realized that it would have to be either thoroughly revised or taken as a basis for agreement and then completely rewritten by some new hand.

I have the notes of all the many criticisms and suggestions for adding new subjects and new lines of argument. These I have not at present sent to you. Salter and I venture to beg you to consider whether you would, having read these documents, produce for joint signature and ultimate publication the right kind of document. You have the literary genius which I do not possess. You have the power of temperately expressing a new policy which would probably carry the support of many distinguished people.

We earnestly beg you to consider whether you would undertake this notable service to international thought, at what is perhaps one of the most critical moments since the beginning of the period represented by the League of Nations. We know it is a formidable task, but we believe you may consent, having regard to its importance. In the event, Salter and I would place ourselves at your disposal and come down to see you, if we may, for several hours talk after you have digested the documents. We even go so far as to suggest that we might perhaps come to see you on Friday next, May 27. May I earnestly beg you to agree? I feel that you must realise, as we all do, that unless some new statement is put out for public opinion, grievous injury to wise thinking and good policy may be done.

Wint to Allen, 24 May 1938
(Allen papers, box 15, correspondence, 1937–1938)

I hope you will be seeing Salter in the very near future. We have not yet data for judgement: but may this not turn out to be the moment to which the group has looked forward as really opening up the possibility of negotiation, i.e. we have made a show of strength, Goering and the extremists have lost face (barring new developments)? These, surely, were the conditions the group regarded as vital for a constructive advance.

Murray to Allen, 24 May 1938 (ms. Murray 232, fo. 197)

[. . .] HMG's policy about Czechoslovakia seems to have altered the whole atmosphere. We have shown at last that we are prepared to stand up for something, and as far as one can judge at present the effect has been extraordinary, both in deterring Hitler from open aggression and in restoring confidence among the small nations. I hope you agree.

Of course I am still a little nervous in case we may make the Czechs concede too much.[24]

Murray to Cecil, 24 May 1938 (ms. Murray 232, fo. 198)

I have got flu or something, and the doctor says I must not come to town on Thursday.

I think our policy about Czechoslovakia is right, and shows the immense value of firmness in dealing with Germany. I should be quite in favour of congratulating HMG, though of course congratulations may be premature [. . .].

Liddell Hart to Toynbee, 25 May 1938 (Liddell Hart papers, LH 1/698)

[. . .] I am sorry you were not at All Souls the weekend before last. An extract from your letter – about your conclusion that you would

[24] Such fears had motivated Murray's letter to *The Times*, 18 May 1938.

stand, in the ultimate issue, on the moral ground – created much commotion there. Murray, Nicolson, and myself were the only people who expressed agreement with it. Lionel Curtis, especially, remarked that twenty years of peace were worth any price. Can you tell me the exact words you used – I should like to recall them exactly.[25]

Toynbee to Liddell Hart, 26 May 1938 (Liddell Hart papers, LH 1/698)

[. . .] I am much amused that my letter to Lord Allen made a flutter. I am enclosing a copy.

Liddell Hart to Toynbee, 27 May 1938 (Liddell Hart papers, LH 1/698)

[. . .] After reading it in full I am still more in agreement with your view.

Murray to Liddell Hart, 27 May 1938 (Liddell Hart papers, LH 1/538)

Have you by any chance lately read Demosthenes' *Third Philippic*? I have just been reading it, and at every turn was reminded of the present condition of things, with the democracies as Athens and the dictators as Philip. He even says 'You say you are at peace, and do not wish to break it. You do not see that he has already begun his war against you, and gained such-and-such advantages.'[26] It reminded me of your remarks about Spain.

[25] At the time Toynbee was consulting Liddell Hart, *inter alia*, about the Spanish Civil War for the 1937 volume of the Chatham House *Survey of International Affairs*. See further correspondence on this in Liddell Hart papers, LH 1/698.

[26] Philip II, King of Macedonia 359–336, father of Alexander III (the Great).

In late May Allen undertook a letter-writing campaign, in particular to the editors of the Manchester Guardian *and* The Times. *Geoffrey Dawson, the editor of* The Times, *and some of his staff were very sympathetic to Allen's views and gave him access to the letter columns of the newspaper.*[27]

Allen to *The Times*, 30 May 1938[28]

It has been asserted over and over again that peace in Europe could be maintained and increased if only collective action were taken on two fronts simultaneously – conciliation and revision of the status quo on the one hand; the display of strength to protect lawful procedure on the other hand.

This dual process is being applied today to the German–Czechoslovak problem. It would seem to offer some hope of an honourable settlement. Surely, therefore, it is most earnestly to be desired that those of us who believe in collective action should guard our words in writing and speech so that no provocation may impede success.

It does not help the conciliator, the arbitrator, the policeman, or the judge to be surrounded by a crowd emitting either angry or exulting cheers. It certainly did not help at Versailles in 1919.

There is everything to be said for allowing the process of law and conciliation to take its beneficent course unhampered.

[27] On Allen's relationship with *The Times* and its editors, see Marwick, *Clifford Allen*, pp. 176–177.

[28] Letters from Allen along similar lines appeared in the *Manchester Guardian*, 30 May 1938, and *The Spectator*, 160 (10 June 1938), p. 1060.

CHAPTER 4

'HOURS AND HOURS OF TALK', JUNE 1938–MARCH 1939

A meeting at All Souls, planned for Sunday and Monday, 5–6 June 1938, never took place, likely because of Allen's ill-health. In the meantime, the divisions within the group continued to grow.

Murray to Bevan,[1] 1 June 1938 (ms. Murray 233, fo. 3)

[. . .] A group has been meeting in Salter's rooms at All Souls, with Allen as Chairman, discussing the whole question of foreign policy. It shows, however, a tendency to split, Allen taking the line that the way to peace is to satisfy Germany; most of us thinking that resistance, and the maintenance of international law, more important. He would let Hitler have whatever he wants in eastern Europe and more than Germany's original possessions in Africa.

Mary Spender to Allen, 1 June 1938 (Allen papers, box 16, miscellaneous materials)

[. . .] My husband enjoyed your and Sir Arthur Salter's visit so much, so did I, we both hope you will come again.

There is nothing we should like better than to stay with the Warden of All Souls. Alfred always loves going to Oxford, and I know how

[1] Edwyn Robert Bevan (1870–1943) classical scholar and Honorary Fellow of New College, Oxford; with Department of Political Intelligence, Foreign Office, 1918–1919. Bevan and Murray exchanged conflicting views of collective security in *The Spectator*, 160–161 (24 June, 1 July 1938), pp. 1136–1137, 11–12. Spender took both to task in the *Spectator*, 161 (8 July 1938), p. 52. For more on Murray's views of Bevan, see Bevan to Rowse, 25 August 1937, Rowse papers, EUL MS 113/3/temp/box 166.

much he would have enjoyed staying there, it was so kind of you to think of it.

This letter gives me an opportunity to explain things. I am constantly in the painful position of being forced to object to his doing the things he cares most about, without giving a reason. He does not know how seriously ill he is, I pray that he never may.

In February a very clever doctor and the London specialists he sent us to, discovered that he has a large hernia of some standing, and also a large growth which must have been in existence some time. Anyhow it is too late to operate, and he is too old – Alas. They only told him of the hernia. I do mind so desperately having to hold him back [. . .].

We had a perfectly normal life and I hope it may always be so. He wrote long years ago in Bagshott, 'life is meant to be spent, not hoarded'. And tho. I think that perhaps he does too much, still, I believe it is what he would wish, even if he knew, without the dread shock of it.

Please do not write me a kind letter – the strain and the anguish are almost unbearable – and please tell no one except Sir Arthur, *in the strictest confidence* – we have mutual friends, I am so terrified of a word of sympathy to *him*, or its being generally known.

He is very keen about the whole matter and would love to continue to do anything he could. He is finishing the writing of his book this week, or next, so will easily have time. And this week Longmans and Cassell have written suggesting books – the latter 800 pages!!! He would like to do the latter. What can I say?

We have had such a wonderful forty-five years, he is so perfect as a husband. It is so kind of you and Sir Arthur not to mind coming here. I am afraid this is rather incoherent – but it is difficult to be coherent.

Allen to Wint, 3 June 1938 (Allen papers, box 15, correspondence, 1937–1938)

I am afraid you will feel that I am treating you very badly in not sending back the summary of our last discussion with my revisions. I have been ill in bed nearly all week, but I hope to get down to it during the Whitsun weekend.

I am so glad you approve of my two letters in the press.

My own feeling now is that the group can do nothing, so far as issuing interim statements, until Salter has tried his hand at producing a comprehensive document and we have checked this with Spender's draft and my own. Indeed, I think we might irritate some members of the group until this major task is concluded, if we try to make them commit themselves to a lot of interim statements. I am afraid the machinery is moving slowly, but if we are cautious I think we may in the end produce something very notable.

By the way, how is Hudson getting on with his section on Czechoslovakia? Do you know?

Forgive me for being so cautious and discreet.

'Memorandum on Czechoslovakia' by Hudson, 8 June 1938 (Liddell Hart papers, LH 5/1)

Foreword

The following memorandum is an expression of personal views and is intended as a basis for further discussion of the question by the group, not as a draft manifesto for publication. Though I had no precise terms of reference, the group, I believe, wished me to produce a document of the latter type. After an attempt to write it on publicity lines, however, I came to the conclusion that such a manifesto could only be drafted after the whole problem had been discussed by us much more thoroughly than hitherto, and it had been ascertained how much agreement there was among us on essential points. My memorandum, therefore, in its final form, is meant simply as a statement of the facts in the case as they appear to me, and as a starting-point for discussion.

CONFIDENTIAL

Composition of Czechoslovakia

Czechoslovakia is composed of four provinces:

(1) Bohemia;
(2) Moravia and Silesia;
(3) Slovakia;
(4) Ruthenia;

of which the first two, as 'lands of the Bohemian Crown', were reckoned as provinces of Austria in the old Austria-Hungary, while the latter two were integral parts of Hungary – 'lands of the Crown of St Stephen'.

The ethnic composition of Czechoslovakia, according to the 1930 census, is as follows:

Czechoslovaks	9,756,604	} Czechs about 7.25 millions
		} Slovaks about 2.5 millions
Germans	3,318,445	
Magyars	719,569	
Ruthenes	568,941	
Jews	204,779	} Jews by 'nationality'
		} Jews by religion numbered 336,830
Poles	100,322	
Other	50,876	} including gypsies
TOTAL	14,729,536	

It will be seen from the above table that the Czechoslovaks only form two-thirds of the total population thus classified, and the Czechs by themselves approximately half, while the Germans are just under a quarter of the whole.

The making of the Czechoslovak state

The making of the state may be considered under two aspects: (1) the actual seizure of the territories concerned, and (2) the decisions of the Paris peace conference. As regards (1), the course of events was quite different in the Austrian provinces (Bohemia and Moravia) from what it was in the Hungarian provinces (Slovakia and Ruthenia). In October 1918, with the final breakdown of the authority of the old dual monarchy, Czech forces under the direction of the *Narodni Vybor* in Prague took over control throughout Bohemia and Moravia, including the German districts, without meeting with armed resistance. The Czech population was permeated with intense nationalist enthusiasm, and the coup had been carefully prepared in advance. In Slovakia, on the other hand, Czechoslovak nationalism was confined to a small group, and the idea of breaking away from Hungary was not widespread; there was no general rising, and the Hungarians with four divisions of their army routed a Czech force which entered Slovakia from Moravia. The Czechs then appealed to the Allies, who ordered Hungary to withdraw her troops south of an appointed line, thus enabling the Czechs to carry out a military occupation of Slovakia and afterwards of Ruthenia.

The Czechoslovak national revolution was thus achieved in the Austrian (which were also the Czech) provinces by the Czechs themselves, but in northern Hungary it was only made possible by the direct intervention of the allied powers. There is no reason to believe that Slovakia and Ruthenia could have been detached from Hungary without such intervention, and this should be emphasized, in view of the belief in some quarters that the Allies merely recognized accomplished facts in the breaking up of Austria-Hungary, and that the Czechoslovaks emancipated themselves entirely by their own efforts. As to the action of the Allies, on the other hand, it is clear that they had no option but to order the Hungarians out of Slovakia after the promises which had been made to the Czechoslovak National Council during the war; these promises certainly committed the Allies to obtain independence from Austria and Hungary for both the Czechs and the Slovaks, though they were not bound to incorporate in their state areas of predominantly non-Czechoslovak population.

The decisions of the peace conference

The peace conference laid down the frontiers of Czechoslovakia on two diametrically opposite principles. On the one hand, appeal was made to historic right and geographical-economic unity for preserving the integrity of Bohemia and Moravia-Silesia and ignoring the ethnographical line between Czech and German; on the other hand, the ethnographical principle was asserted for the Slovaks and Ruthenes, in defiance of the historic right and geographical-economic unity of Hungary. The logical application of the arguments used for including the 3 million *Sudeten* Germans in a new state would have left the 3 million Slovaks and Ruthenes inside Hungary, and conversely the ethnic separatist doctrine used to disrupt Hungary would logically have justified the union of the *Sudetens* with the German *Reich*.

The fact that the frontiers of Czechoslovakia were not drawn on any consistent principle is not surprising in view of the aims of French policy which mainly determined the form of the peace settlement in central Europe. France had two objectives: first, to make the two states, Poland and Czechoslovakia, as strong as possible in order that they might in future 'contain' Germany on her eastern frontier; and second, to ensure that the 10-million-strong German residue of the dissolved Austria-Hungary should not be added to the German *Reich*. Both these purposes were served by incorporating the *Sudeten Deutsch* in Czechoslovakia. The Germans of Austria proper could form a separate state, and by the ban on the *Anschluss* they were, therefore, compelled to be 'independent'. But the *Sudetens*, for obvious geographical reasons, could neither form a state of their own nor could they join the new Austrian state (since the vast majority of them were contiguous with, not Austria, but Bavaria, Saxony, and Silesia); they must either attach themselves to the German *Reich* or be incorporated in Czechoslovakia, and since they could not be allowed to do the former, the latter course was adopted.

It may be mentioned that the deputies of the German districts of Bohemia and Moravia were included in the National Assembly formed by the German members of the Austrian *Reichsrat* on 21 October 1918, to organize a state for 'the German people in Austria'. In addressing the Assembly, the Socialist leader, Adler, declared:

> The German people in Austria will form its own democratic state [...] which is freely to decide its relations with the neighbouring nationalities and with the German Reich. It will form a free confederation with the neighbouring nationalities, if they wish it. Should they refuse, or make conditions incompatible with the economic and national interests of the German people, the German-Austrian state, which by itself is an economically impossible formation, will be compelled to enter the German Reich. We demand for the German-Austrian state full freedom to choose between these two possible connections.

'A second Switzerland'

Dr Benesh, at the peace conference, used the phrase 'a second Switzerland' in giving an account of the intentions of the Czechs for their new state. This certainly implied some kind of local autonomy and federalism corresponding to that of the Swiss cantons. In fact, however, Czechoslovakia, though genuinely democratic in its constitution, has from the beginning been a highly centralized, unitary state on the French model.

The democracy of the Czech state and the relatively humane and uncorrupt character of its administration are often held to sustain the view that the grievances of the German and other minorities are mainly fictitious. The Czechs should, indeed, be given full credit for the virtues of their rule, but it must be realized that for national minority problems decentralization is much more important than democracy. As between two racial elements whose numerical ratio is more or less fixed there is no 'floating vote' such as promotes compromise and adjustment in ordinary party politics: the majority nationality has a permanent majority position in the central legislature and can discriminate in all kinds of ways against minorities without ever violating democratic principles. It is, indeed, against the 'democratic' racial majority that the racial minority needs protection, and such a minority seeks through local and regional autonomy the satisfaction which it cannot hope to obtain through the central legislature, however freely elected. An Englishman may think that Irish national aspirations were adequately met by the right to send representatives to Westminister; the fact remains, however, that the Irish have always struggled for autonomy or independence for Ireland, and have never been content merely with enjoyment of a universal franchise within the United Kingdom.

The Czechs have always taken the view that centralized government is essential to the integrity of Czechoslovakia and that local self-government in the minority areas would lead to a disruption of the state. This argument, however, involves indirectly an admission of the extreme artificiality of the 'nation' formed in 1919, and points the contrast between Czechoslovakia and Switzerland. Switzerland is by origin a voluntary federation of cantons, and just because of this basis of a voluntary association, strengthened by centuries of common political life, does not need a unitary state in order to preserve its unity. In Czechoslovakia, on the other hand, the Czechs themselves are the only real *Staatsvolk*; the German and Magyar minorities, numbering over a quarter of the population, have been incorporated in the state by *force majeure*, while the Slovaks and Ruthenes are by no means firm[?] in their attachment to it. In these circumstances the Czechs dare not 'cantonalize' the state lest it should fall to pieces.

The Slovaks and Ruthenes

Apart from the vague references to Switzerland in the Czech declaration of intentions at the peace conference, no definite promise of autonomy was ever made by the Czechs as regards the German and Magyar minorities. Such promises were, however, made to the Slovaks and the Ruthenes as part of the bargains by which their leaders were induced to join the Czechs; in neither case has the promise of autonomy been kept.

Autonomy with a separate regional parliament, administration, and judiciary, was promised to the Slovaks in the so-called Pittsburgh Convention, concluded in the spring of 1918 between societies representing the Czech and Slovak emigrants in America. On these terms the Slovak League joined in setting up the Czechoslovak National Council, which negotiated with the Allies in the name of the Czechoslovak nation. The Pittsburg Convention was apparently endorsed by the first Czechoslovak government in Prague, which expressly recognized as valid all agreements concluded by Masaryk during the revolutionary period. In spite of this, however, Slovakia was treated as part of a unitary state, and no autonomy has ever been conceded. The fulfilment of the Pittsburg Convention is vigorously demanded by the Slovak Clerical (People's) Party led by Father Hlinka, and the agitation has recently been brought to a head by the arrival of a delegation of American Slovaks, bringing with them the original document, a huge reproduction of which, mounted on a motor lorry, headed a procession of 70,000 to 80,000 (*Daily Telegraph* correspondent's estimate) autonomists through Bratislava. To the charge of bad faith (which cannot directly be refuted) the Czechs and the Slovak centralists, including the Prime Minister, M. Hodza, reply that the Hlinka Party has not so far obtained more than a minority of Slovak votes, and that most of the Slovaks are today content with the unitary state.

It appears to be true that the autonomy demand is at present confined to a minority among the Slovaks, and also that the Hlinka Party desires only autonomy and not secession from Czechoslovakia. The movement is, nevertheless, a serious element of weakness in Czechoslovakia's position vis à vis Germany and reflects the divergence of sentiment and interest which, despite so many asservations [*sic*] of identity, undoubtedly exists between the two sections of the Czechoslovak nationality. Whereas for a Czech the German is traditionally the enemy, the Slovaks have never hitherto been involved in the struggle against *Deutschtum* and have no anti-German feeling; they tend to regard the quarrel over the *Sudetenland* as no business of the Slovaks, and the more conservative among them do not feel any great enthusiasm at the prospect of the arrival of the Red Army from the Soviet Union in case of a war with Germany. Especially significant is the Hlinka Party's demand for 'Slovak soldiers to serve only in formations stationed in Slovakia' – a condition which, if allowed, would enable the Slovaks to detach themselves and go their own way in the event of a European war. The Slovak autonomists are believed to maintain secret relations with both Poland and Hungary, and in certain circumstances might incline towards secession from Czechoslovakia and a federal tie with whichever of the two neighbour states offered the more favourable terms.

The position of the Ruthenes is rather different. They are linguistically a fragment of the 40-million-strong Ukrainian nationality, and if a fully independent Ukrainian state were to be formed, they would probably wish to join it. But the great majority of them, under Uniate or Orthodox clerical influences, have no inclination towards the Soviet Union, and consider themselves much better off in Czechoslovakia than are their co-racials in Poland and Romania. They do not seem to be actively discontented with Czech rule. On the other hand, they are even less interested than the Slovaks in preserving the inheritance of the Bohemian crown for the Czechs (with whom they never had any connection before 1919), and economic geography pulls them towards Hungary; moreover, they have the same grievance as the Slovaks in that autonomy was promised, but never given them, by the Czechs. It is doubtful whether their loyalty to Czechoslovakia would stand any severe strain.

Strategically, Ruthenia is of special importance as it forms a corridor between Poland and Hungary by which Czechoslovakia maintains communication with Romania and the Black Sea. The railway line into Romania is extremely vulnerable to attack from Hungary, and if, in a war, it were cut while the Soviet forces were unable to force a passage through Poland, Czechoslovakia might be driven to surrender, even though the great fortified lines enclosing Bohemia and Moravia remained intact.

The German and Magyar minorities

The large German and Magyar minorities involve Czechoslovakia in conflicts with the states of their co-racials, Germany and Hungary. Today the tension over the *Sudeten Deutsch* puts all other issues into the background, but up to three years ago Czechoslovakia was the object of much more bitter antagonism from the Hungarian than from the German side. This was quite natural if the historical antecedents are taken into consideration. Hungary was mutilated by the Treaty of Trianon, and both the Slovaks and Ruthenes and the large blocks of Magyar population which were included in Czechoslovakia were cut out of an existing political unity. The *Sudeten* Germans, on the other hand, were lost, not to Germany as constituted in 1918, but to the dissolved Hapsburg Empire, and before the reign of Hitler most Germans felt themselves touched by the wounds of St Germain much less than by those of Versailles. German feeling up to 1934 was certainly much more favourable to the Czechs than to the Poles. The 'Polish corridor' was Germany's principal grievance, and an observer writing from central Europe in 1925 remarked:

> I noticed no hate (in Germany) for the new nations, but there was an even more significant contempt, especially for the Poles, a conviction that they will come to nothing of their own selves. I heard respect expressed only for the Czechs. (*The Letters of John Dove*, p. 211).

Even now, there is a contrast between publicly expressed German and Hungarian aspirations, for, whereas Hungarian revisionism openly claims territorial retrocession, with the Magyar-inhabited districts as a minimum and the whole of Slovakia and Ruthenia as a maximum, Hitler and other Nazi leaders have so far avoided making any demand for the inclusion of the *Sudetenland* in the German *Reich*; their claim is rather to a protectorate over all German communities outside the *Reich*, a right overriding, but not annulling, state frontiers. It is true that actual annexation would be a logical corollary of the principle 'One people, one *Reich*', and demands for territorial cession may be merely reserved until a later stage. But it seems quite likely that the Nazis would really prefer to have the *Sudeten Deutsch* as a pro-German *imperium in imperio* inside Czechoslovakia, rather than to take them (with their numerous unemployed) into the *Reich*. The main purpose of German policy is to bring the countries of east central Europe into a German orbit, and this does not necessarily involve territorial expansion. The Hungarians, on the other hand, cannot aspire to such a hegemony and their one idea is to obtain frontier revision.

Czechoslovakia and Poland

If Czechoslovakia were faced with hostility only from Germany and Hungary, her situation would be serious enough, but she has also to reckon with the enmity of Poland. The first reason for this is Poland's old grudge over the division of the Duchy of Teschen in 1920, which gave the very important Karvin coalfield to Czechoslovakia. The partition was determined by the Conference of Ambassadors, but the Poles blamed the Czechs for their fait accompli of military occupation of part of the area in February 1919 – an action which the Poles themselves imitated very successfully at Vilna in the following year. Though the Poles formally accepted the Paris settlement of the Teschen dispute – being greatly weakened at the time by their war with Russia – they have never ceased to hope that events might provide them with an opportunity to reassert their claim to the Karvin area, and with this in mind have paid extraordinary attention to the rights of the small Polish minority in Czechoslovakia – a minority which, unlike the big non-Slavonic German and Magyar elements, would not be a serious problem for Czechoslovakia but for the external stimulus.

The conservation of the Polish minority has needed a special effort, for most of the inhabitants of the Duchy of Teschen (known as Slonzaks) formerly spoke a dialect intermediate between Czech and Polish, and their children could therefore easily be made into Czechs or Poles according to the language used in the local schools; the distinction here between Czechs and Poles presents great difficulties and leads to much recrimination. There is no doubt that a German is a German and a Magyar is a Magyar, but the Slonzaks, like the

Macedonian Slavs, were formerly of indeterminate nationality, and still find themselves hard to classify, though the governments of Prague and Warsaw are so anxious that one or other of two labels shall be attached to every individual.

The second reason for Polish hostility to Czechoslovakia is the Czecho-Soviet pact. The traditional pro-Russian sentiment of the Czechs, combined with the menace from Germany and Hungary, conceals the anti-Bolshevik inclination of the Czech bourgeois, but the Pole by habit and tradition hates the Russian as a Russian, quite apart from his feelings about Bolshevism. Since the obvious road for the Red Army either to reinforce Czechoslovakia or to invade Germany lies through Poland, the Poles regard the Czecho-Soviet pact as directed against themselves and are resolved to thwart its execution in case of a Czecho-German war.

Both Poland and Czechoslovakia are allies of France, but they have never had any alliance with each other. Recently, France is alleged to have informed Poland that the Franco-Polish alliance would be nullified if Czechoslovakia were to be crushed by Germany with Poland as a neutral. The Poles desire to retain their friendship with France, but decline to be party to any arrangement which involves the passage of Russian troops through Poland, as demanded by the Czech General Staff.

The **Sudeten** *Germans and Czech foreign policy*

Czechoslovakia is now bound by mutual assistance pacts to France and Russia, and is thus, in the eyes of the *Sudeten* Germans, 'in the camp of the enemies of Germany'. The foreign policy issue is, perhaps, more than anything else, destructive of the foundations of the Czechoslovak state as far as the loyalty of the German minority is concerned. It is, of course, impossible to argue theoretically that a minority in a democracy has a right to dictate foreign policy. But, in practice, a majority policy which commits a 22 per cent minority to war against their racial kinsmen because of an alliance obligation to another country is putting a strain on internal solidarity which threatens to lead to civil war, even before an international crisis has been reached. If there were 10 million French-speaking inhabitants of England (a minority in the same ratio to the whole population as the Germans in Czechoslovakia), it would hardly be the best way to internal peace for the English majority to make an alliance with Germany against France. In a war in which Czechoslovakia acted as an ally of either France or the Soviet Union against Germany, a *Sudeten* must be 'a traitor either to his state or his race', and if it is argued that the alliance will never operate unless

Germany launches a war of aggression, it must be admitted that the history of 'defensive' alliances is not reassuring.

Apart from their constitutional right to conclude any alliances they please, the Czechs argue that without the French and Soviet alliances Czechoslovakia could not hope to retain her integrity and independence as a state. Yet with these alliances Czechoslovakia can never hope to obtain the loyal co-operation of nearly a quarter of her citizens, who, whether or not they wish to enter the German *Reich*, will not be willing to take part in war against it on behalf of France or the Soviet Union, any more than the Czechs themselves in the old Austria-Hungary were willing to fight against Russia.

The neutralization proposal

In view of the tension produced by the existing system of alliances, suggestions have been put forward for a 'neutralization' of Czechoslovakia. Under such a scheme, Czechoslovakia would pledge herself to permanent neutrality and would receive a guarantee from all the great powers of Europe, including Germany. Her position would then resemble that of pre-war Belgium rather than that of Switzerland, for Swiss neutrality is not guaranteed but is simply a matter of Switzerland's own declared policy. It is claimed that a neutralized Czechoslovakia thus guaranteed would have at least as much security as now while, being released from alliance obligations to France and Russia, it would more easily be able to reach a *modus vivendi* with the *Sudetens* and would cease to stimulate German jingoism by its strategic threat to the heart of Germany.

This solution is admirable in theory, but it cannot be regarded as practical politics. Even if Germany were to consent to become a guarantor, it is not to be expected that either France or Russia would continue to assume the liabilities without the benefits of their alliances. The Czech army, and Bohemia as an advanced air base for operations against Germany are an essential part of French and Russian military calculations. Czechoslovakia was created to be an ally of France, and the French, who take no interest in distant countries except as possible allies or enemies, would have no inducement to risk war in defence of a country which did not promise them any aid in return. If Czechoslovakia were not a military ally of France, the French could not even count on her resources being withheld from Germany in time of war; her remoter markets would almost inevitably be cut off, and she would probably sell both food stuffs and munitions to Germany to the limit of the latter's purchasing power.

The new nationalities statute

According to a report in today's *Times* (June 8), Dr Derer, the Czechoslovak Minister of Justice, has stated in an interview that the new nationalities statute 'will not provide for any territorial autonomy'. If this is correct, the statute will not go far towards meeting the demands of the *Sudeten Deutsch* (Henlein) Party, in which the demand for regional autonomy is the central feature. It is likely, therefore, that even though minor grievances are remedied, the conflict will become more acute.

The Czech government has reached a point where it must either go forward or back; things cannot remain as they are. Czechoslovakia must either grant something like home rule to the *Sudetens* or it must adopt increasingly repressive measures against them, so as to maintain the authority of the state. The indications now are that the latter course will be followed after a preliminary gesture of making concessions. It is not generally realized that, in spite of its democratic constitution and guaranteed civil liberties, Czechoslovakia already possesses the legal cover for the most drastic measures of repression, whenever it is decided to adopt them. The Law for the Defence of the State, promulgated in May 1936 (analysed in detail by C.A. Macartney, *Hungary and Her Successors*, pp. 178–180), which is applicable in time of peace as well as during war, gives to the government, in effect, all the powers of a totalitarian regime.

According to an article from a correspondent in Prague appearing in the *New Statesman* of June 4:

> On May 20 General Krejci, the Commander-in-Chief of the Czechoslovakia army, presented an ultimatum to the Prague government; he refused to accept responsibility for the consequences unless a number of the reserves were called up at once [...]. The calling up of the Czechoslovak reserves has underlined the alliance of the army with the people against the Germanophile policy of at least the right wing of the Agrarian Party. The communal elections which have been taking place may be said to confirm this assertion in the swing to the left which is evident in the Czech interior of the country [...]. The increase in the Communist vote in Prague is primarily a Slavonic tribute to Russia. It has long become traditional for Pan-German extremism to evoke Pan-Slav sentiments among the Czechs [...]. Though they seldom admit it in public, the Czechs are becoming embittered by the behaviour of Great Britain and even of France, who have urged them to endanger the existence of their state ostensibly in the interests of the *Sudeten* Germans, who are generally admitted to be the best treated minority in Europe. The old 'big brother Russia' feeling has been fortified by the absolute confidence felt by the Czechs that, when it is necessary, Russia will come to their help, and that she will

do so without imposing conditions, indeed without imposing any conditions at all. If these are indeed the sentiments of the Czechs, the similarity of the whole situation to that which existed in Central Europe in 1914, is appallingly close.

Allen to *The Times*, 8 June 1938

I would not have troubled you with this letter were it not for one sentence in Mr Wickham Steed's[2] communication [*letter to* The Times, *4 June 1938*]. That sentence uncovers at last the real disease that has infected the minds of the most devoted servants of the League of Nations since the Treaty of Versailles:

> But among those who have studied and reflected upon it most carefully for the longest time there is a remarkable unanimity that the surest way to bring on a major European war would be to allow a feeling of uncertainty to spread upon the permanence and the inviolability of national frontiers.

[. . .] Had Mr Wickham Steed said that the vital need of this new age of international collaboration was that in future all changes must be effected by lawful and peaceful procedure, I could have understood him and applauded. But that is not what he says in his letter.

'Permanence!'

What, then, becomes of Article XIX of the League Covenant? Has our belief in that article of peaceful change been all the time an empty mockery?

Allen to Curtis, 8 June 1938 (ms. Curtis 12, fo. 162)

I wonder if you have seen my outburst in *The Times* this morning? I feel almost passionately indignant on behalf of the younger generation

[2] Henry Wickham Steed (1871–1956) Foreign Editor, *The Times*, 1914–1919; then Editor, 1919–1922; Lecturer, King's College, London, 1925–1938; publications include *The Meaning of Hitlerism* (London, 1934), *The Press* (London, 1938), *Our War Aims* (London, 1939), *That Bad Man* (London, 1942), and his autobiography, *Through The Years*, 2 vols (London, 1924).

at this war-lust of men like Wickham Steed, who seem incapable of thinking of the League as an instrument of growth. I expect Wickham Steed will fall upon me with great ferocity. There are few people living at the moment who have a more sensitive approach to the League idea than yourself. A few words from you to *The Times* would carry great weight in this controversy. Please forgive my arrogance in suggesting you should intervene.

Spender to Allen, 8 June 1938 (Allen papers, box 15, correspondence, 1937–1938)

I feel apologetic about this, but I haven't had time to work it out in the proper form. It is submitted merely as material to be knocked into shape by discussion.

I wish I could come to Oxford but everything is against my breaking bounds at present.

Congratulations on your letter to *The Times*. Steed has become one of the most bellicose of the champions of peace in recent months. Norman Angell hurt[?] him hard.

Memorandum by Spender, 8 June 1938 (Liddell Hart papers, LH 5/1)

CONFIDENTIAL

We have watched with concern the increase of recrimination between parties on foreign affairs at a time when as much unity as possible is to be desired. Many critics of the government have lent themselves to a version of history since the war which throws the whole blame for everything that has gone wrong on this country, and almost entirely leaves out of account the part played by other governments. The time for writing the history of these years in a manner which will make an allowance for inherent difficulties and distribute the responsibilities fairly between the different nations is not yet, and in the meantime nothing could be less desirable than that there should be controversies between friendly nations as to their respective shortcomings. But while judgement is to this extent in suspense, it seems to us unnecessary and unfair for British speakers and writers to throw the whole blame for past failures and mistakes upon British governments and statesmen.

The history of the League of Nations is an example of the difficulty of fixing the responsibilities. All people of peaceable disposition are agreed that the great ideal of the League should be kept alive, and that British governments should make the establishment of 'collective security' one of the cardinal aims of their policy. But if the failure of the existing League is attributed solely to the weakness or vacillation of British governments or British statesmen the real difficulties of the problem are obscured, and the prospect of overcoming them becomes the more remote.

As contemplated by its founders, the 'collective security' guaranteed by the League was to be a security for all against war and for each against aggression. It was hoped that the United States would be a member and that within a few years all the great European governments would come in. The 'aggressor', convicted as such by the League, would thus be helpless against overwhelming force and if he did not immediately give way, economic sanctions without war would bring him to reason.

Unfortunately the sequel disappointed these hopes. The United States declined to join; Germany came in for a time but withdrew, Japan and Italy resisted and seceded when the League endeavoured to restrain them. It may be said that the League powers should have persisted in their efforts to coerce these two powers, and there is much room for legitimate criticism of the decision followed by retreat which discredited the League and the powers associated with it.

But it is fair to remember that the situation with which the League powers were confronted in 1932 in the case of Japan, and in 1935–1936 in the case of Italy was entirely different from any contemplated by the founders of the League. In neither of these cases was such overwhelming force massed against an aggressor as to lead automatically to his submission. In 1932 there was a great preponderance of power at least temporarily on the side of Japan; in 1936 there was least a risk, in view of the rearmament of Germany and the possibility that she would join forces with Italy, that the enforcement of sanctions would lead to a general war. Many opinions may be held about the degree of this risk, but it cannot be said that in either 1932 or 1936 the situation at all corresponded to what was understood by 'collective security' when the League was founded.

It is of the greatest importance that these circumstances should be understood, since, so long as they continue, there can be no chance of making 'collective security' what it was intended to be, viz. the maintenance of peace through the co-operation of the great majority, if not all, of the great powers. On any other conditions, attempts by the League powers to coerce an aggressor must run the risk of precipitating a war between groups of allied powers. If therefore we now proceed to boycott the powers which the League has failed to coerce and to refuse to make treaties or agreements with them, the idea of 'collective security' will have to be abandoned. Since it is quite certain that these powers will not publicly recant to restore the territory they have conquered, there would in that case be a permanent cleavage between the League powers and Italy, Germany, and Japan. The failure of the League would then have left the world with a legacy of unappeasable quarrels. If that were indeed an inevitable result the League would have created a new and fatal obstacle to peace.

It is not in our opinion an inevitable result, and if any principles or any conscientious scruples seem to lead to such a conclusion, they need, in our view, to be very carefully examined. The League has done great services to the world in the years since the war, but it has not succeeded in placing itself in a position in which its judgements on the affairs of nations have the unchallengeable authority which would be binding on conscience. It failed to reduce armaments while Germany was yet disarmed, and took no steps for the peaceful remedying of the grievances that she has since dealt with by an assertion of her power. Its authority was used to prevent the inclusion of Austria in the German *Reich* at a time when the peaceful concession of it might have done much to promote conciliation and strengthen the then democratic German government. There are, no doubt, many explanations of these failures, but in the circumstances we do not think it can reasonably be claimed for the League that it should enjoy a monopoly of efforts to advance the cause of peace, or that no alternative methods should be permitted when it has failed.

For these reasons we cannot share the view that it is 'disgraceful' to enter into negotiations with Italy after her aggression in Abyssinia. It would, in our opinion, be a most serious hindrance to good relations between nations if they passed these judgements upon one another and thought it necessary to ostracize those whose conduct they condemned. International, as well as civil, life would be brought to a standstill if it were deemed immoral to recognize facts that are beyond recall. A statute of limitation at the end of which the judgement is left to history is necessary to the peace of the world.

It is, in our view, the failure to understand this situation which has led so many sincere supporters of the League of Nations into the paradoxical position of seeming to demand war in the name of an institution which was intended to maintain peace. Under a perfect League of Nations system there could be no breach of covenant or treaty by any nation which would not be the concern of other nations. Nothing ultimately is more to be desired than that there should be this joint and several responsibility for world affairs. There would then be no question of the duty of all the powers to place their resources at the disposal of the authority which was entrusted with the task of keeping the peace. To keep this idea in view, an ultimate aim when we speak of 'collective security' is greatly to be desired. But in the absence of such an authority it is, not, in our opinion, reasonable to expect one nation to take upon itself the task of doing this collective work.

For this reason we cannot think the reproaches so often raised against the government for its failure to assist the Chinese against the aggression of Japan, to prevent the intervention of other powers in Spain, or to solve the problems of central Europe are well founded. It is right that the British government should do its utmost to mediate and pacify, to limit the areas of conflict, to prevent cruelty and inhumanity in war; and it would lay itself open to legitimate criticism if it were not ready to take a bold initiative in these respects. But it cannot be expected to do single-handed what the powers collectively have failed to do; and to approach it as if it were guilty of a dereliction of moral duty when it declined this responsibility, seems to us unfair and unnecessarily lowering to the good name of Great Britain in other countries.

There is all the time going on in the world today a veiled conflict between the free countries and those which are under the control of dictatorships. Superficially the dictatorships have many advantages. They can act swiftly and secretly without consulting parliament or arguing with critics. They can require their workers to do any work on any conditions that they prescribe. They can tune their press and make it appear that they have a unanimous country behind them.

These conditions are a denial of what makes life most worth living for free Englishmen, and we believe that, in the long run, the advantages will be on the side of the countries whose governments are based on the free-will support and consent of their citizens. But if they are to hold their own in the stress of immediate circumstances the free countries will need to show that they are capable of submitting voluntarily to some part of the discipline which is imposed compulsorily on the other countries. In such circumstances, it seems to us that political parties may fairly be asked to refrain from the kind of recrimination which gives the false impression that Great Britain is deeply divided in aims and methods, and incapable of the restraint which would enable her to meet the officially disciplined countries on equal terms.

From this point of view, we specially deprecate the criticism which suggests that the British government is hypocritical in its professions of attachment to free institutions and that it is actuated by a secret sympathy with fascism in its European policy. There is, we believe, no foundation whatever for these suspicious. Many faults may legitimately be found with the execution of British policy in recent times, but the imputation of sinister motives is, we believe, unfair and unfounded. Whatever faults, for example, may be found with the non-intervention policy in Spain, we are convinced that the British and French governments, who are equally responsible for that policy, have had nothing but the honest intention of preventing the civil war in that country from becoming a general war between European powers.

But especially we would deprecate the idea that there is something ignominious or cowardly in efforts to keep the peace in these times. The idea that war is inevitable and that it had better come quickly, which has gained currency among some critics of the government, seems to us to differ little, if at all, from the much condemned doctrine of preventive war, which even Bismarck said was a usurpation of the functions of providence. Many wars which seemed inevitable have been avoided by having been postponed. Those of us whose memories go back fifty years can remember a time when wars were said to be inevitable between Britain and Russia, and between Britain and France. Again and again in the course of quite recent history, unforeseen events have changed the whole aspect of foreign affairs, and the attitudes of some of the leading powers.

Peace is, we believe, in present circumstances the greatest interest not only of the British Empire and Commonwealth but of the entire cause of freedom and democracy. There never was a time when the hazards of war were more incalculable, but if any result can be predicted with certainty, it is that the cause of freedom and democracy would be wrecked in the chaos that would follow even a successful war. It is a deplorable fact that the hope of peace should be founded, as it is at present, mainly on the fear of armaments, but in face of the warnings on this subject and the manifest difficulty of the strategic problems of the British Empire, it seems to us that critics of the government exceed their province when they urge it in a warlike direction, or reproach it for being reluctant to take the risk of war. The government alone knows what state of preparedness, what allies it can depend upon, how far it could carry the dominions with it on any given line of policy.

The responsibilities of the British government are immense. Its policy may decide the fate of India, of six self-governing nations, of Egypt, of Palestine, and immense regions of Asia and tropical Africa. It is not entitled to risk all these on interventions in the affairs of other nations, which are not either vital to Britain interests or obligatory by reason of treaty engagements. There are limits to its power which it could not exceed without disaster, and its first duty is to be clear about these and to govern its action accordingly. This often requires a distinction between what it desirable and what is possible, which is extremely distasteful to men and women of generous instincts. Large numbers of the British people have greatly desired to assist the Spanish government, to help the Chinese against Japanese aggression, to prevent the forcible annexation of Austria, and then save the other small states of central Europe from aggressive action by Germany. But however desirable these aims and objects may be in themselves, the combination of them in a British policy of action is manifestly outside the limits of British power and would lead to a scattering of British commitments and resources which would almost certainly end in disaster. It should not, in our opinion, be made a reproach to the British government that it is unable to take action entailing the risk of war in some of these affairs.

British policy should, in our opinion, be one of peace with all who are willing to make peace, irrespective of their internal forms of government, or what we may consider to have been their misdemeanours in the past, and an unceasing endeavour to remedy any just grievances, territorial or economic, even if for the time being they may require certain sacrifices on our part. On these lines, we believe the preservation of peace to be not only possible but probable. But if, in spite of all efforts, war should be unavoidable, we should then be in the strongest position to wage it successfully and to obtain the largest measure of support from the Empire and Commonwealth, and from our European friends and allies.

We would add that, in our opinion, greater efforts should be made by the government to keep the opposition parties informed about the facts of the European and world situation. These are times of exceptional difficulty in which no government can expect to be immune from criticism. But they are also times in which the appearance of a breach between government and opposition on the main issues of policy ought, if possible, to be avoided. They can hardly be avoided if opposition policies are founded on wishes and desires divorced from a knowledge of facts which make their realization difficult or impossible. Most of those who subscribe to this memorandum are wholly in sympathy with these wishes and desires, when stated as abstract propositions; and if it were merely a question of registering sympathies, they would have no hesitation in voting for them. But the serious questions for governments and for oppositions which present themselves as alternative governments are whether the facts are such as enable them to be realized, whether their realization is within the limits of British power, whether the British government would be justified in risking the immense interests committed to its charge for their attainment.

Recent debates and public speeches seem to us to point to the need of a much greater pooling of knowledge about the facts which govern and limit British policy in these times. We are persuaded that a fuller knowledge of the facts would go far to prevent the cross-purposes and misunderstandings, the reproaches and recriminations which have embittered the relations of government and opposition in recent months.[3]

Curtis to Allen, 10 June 1938 (ms. Curtis 12, fos 163–164)

I read your letter to *The Times* with the deepest satisfaction and must congratulate you most heartily upon it. I am very chary of writing letters to *The Times* on international questions for a variety of reasons; but one of them is I have spread myself so wide on them in the second volume of *Civitas Dei*. My field, as I was always reminding you at our 'Soviet', is the far future, to which I am trying to get people to direct their eyes, because my conviction is that people will only begin to find their way about the immediate future when they have made up their minds as to the goal at which we ought to aim in the far future. I am reluctant, therefore, to get involved in controversies about the immediate future, which is not my special field.

If it were not for this inhibition the old Adam in me would love to ask Wickham Steed, in reply to his letter, what he did to discourage the French from violating the German frontier and marching into the Ruhr. In those days he was right in the counsels of the Quai d'Orsay, and on one occasion at least turned up at an international conference with the French ministers and officials. It is astonishing how little the League of Nations fanatics realize that they have now become the war party and the exponents of the principle of preventive war. The fact that they found themselves in the same camp with Winston Churchill and Harold Nicolson might, one would have thought, have opened their eyes to their own position.

[3] This memorandum echoes conclusions reached in Spender's *Between Two Wars* (London, 1943), which his biographer deemed 'the best existing defence of the Munich policy'. See Wilson Harris, *J.A. Spender* (London, 1946), p. 187. Cf. the portrait of Chamberlain in Spender's *Last Essays* (London, 1944), pp. 43–45.

Murray to Wickham Steed, 10 June 1938 (ms. Murray 233, fo. 32)

[...] Allen's nerves are evidently upset. He says different things on different days, and his attack on you was clearly hysterical. I mentioned it in a letter I have sent to *The Times*, and in my first draft referred to him as 'infelix puer, atque impar congressus Achilli' which I regretfully omitted in the final form, because I did not want to tease him too much.

I was already suspecting that Germany was trying to pay us out in Spain for her defeat in Czechoslovakia.

Allen to Catchpool, 10 June 1938 (Allen papers, box 15, correspondence, 1937–1938)

I have had quite a nasty turn since you left this house, and am leaving for a fortnight's holiday this afternoon. I feel I ought to make it clear, however reluctantly, that whether I am physically able to carry through the suggestion we discussed together must depend upon what the doctor says when I get back. You know how much I want to be of service, but with my health in its present state, it is clear I must know what effect this fortnight's holiday will have upon me. If leaving the matter in this state of uncertainty seems to you serious, then I feel perhaps you ought to think of some other person who would go abroad.

Salter to Liddell Hart, 20 June 1938[4] (Liddell Hart papers, LH 5/1)

I am sorry not to have written before [...]. We shall be arranging another foreign affairs meeting soon, which I hope you will be able to attend.

[4] This letter largely focused on the subject of the peacetime storage of food and raw materials. See also Salter to *The Times*, 21 January, 11 February, 7 March, and 9 July 1938, and Salter to Liddell Hart, 5 July 1938, Liddell Hart papers, LH 5/1.

Hole to Liddell Hart, 28 June 1938[5] (Liddell Hart papers, LH 5/1)

It has been decided to hold one more meeting of the Foreign Affairs Group before the summer holidays, and this has been fixed for Saturday, July 16 at All Souls, beginning at 12 noon, and ending the same day.

Hole to members of the All Souls Group, 29 June 1938 (Liddell Hart papers, LH 5/1)

The enclosed two documents – one by Mr G.F. Hudson, and one by Mr J.A. Spender – are being circulated to members of the Foreign Affairs Group. Members are asked to treat them as confidential.[6]

Hole to Liddell Hart, 4 July 1938 (Liddell Hart papers, LH 5/1)

Owing to the fact that a number of the members are away,[7] and are therefore unable to be present at the meeting of the Foreign Affairs Group on July 16, Lord Allen and Sir Arthur Salter have thought it wiser to postpone this to a more convenient date, which will be fixed later.

[5] This letter also included copies of the Spender and Hudson memoranda of 8 June 1938.

[6] The two documents are those of 8 June 1938 reproduced above, pp. 193–204, 205–211.

[7] Among the several absentees was Rowse, who had surgery in mid-May for his duodenal ulcer and spent many weeks recuperating. To assist in his recovery, Salter took Rowse in August on a motoring trip through Wales. See Rowse papers, EUL MS 113/2/5/6, summer-autumn 1938, manuscript transcripts from notebooks and typescripts, and Salter to Rowse, 16 July, 19 August 1938 in EUL MS 113/3/1/Corr.S. Also absent was Walter Layton, who was visiting Prague in the company, among others, of Wickham Steed and the Duchess of Atholl; David Hubback, *No Ordinary Press Baron: A Life of Walter Layton* (London, 1985), p. 156.

Curtis to Allen, 11 July 1938 (ms. Curtis 12, fo. 219)

You know that I have always expressed doubts whether the members of the group meeting at All Souls over which you have presided since last November, could ever succeed in producing a memorandum on foreign affairs to which most of them could subscribe. I have just read the confidential draft memorandum by J.A. Spender, dated June 1938, and find, to my own great astonishment, that I could have subscribed to this memorandum myself if I had not been just leaving this country for Australia. Indeed, I feel that if any important number of the group were willing to sign and publish this memorandum as it stands without mutilation they would have succeeded in making a really important contribution to public interests.

I am wondering whether you could not send a copy of this memorandum as it now stands to Halifax for his private information, enclosing, if you care to, this letter with it. It impresses me as one of the wisest documents I have ever read.

Allen to Curtis, 13 July 1938 (ms. Curtis 12, fo. 224)

I very much appreciated your letter. I agree with you as to the fine quality of Spender's memorandum, though in some ways I think it was not quite comprehensive. I will certainly consider letting Halifax have a look at it and sending your own helpful letter as an accompaniment.

Salter is coming to spend the weekend with me, and I hope we shall be able to arrive at some decision about the future of the group.

In some ways I am sorry to hear that you are off to Australia, though I know the good work you are going to do there. I presume this means we shall not be able to have your helpful spirit in our group until about October.

Events and a desire for more tangible results overtook some of the group. As early as 4 May 1938, Wint had proposed that the crisis in central Europe demanded intervention by a British intermediary. He suggested Salter, who demurred, citing his long experience of international negotiations which had taught him the benefit of meticulous advance preparations. On the other hand, the proposal appealed to Allen, and he and his Quaker colleague, Corder Catchpool, went ahead with plans for a personal visit to Germany.[8] *At the same time, however, Allen and Salter tried a different tack.*

Allen to Fisher, 20 July 1938 (ms. Fisher 77, fo. 30)

Sir Arthur Salter has been spending the weekend with me, and we both feel it essential that some useful letter should be sent to *The Times* at this critical moment about Czechoslovakia. You will realize that the draft which we submit to you studiously avoids all the usual ferocious demands that the British government should commit itself in any form whatever. On the other hand, it makes a practical proposal which we believe would be of enormous service both to our own government and the government of Czechoslovakia.

I enclose the list of the people[9] to whom we have submitted the letter, and we both feel it should be headed [. . .] by your own name as by far the most eminent amongst us.

I should esteem it a very great favour if you could let me have your answer by return of post.

Allen to Nicolson, 20 July 1938 (Liddell Hart papers, LH 5/1)

Sir Arthur Salter has been discussing with me whether any helpful contribution could be made to the solution of the Czechoslovakian crisis by means of a jointly signed letter to *The Times*. We are submitting for your consideration the enclosed letter [*not reproduced*] together with the list of those to whom we have sent it. The list is of value in so far as it unites many schools of thought.

We very much hope that you will sign, and that you will be good enough to let us have an answer immediately. Naturally we also hope that you will not feel it necessary to make any textual alterations.

[8] See Allen to Corder Catchpool, 13 July 1938; Allen to Sir Robert Vansittart, 14 July 1938; Vansittart to Allen, 15 July 1938; and Corder Catchpool to Allen, 15 and 16 July 1938, in Allen papers, box 15, correspondence, 1937–1938; and FO371/21782, C8072/8072/18.

[9] The list is not preserved here, but see the following letter to Nicolson.

The Rt. Hon. H.A.L. Fisher, Lord Allen, Lord Astor, Lord Cecil, Lionel Curtis, J.A. Hobson, Lord Lothian, Lord Lytton, Dr Gilbert Murray, The Hon. Harold Nicolson MP, Lord Noel-Buxton, Sir Arthur Salter MP, Lord Samuel, J.A. Spender, Sir John Fischer Williams.

Allen to Wint, 21 July 1938 (Allen papers, box 15, correspondence, 1937–1938)

I have read through with profound admiration your outline sketch of a study on India. If I may say so, it suggests an exceedingly valuable and helpful book, especially at a moment when democracy is so much under discussion and when people question whether the British Commonwealth has the power to extend that principle in such cases as India. It has always seemed to me quite magnificent that at a moment in history when liberty was being limited in so many quarters, Britain should have set about extending freedom and self-government in India.

But it is no good my trying to comment in a letter on this exciting task of yours. What I should like to do would be to have another talk with you about this and other subjects in the early part of August. I am likely to be going to Germany and Czechoslovakia next week, but I shall be within reach of London between August 7 and August 20. Will you please telephone to me and suggest when we could meet? I feel I have treated you very badly recently.

Curtis to Allen, 21 July 1938 (ms. Curtis 12, fo. 225)

Your letter reached me just as I am off to Australia so I must be short. I think it might have helped the situation if two months ago we could have produced a memorandum saying what the Swiss solution might mean as applied to Czechoslovakia. At the moment the boat is entering the rapids. My own feeling is that the passengers had better abstain from offering suggestions to the man at the wheel while he is looking out for the rocks and doing his best to dodge them. Personally, I feel that we are fortunate in having so imperturbable and conciliatory a person as Halifax at the wheel at this juncture.

I should like to take this opportunity of saying that I feel that our consultations at All Souls under your masterly direction have been most useful. You know the old fable of the dying man who told his sons to dig for treasure in the garden.

Spender to Allen, 21 July 1938 (Allen papers, box 15, correspondence, 1937–1938)

The Nazi view is that the question of the *Sudeten* Germans is one to be settled between Germans without outside intervention. We shall have to break it down but our best hope is to do it quietly by pressure behind the scenes. A public proposal to submit it to third-party arbitration would almost certainly be interpreted in Germany as an effort to put them in the wrong.

Samuel[10] to Allen, 22 July 1938 (Allen papers, box 15, correspondence, 1937–1938)

I doubt whether this is the right moment to attempt to intervene. I think that public opinion here would be disposed to await the results of the negotiations which are now actively proceeding before supporting any suggestion of action to be taken in the event of a breakdown. If and when a breakdown appeared to be imminent would be the time to make a suggestion.

Lothian to Allen, 22 July 1938 (Allen papers, box 15, correspondence, 1937–1938)

A third-party decision to a German means a decision by the League of Nations or by somebody else who is prejudiced against the German

[10] 1st Viscount Samuel (1870–1963) MP, 1902–1918, 1929–1935; High Commissioner, Palestine, 1920–1925; Secretary of State for Home Affairs, 1931–1932; leader of Liberal Parliamentary Party, 1931–1935; author of numerous works on liberalism, war, and ethics; *Memoirs* (London, 1945).

nation [. . .]. It is when people feel that they are beginning to enter upon the rapids that a precise, concrete proposal of this kind [. . .] might be effective.

Cecil to Allen, 22 July 1938
(Allen papers, box 15, correspondence, 1937–1938)

It is, of course, rather a strong order asking a country to submit to outside judgement an internal dispute [. . .]. I should not wish to be associated with any move of this kind unless I felt sure that the Foreign Secretary regarded it as, at any rate, likely to do no harm. My signature, therefore, must be subject to the condition that the Foreign Secretary be approached and asked to give his agreement to the extent I have mentioned.

Spender to Allen, 24 July 1938
(Allen papers, box 15, correspondence, 1937–1938)

If you told me that Halifax thought the publication of the letter would be useful, I would certainly not withhold my signature.

Allen to Salter, 26 July 1938
(Allen papers, box 15, correspondence, 1937–1938)

It may well be that in view of [. . .] the possibility of Runciman going to Prague, that we have missed the boat.

Allen to Halifax, 26 July 1937
(FO371/21730, C7766/1941/18)

Some of us have been wondering whether we could say anything helpful on the subject of Czechoslovakia through the medium of a jointly-signed letter to *The Times*. Sir Arthur Salter and I have consulted a number of friends who include: Sir John Fischer Williams, J.A. Spender, Harold Nicolson, J.A. Hobson, Lord Cecil, Lord Lytton, Gilbert Murray.

Most of them would be willing to join in such a letter, but we all feel that we ought not to take such a step without ascertaining whether you think it would be helpful, or at least not harmful. Naturally, in consulting you, we do not wish in any way to imply that you should bear the responsibility for our action, but we do wish to abstain from any step which would be definitely harmful. We feel that there might be some advantage in this proposition being published in *The Times* signed as it would be, by people of such manifold opinions on foreign policy, that is to say supporters and critics of the government.

I wonder if you could just give me a hint as to what you feel on the subject.

Draft letter to the Editor, *The Times*

Will you allow us to make a suggestion in regard to Czechoslovakia?

During the last few months negotiations have been in progress between the government of that country and the various parties and racial groupings within it. It is earnestly to be hoped that these will result in agreement. Nonetheless, Europe must not be caught unawares if they fail; for in that case one country after another, first Czechoslovakia, then Germany, France, Russia, Great Britain, and others may in rapid succession be compelled to take the most urgent decisions on their own course of action.

The present negotiations are taking place in an environment created by successive declarations of policy by statesmen of other countries, including notably that made by the British Prime Minister on March 24.

In this he said that the British government could give a prior guarantee of the kind that some had suggested, but that, if war broke out, 'it would be well within the bounds of probability that other countries, besides those which were parties to the original dispute, would almost immediately become involved. This is especially true in the case of two countries like Great Britain and France'. He also said, in the same speech,

> I cannot but feel that the course and development of any dispute, should such unhappily arise, would be greatly influenced by the knowledge that such action

as it may be in the power of Great Britain to take will be determined by HM Government of the day in accordance with the principles laid down in the Covenant.

If this declaration still leaves those concerned in some uncertainty as to what Great Britain would do in a particular eventuality, it at least makes clear that the attitude of the disputants before the outbreak of any actual conflict would have a very material bearing upon the ultimate decision of Great Britain, if that conflict occurs. It may be presumed that this is true of other countries also.

In these circumstances, we venture to express the hope that, if agreement is not reached by direct negotiation, the parties concerned may, before the tension increases, declare their readiness to invite, through some suitable procedure, a third-party opinion as to the best solution, without necessarily binding themselves to accept the opinion so obtained. This would, we suggest, offer substantial advantages from the point of view of all concerned. The further time afforded, and the objective discussion and report on a question of exceptional complexity by those not directly interested, would give the parties themselves an additional chance of reaching an agreed settlement.

But beyond that, it must be clear to each of the disputants, as they contemplate what would happen should the attempt at agreement fail, that if one of them had publicly agreed to invite a third-party opinion, it would greatly improve its position in regard to the outside world, just as it would greatly impair its position if it had refused to do so.

Halifax to Allen, 29 July 1938 (FO371/21730, C7766/1941/18)[11]

Thank you very much for your letter of July 26 about your proposal to send a letter to *The Times* on the subject of Czechoslovakia. I am much obliged to you for letting me see the text of your proposed letter and for consulting me in the matter. As far as I am concerned, I take no objection to the thought that the letter expresses. At the same time I cannot help feeling that although the proposal made in the letter differs, of course, from the mission which Lord Runciman has undertaken, the fact that Runciman is about to leave for Prague with the apparent good will of both the disputants, puts rather a different

[11] This letter was based on a minute by William Strang, 27 July 1938, FO371/21730, C7766/1941/18.

light on it, and inevitably rather detracts from the value of the letter in its present form.

Allen to Spender, 2 August 1938 (Allen papers, box 15, correspondence, 1937–1938)

I thought perhaps you might like to know what has happened about the proposed letter to *The Times*. I consulted Halifax and had a talk with him. He had no objection whatever to the letter, but we both felt that now Runciman was going to Czechoslovakia, the argument set out in the letter had in fact been met. Consequently I am sure you will agree that there is no case now in favour of pushing a suggestion which has already been carried into practice.

If any opportunity of intervening arises, I will venture to let you know. I am myself off to Germany this week, and I hope to see members of the German government.

The letter was withdrawn. Some members of the group continued to warn the government of Germany's warlike intentions.[12] *Others began to clash openly in print as the crisis deepened.*[13] *Meanwhile, Allen pressed forward in what had now become a personal mission with a somewhat more private agenda. On 27 July he stood in the House of Lords for what was to be his last speech there. He pleaded for a more humanitarian regime in Germany, in particular with regard to the persecution of Jews and the treatment of refugees. Allen also repeated his wish for 'good will and understanding' between Germany and Britain.*[14] *From 6 to 15 August he visited Germany and Czechoslovakia. One result, as he noted afterwards, was 'hours and hours of talk and NOTHING else whatever'.*[15] *But another version soon took root.*

[12] See e.g. Dudley to Leeper, 9 August 1938, FO371/22500, W11083/971/50; Dudley to Leeper, 23 August 1938, FO371/22500, W11766/971/50; Layton to Halifax, 19 August 1938, FO371/21664, C8666/62/18; and Nicolson to Halifax, 26 August 1938, FO371/22289, N4317/97/38.

[13] See, for example, the acrimonious exchange between Murray and Spender in *The Spectator*, 161 (8 July, 19 August 1938), pp. 52, 304.

[14] *Parliamentary Debates, House of Lords*, fifth series, CX, 27 July 1938, cols 1224–1230.

[15] Gilbert, *Plough My Own Furrow*, pp. 405–412; Marwick, *Clifford Allen*, pp. 178–185; Newton to Halifax, 13 August 1938, FO371/21731, C8301/1941/18; correspondence in Allen papers, box 15, correspondence, 1937–1938; and *Documents on German Foreign Policy, 1918–1945*, series D, II (London, 1949), Hencke to Foreign Ministry, 13 August 1938, no. 351, 557–558, and Bürgen to Foreign Ministry, 17 August 1939, no. 366, 577–582.

Wint to Allen, 14 September 1938 (Allen papers, box 15, correspondence, 1937–1938)

Is it too late to persuade the government (a) to get the Czechs to agree to the cession of the *Sudetenland* by (b) giving a guarantee to the Czechs for what remains?

Collective security has once more brought us to the verge of war, and if it comes to war we shall be fighting on the worst ground strategically and morally. To suit the French General Staff we are flagrantly to go against the Wilson tradition. Surely nobody can think that it is now possible for Germany to retreat. If this is so – and perhaps I am mistaken – peace can then only be saved by a change in English policy.

Allen to Wint, 14 September 1938 (Allen papers, box 15, correspondence, 1937–1938)

The two points you mention are to my judgement vital. Since my return from Germany and Czechoslovakia I have already communicated the idea to the government. I also discussed it in both countries.

Allen to *The Times*, 19 September 1938

It would be monstrous if for the second time in twenty-five years Britain and Germany were plunged into war. It would be a terrible commentary on the peace treaties of 1919 and on statesmanship thereafter. It compels us to ask whether we are sure that we have canvassed every proposal that might, even at the eleventh hour, give security to the Czechs and justice to the Germans. Hitherto most of us have believed it right to keep silent on this matter, lest we should embarrass the government in its gallant struggle for peace. Now it is imperative that we should all of us express frankly what we believe to represent the attitude of public opinion. May I state the case for the following dual remedy?

(1) Self-determination for the *Sudeten* Germans with international control to supervise whatever procedure to this end is adopted: including, if necessary, the subsequent transfer of minorities.
(2) An international guarantee, including that of Great Britain, of the new boundaries of Czechoslovakia that might in consequence have to be drawn.

I realize only too well, after discussions in Germany and then in Prague, how manifold are the difficulties and how considerable the opposition this procedure creates. I would only reply by a reminder that the alternative may be a world war [. . .].

Murray to *The Times*, 22 September 1938

The emotions of the country have seldom been so deeply stirred as by what is called 'the betrayal' of Czechoslovakia. They give Mr Chamberlain credit for his vigour; they are ready to believe that there are facts unknown to the public which have exercised a justifiable influence upon him. But the question they ask is: 'Is the government honest, or is it merely agreeing to weaken Czechoslovakia now in order to betray her to complete destruction later on, as soon as Hitler requires it?'

The proposal to have Czechoslovakia 'neutralized', disarmed, and then guaranteed by her principal enemies, with England and France playing the same protecting role as at present, is not calculated to inspire confidence.

If the Prime Minister or Foreign Secretary would give, in unmistakable language, an assurance that if the Czechs, trusting in British promises, assent to the amputation of their territory and are then attacked by Germany, this country would really join in all necessary measures to defend them, even including war, a large part of the bitter suspicion with which the government is now regarded would disappear.

[. . .]. Surely the world can be shown that at some point somewhere Great Britain will keep her covenants and protect those who trust in her.

Hudson to *The Times*, 26 September 1938

For better or worse, the government of Czechoslovakia has accepted the Anglo-French plan, which, according to general belief, provides in principle for the cession of the *Sudetenland* to Germany. On the wisdom of the British and French governments in pressing this plan on Czechoslovakia opinions violently differ, but now that the plan has been accepted it would be fantastic if war were nevertheless to result from a conflict over the time schedule of evacuation. Yet it seems possible that war may come in just this way.

Why does Germany, having obtained the cession of the *Sudetenland* in principle, now insist on immediate evacuation, even at the risk of a European war? If Hitler desires a European war, such insistence must be merely to provide a pretext. But if he does not, there is still, on Nazi political premises, every reason for regarding the time schedule as of vital importance.

[. . .] In the international anarchy which continues to reign in Europe, possession is at least nine points of the law, and, granted the principle of a territorial transfer, the logical course appears to be agreement on an immediate German occupation of the high-percentage *Sudeten* areas to be carried out simultaneously with German and Czech demobilization and to precede a final, detailed settlement of frontiers, exchanges of minorities, and economic claims.

Allen to Peet,[16] 3 October 1938 (Allen papers, box 15, correspondence 1937–1938)

[. . .] You know that I went to Berlin and Prague during August and had hours of vital negotiation with Ribbentrop, Benes, Hodza, the *Sudeten* German and all parties both sides of the frontier. It was out of these negotiations that emerged the proposal to use a conference of the four powers if a final deadlock occurred. It was a highly controversial technique but it had the supreme advantage of preventing the actual invasion of Czechoslovakia, stopping a world war, and perhaps bringing Germany back into international consultation. I flew back at once and reported to Lord Halifax and as you all now know the device was the one ultimately employed.[17]

[16] Hubert William Peet (1886–1951) joint Editor of *The Ploughshare*, 1916–1919; imprisoned for twenty-eight months as a conscientious objector; editor of the Quaker weekly, *The Friend*, 1932–1949.

[17] On the question of whether Allen was the true architect of the four-power conference idea, compare Marwick, *Clifford Allen*, p. 202, and Kennedy, '"Peace in our time"', p. 233.

Allen to Salter, 19 October 1938 (Allen papers, box 15, correspondence, 1937–1938)

I cannot tell you how touched I was by the extraordinarily kind way you wrote about my illness and the struggle which preceded it. I am afraid it was the visit abroad to Berlin and Prague which finally knocked me out. I am still in bed, and imagine I shall be here for sometime.

I entirely understand what you say about your pamphlet,[18] and I should be the last person to advise anyone exactly in what manner to make his own contribution to the rebuilding of the peace movement at present. I am quite certain your pamphlet is going to be extraordinarily helpful, and I look forward to having a copy very much.

As for myself, I feel I must take a slightly different line, which is principally concerned with the urgent necessity of being really practical and not sentimental when we talk about appeasement and a new peace settlement. The rubbish that is talked on this subject by idealists is beyond imagination, and yet it is a vital topic, and if we do not think it out amongst ourselves all that will happen will be that we shall rearm the government – a good thing in itself – and still not be able to capture the reins of office so as to direct the policy of appeasement.

While I have been lying here day after day, I have been reading a great deal of Czechoslovak history, not so much the history of the formation of the state as the history of the foreign policy of that country and France between 1920 and 1925. It is really a monstrous record, enough to drive any nation, especially one like Germany, into a madhouse. Thus I am quite unrepentant, now that I have refreshed my memory, in having used the word 'justice' in relation to Germany in my *Times* letter.

I am longing for the time when I can be up and about and join discussions at All Souls, if any more are held. I feel, as I have ever since 1919, that whilst people like yourself are making the country strong so that we can have a policy of appeasement, others, like myself, must think out in the most minute and practical detail what appeasement means.

I feel, in this rather unhappy time of illness, very much gratitude to you for the friendship of your letters.

[18] Arthur Salter, *Is It Peace? The Nettle and the Flower* (London, 1938).

Salter to Liddell Hart, 21 November 1938 (Liddell Hart papers, LH 5/1)

We are now well advanced with the project for the Air Raid Defence League, about which I think I spoke to you some time ago. Lord Hailey is coming on to the working committee, and Sir John Anderson warmly welcomes the project, as will be seen by the enclosed copy of his letter. Before sending out a public appeal, we want to obtain names of personalities of distinction in different spheres of national life who will allow their use in this connection. May we include yours? I enclose a note indicating the general purposes of the League.[19] Acceptance of this invitation involves nothing more, but I would like to have a word with you later on as to whether you would be able to come on to the Executive Committee. That, however, is a separate matter, and agreement with what I am now asking in no way involves you in that.

Liddell Hart to Salter, 25 November 1938 (Liddell Hart papers, LH 5/1)

Many thanks for your letter of the 21st.

I shall be glad to help the project in any way that you wish.

Curtis to Macadam, 20 January 1939 (Royal Institute of International Affairs archive, 4/CURT)

I have just been spending three hours with Salter and Sir Ralph Wedgewood, General Manager of the North Eastern Railway, over the Air Raid Defence League. As I anticipated, they wanted me to make it a major claim on my time which I firmly declined to do. I said that I would sit on a small executive committee under Hailey's chairmanship, and I believed that you would be prepared to do the same [. . .].

[19] The enclosure is not preserved.

Salter's obituary appreciation of Allen (*The Times*, 11 March 1939)[20]

For most of those who knew him the memory of Clifford Allen is inevitably coloured by the political crisis of 1931. I did not know him at that date, but was in intimate contact with him during the last five years of his life. As I saw him during this period he combined moral with physical courage, a lofty idealism with a knowledge of the technique of organization, and a strong will with sympathetic responsiveness to others – in a degree I have scarcely seen equalled. An ideal chairman, he could rapidly lead a difficult committee to agreement while making each member feel that he had been given a fair share in the result. An eloquent and persuasive speaker, he could hold a popular audience in rapt attention to a lofty theme without the relief of anecdote, humour, or personal allusions. With an unshakeable purpose in his main objectives, he had great flexibility of method and skill in persuasion. And he so dominated his physical disabilities that his visible frailty rather added to the force of his appeal than weakened it [...] he was given the choice of conserving his life or spending the last remnants of his strength in the service of the public purposes to which he was devoted [...] he took the heroic course. He was clearly warned of the great danger to him of his visit to Europe last summer under the physical conditions of abnormal heat and flight at a great altitude. He then signed his death warrant, as he knew he might be doing, with only a short reprieve. This was a characteristic climax.

[20] Lord Allen of Hurtwood died on 3 March 1939 in Switzerland. On 30 March a memorial service was held at St Martin-in-the-Fields. Salter read the lesson. Tributes from some participants in the All Souls Foreign Affairs Group – Macmillan, Fisher, Angell, and Arnold-Forster – are in Gilbert, *Plough My Own Furrow*, pp. 426–429. Alfred Barratt Brown placed a notice in *The Spectator*, 7 July 1939, asking for materials in order to write a life of Allen. Nothing was, in fact, done on Allen until the studies by Marwick (1964) and Gilbert (1965).

CONCLUSION

'BETWEEN RESISTANCE AND RETREAT'

On returning from his visit to Germany and Czechoslovakia from 6 to 15 August 1938, Lord Allen wrote that he had engaged in 'hours and hours of talk and NOTHING else whatever'.[1] Could the same assessment also be true of the All Souls Foreign Affairs Group? The group, in fact, never reconvened after the postponement notice sent out on 4 July 1938.[2] What then can be asserted with regard to the impact and historical significance of the All Souls Foreign Affairs Group? Indeed, what was its 'true character and influence'? Although its history was documented in the papers accumulated during the nine meetings from 18 December 1937 to 15 May 1938, what subsequent role did the more prominent members play in the period leading up to the outbreak of World War II? In reality, the group served precisely the purposes designed by Salter and Allen, essentially acting as a 'Brains Trust'. The discussions helped the individual members, with diverse experience and with divergent views, to clarify their positions on foreign and domestic policy. They then spoke, wrote publicly, and lobbied the press and the Foreign Office, confident that the issues had been analysed by some of the best elite minds of the period.

The All Souls Foreign Affairs Group agreed quickly on a dual policy of firmness and conciliation. However, the weighting of these two elements and their global application proved to be very contentious. Economic or political appeasers with regard to Europe could also be resistors when contemplating the Mediterranean and the Far East, and vice versa. Under the impact of a deteriorating situation in Europe, the Mediterranean, and the Far East, and especially after the *Anschluss*, the group faltered. The future of Czechoslovakia was a non-issue, as most members agreed that its neutralization in some form was inevitable. Rather, the group never succeeded in formulating an agreed public statement on foreign affairs. This was partially due to the state of international affairs. Their discussions were usually overtaken by the daily crises headlined in the press and radio. As well, by design

[1] Gilbert, *Plough My Own Furrow*, pp. 405–412; Marwick, *Clifford Allen*, pp. 178–185; Newton to Halifax, 13 August 1938, FO371/21731, C8301/1941/18.

[2] See Allen to Salter, 19 October 1938, Allen papers, box 15, correspondence, 1937–1938.

the group encompassed much of the political spectrum, without the extreme right or left. This allowed for agreement on such issues as taking a hard line in the Far East and the Mediterranean, hastening rearmament, and more co-operation with the USSR. Ultimately, the Allen prescription on 15 May 1938 of 'peace at any price' was never accepted by the group. What stymied members, however, were two related questions. The first, as put by Arnold Toynbee on 10 March 1938, was: 'Would firmness on our part [. . .] daunt the dictators, or would it madden them [. . .] [and] swell their ambitions to outrageous dimensions?'[3] The second was the daunting question to where and how to make a stand. On this issue 'the realists and the moralists', as Nicolson termed them, understandably split. Indeed, the group never resolved the dilemma as to whether there was 'a middle policy between resistance and retreat'. Failure to agree on this fundamental question, to what purpose and with what allies would British power be used, made it finally impossible to produce the published document.

The demise of the All Souls Foreign Affairs Group, however, still left several of the leading participants as active contributors to the ongoing debate about appeasement. The parliamentarians in the group, Lords Arnold and Allen and MPs Macmillan, Salter, and Nicolson weighed in after the Munich conference and during the months leading to the outbreak of the World War II. Lord Arnold had always been a strong supporter of Chamberlain's policy of appeasement, and consistent in his view that an agreement with Germany was mandatory, and that Czechoslovakia was not worth a war. In the wake of the Munich agreement, Arnold was convinced that the Prime Minister 'had done more for the future of peace in fourteen days than the League of Nations and all the Chanceries of Europe had done in nineteen years'. He shared the view of a range of supporters that 'the Munich Agreement was nothing more than a rectification of one of the most flagrant injustices of the Peace Treaties', and looked forward to 'the promise of a new era'.[4] As late as 7 March 1940 Arnold was still asking for a negotiated peace with Germany. Lord Allen, although in poor health, continued to concentrate his mind on what concerned him most, not rearmament but the rebuilding of the peace movement. In a lengthy letter to the *Manchester Guardian* on 20 October 1938, he argued that 'we have all sinned': the Versailles treaty-makers,

[3] Record of meeting, 'The issues of British foreign policy', Royal Institute of International Affairs archive, box 33.

[4] See for example, Arnold's speech in the House of Lords, 18 May 1938, quoted in *The Times*, 19 May 1938; his letter to *The Times*, 14 September 1938; his speech in the House of Lords, 5 October 1938, quoted in *The Times*, 6 October 1938; and Arnold and others, letter to *The Times*, 12 October 1938.

the Czechs for their insistence on an enlarged state, the French foreign policy elite, and the National Government. All this confronted Chamberlain in September 'with a choice of catastrophes', and for Allen it was right to yield to 'improper procedures' rather than go to war. A renewed appeasement effort was mandatory, he urged, with emphasis on 'economic and colonial readjustments', arms limitations, and better treatment for native peoples. Finally, he wished to see the League enlarged with United States entry, even if that required revisions to the covenant.[5] Allen followed this with another letter to *The Times*, emphasizing that the post-Munich period required placing 'as much emphasis upon the outline of a constructive peace policy as upon rearmament', accompanied by the entry of the United States into a restructured League.[6]

Harold Macmillan became increasingly associated with several groups of discontented parliamentarians, clustered around the former Foreign Secretary, Anthony Eden, Winston Churchill, and some contact with members of the Labour Party. Macmillan publicly supported the candidacy of A.D. Lindsay, the anti-Munich Independent candidate, in the Oxford by-election of October 1938. In addition, he took a pro-active role in lobbying the Foreign Office on the plight of refugees displaced in the wake of the Munich agreement.[7] In order, as he put it, 'to try to clarify my own mind and that of others', Macmillan wrote a pamphlet in October, *The Price of Peace: Notes on the World Crisis*, which he circulated privately and widely. After surveying government policy since the general election of 1935, he called not only for a reinvigorated rearmament programme, but also a revival of the League of Nations and closer relations with France and the USSR, and purposive economic planning to support rearmament and collective security.[8] Macmillan followed this in February 1939 with *Economic Aspects of Defence*, in which he advised immediate industrial reconstruction, the storage of raw materials, state assistance for foreign trade, and a Ministry of Supply.

Harold Nicolson maintained his ongoing opposition to appeasement both in parliament and the press. He took it as a given that 'Germany has secured a resounding diplomatic victory and a tremendous accretion of power'. The issue was not just about a boundary revision, but a German bid for continental domination,

[5] Letter to the *Manchester Guardian*, 20 October 1938.

[6] Letter to *The Times*, 24 October 1938.

[7] Memorandum by R.A. Butler, 2 November 1938, Macmillan to Butler, 4 November 1938, FO371/21586, C13639/11896/12.

[8] Harold Macmillan, *The Price of Peace: Notes on the World Crisis* (London, 1938), pp. 1–19; *idem*, *Economic Aspects of Defence* (London, 1939), pp. 1–48; and *idem*, *Memoirs*, I, *Winds of Change, 1914–1939* (London, 1966), pp. 584, 589.

and as a consequence, Britain 'must prepare for the final attack', and at the same time, 'a line should be drawn beyond which we are not prepared to retreat', wherever that might be situated.[9] His major contribution was a Penguin Special, *Why Britain Is at War*, a 50,000-word book which he wrote in two weeks and which was published on 7 November 1939. It sold over 100,000 copies.[10] After an extensive survey of the rise of Nazism and German foreign policy since 1936, Nicolson concentrated on diplomatic events leading up to the outbreak of the war. He emphasized his long-standing distrust of Hitler, the perverse National Government faith in Nazi assurances, and the 'profound shock' to British public opinion by the seizure of the Czech state in March 1939, and the end of appeasement which it signalled. Nicolson argued that the war was not about self-preservation, but had a moral dimension: 'to save humanity' from what he termed 'the rubber truncheon and the concentration camp'. Finally, he addressed those who would argue that war settles nothing. In his view, it was 'a bad peace' which settled nothing. Hence, in the final chapter, he examined the issue of war aims and peacemaking, suggesting that the outcome must produce a genuine linkage between idealism and realism, one which would address both the problem of Germany, ensuring that there would be no imposed peace, and a future world order, based on a new League that would have powers to enforce its decisions, and on a new European federation.[11]

Not surprisingly, Sir Arthur Salter also chose similar themes to explore. His first post-Munich contribution was the pamphlet *Is It Peace? The Nettle and the Flower*. He was very critical of many aspects of recent diplomatic events, describing the process as 'the victory of the threat of force over the process of reason and peaceful negotiation', with 'ominous consequences for the future'. He appealed for a system of collective security with sufficient collective strength to deter or defeat an aggressor. Yet he was not among those who believed that firmness in September would have deterred Hitler, or saved Czechoslovakia. As for what was to be done, Salter expanded on his own agenda. He made an impassioned appeal for rearmament, particularly for the air force, and civilian defence against 'a knock-out blow from the air'. He found it 'intolerable' that the nation *'should have to rely upon a procrastinating and incompetent administration being stimulated into spasmodic and inadequate action by external pressure'*. He appealed

[9] Harold Nicolson, 'After Munich', *The Nineteenth Century and After*, 124 (1938), pp. 513–524.

[10] Nigel Nicolson (ed.), *Vita and Harold: The Letters of Vita Sackville-West and Harold Nicolson* (London, 1992), p. 316.

[11] Harold Nicolson, *Why Britain Is at War* (London, 1939), pp. 97, 103–104, 129–137, 143, 150–160.

for a 'truly national' government, new government departments focused on civilian defence and supply, and industrial reorganization. Finally, Salter reaffirmed his belief in collective defence, based on preponderant strength 'obvious enough not merely to defeat, but to deter, aggression'. As he wrote: 'we need this to be able to resist if appeasement fails'.[12] Salter followed this with a feverish writing spree that resulted in a book which went to press on 20 April 1939: *Security: Can We Retrieve It?* To a degree he expanded on his pamphlet, but he also added some critical, though personally, sympathetic thoughts on Chamberlain and the situation after the German seizure of the rump Czech state in March 1939. Salter doubted whether Chamberlain, 'disillusioned and indignant', had the 'requisite strength and constructive vision' to pursue any policy other than appeasement. In conclusion, Salter returned to his *via media*, despite his fears that his prescriptions might be dismissed as the futile musings of a 'Liberal internationalist'. Given the possibility of some 'reasonable negotiation' with Germany, he proposed that a general settlement with Germany should be made public in a White Paper and be based on a broad range of mutual concessions and firm commitments, or as he wrote: 'A cause worthy of Britain must be more than Britain's cause'.[13]

The non-parliamentarians in the All Souls Group also contributed in somewhat similar vein. Salter's *Is It Peace? The Nettle and the Flower* had originally appeared in *The Spectator*, as one of a six-part, post-Munich series, 'British Policy Now – II'. Another contributor was Norman Angell, who surveyed the course of appeasement since the early 1930s and noted its failure. Given, as he wrote, that Britain is 'at Germany's mercy', he rejected any notion of an alliance with Germany for mutual gain and urged instead a return to 'the collective method', the creation of a Franco-Russian-British combination, followed by 'a system of economic and political right' into which Germany could also enter as a partner. Angell also addressed some of the larger issues looming soon after the outbreak of the war in his *For What Do We Fight?* He singled out the rights of man, collective security, a 'new international order', and what he termed the need for 'moral understanding', in which he included the abolition of 'anarchy' in international relations, and its replacement at once with 'the federal unity of Europe'.[14] J.A. Spender was the last contributor and distanced

[12] Salter, *Is It Peace? The Nettle and the Flower*, pp. 1–16.

[13] Sir Arthur Salter, *Security: Can We Retrieve It?* (London, 1939), pp. 283, 315, 343, 385. The book included 'A draft manifesto of British policy', pp. 345–366. Rowse assisted Salter with the proofs of the book. See Rowse papers, engagement book, 26 April 1939, EUL MS 113/2/6/1.

[14] Sir Norman Angell, 'British policy now – V', *The Spectator*, 161 (11 November 1938), pp. 800–801; Sir Norman Angell, *For What Do We Fight?* (London, 1939), pp. 1–9, 116, 316.

himself from the gloomy opinions proffered by previous writers. He pointed out that there were limits to British power and the government should not be singled out for reproach. Rather the inherent failure was due to the limitations of the League of Nations in the areas of disarmament and treaty revision. Spender described the resolution of the Czech crisis as 'a bad job, which would probably have been a far worse one but for the Prime Minister's courageous intervention'. As for the two alternatives for the future – appeasement versus an anti-German coalition – he tended towards the former in the hope that the general aversion to war would see reason prevail.[15]

On 24 October 1938 E.L. Woodward addressed the Imperial Defence College to offer what he termed 'An historian's outlook on the present state of Europe'. He highlighted the changes in the European distribution of power, which he emphasized were not military resources but 'the social and economic structure of society upon the character of war'. Modern war, or 'totalitarian war', he argued, required 'the mobilization of industry' on an unprecedented scale. He went on to criticize the Versailles treaty and British policy for never making a clear choice subsequently between either conciliating and repressing Germany, or between a policy of realism or idealism. As for the present, Woodward argued that war 'would settle nothing'. However, he espoused a dual policy of maximum defence preparedness combined with a waiting game that in time might bring down the German system of totalitarianism. Despite its prescription of hope, the text was sent to the Foreign Office where it received some approval, was read by the Foreign Secretary and widely circulated.[16]

The other historian in the group, Arnold Toynbee, had become increasingly pessimistic in the wake of the September crisis. A paper which he wrote, 'A turning point in history', was vigorously criticized during a Chatham House meeting on 27 October, with Woodward in the chair and Salter attending. Woodward observed that Toynbee's views were to be 'deplored'.[17] It was a revised version, therefore, that Toynbee read at Chatham House on 15 November 1938, expressing a degree of uncertainty, and raising more questions than answers. He took it as given that the Germans, the largest nation in Europe, now likely enjoyed a complete preponderance over central and eastern Europe. What was Britain to do? As regards passive defence against

[15] J.A. Spender, 'British policy now – VI', *The Spectator*, 161 (18 November 1938), p. 839.

[16] See minutes by Strang, Cadogan, and Halifax, FO371/21627, C14420/95/62 on the paper. In a letter to *The Times*, 4 October 1938, Woodward urged upon the government 'the vital need for us to accelerate our means of active and passive defence'. See also his 'Historians and the crisis', *The Spectator*, 161 (9 September 1938), p. 402.

[17] Crozier, 'Chatham House and appeasement', pp. 234–238.

air attack, time was on the British side. On the question of active resistance, Toynbee regarded both Britain and France as having the advantage in the long term. He also advocated industrial and manpower organization, even at the risk of lowering standards of living. Finally, he pointed out that the nineteenth-century *Pax Britannica* to maintain law and order world-wide still required some alternative, such as the League of Nations.[18] In a following contribution to *Foreign Affairs*, he reiterated much of what he had already offered with some differences. He now termed the events of September 1938 as 'momentous' and 'a turning point [. . .] in world history'. In the event that Germany constructed a *Mittel-Europa* on the continent, what, he asked, should be Britain's response in light of her historical role in the European balance of power? Toynbee admitted 'we have run into a fog in which we cannot yet see beyond our noses'. He also expanded on the moral dilemmas of peacemaking, had war broken out in September 1938, and the likely recurrence of another Cathaginian peace. The principal of nationality had been ironically reasserted, he suggested, but for the future he foresaw no other option but the return 'of some kind of world order', for the alternative was a *Pax Hitleriana*.[19]

Others from the group were more outspoken, in different ways. A.L. Rowse continued to criticize the 'incompetence and duplicity' of the government, 'dominated by a rump, a small Junta, that is totally unrepresentative of this great country', with its policy of 'retreat before aggression'. The way forward, he argued, was the constitution of 'a real National Government', conceivably headed by Eden.[20] His further concern was what he termed the 'regrettable' publicity given in the British press to Hitler's various speeches, 'designed as so much propaganda'.[21] Gilbert Murray was both more circumspect and moderate in tone. He admitted that the terms imposed on Czechoslovakia, 'with needless brutality' may have been unavoidable. But 'we can only tremble to think', he wrote, what was meant by the Prime Minister's assurances of ongoing co-operation with the

[18] The text of the address was published in 'After Munich: the world outlook', *International Affairs*, 18 (1939), pp. 1–19.

[19] Arnold J. Toynbee, 'A turning point in history', *Foreign Affairs*, 17 (1939), pp. 305–320.

[20] A.L. Rowse, letter to the *Manchester Guardian*, 24 October 1938. The editorial of the day largely supported Rowse's suggestion for a national unity government. See also his 'Reflections on the European situation', *Political Quarterly*, 9 (1938), pp. 334–350. In his diary, Rowse lamented what he called 'government by lily-livered Nonconformists [. . .]. Now they are making every concession to Hitler and Mussolini, bringing about the decline of the British Empire, they pretend that the Labour Party wants war. The hypocrisy of it!'; Rowse papers, EUL MS 113/2/5/6, summer–autumn 1938.

[21] See Rowse's unpublished letter to *The Times*, 1 May 1939, and the reply from the editor, Geoffrey Dawson, in Rowse papers, EUL MS 113/3/temp/box 161.

dictators, and asked whether Chamberlain could be trusted. Where Murray did place his trust was 'in a refortified League', given that 'if we do not end war, it will end us'.[22] On the question of the League's future, Murray wrote to Halifax on 8 November, to argue the case that a League, bereft of Article XVI, and thus confined only to social, political, and intellectual questions, would avoid the basic question of 'how to get rid of war'. Such a revised covenant, which he strongly opposed, would lead instead to an alliance system, based on pure self-interest, and would throw morality to the winds.[23]

Basil Liddell Hart published in July 1939 *The Defence of Britain.* He examined, among much else and in great detail, the military and diplomatic situation since Munich, in an attempt 'to face the facts frankly, instead of pretending that it was "peace with honour"'. He was critical of the government for advancing 'weighty arguments for avoiding our obligations – but the fact remains that each surrender led to a worse one, and to a worsening of our situation as well as that of civilization'. He bluntly pointed out that the strategic balance had shifted in Germany's favour. The one certain need was for Britain to strengthen its air defences, including civilian air defence, and engage on a massive rearmament programme. As he succinctly put his extensive military prescriptions, 'If you wish for peace, understand war'.[24] Lionel Curtis continued his passionate commitment to a federalist solution to world disorder. Returning from his travels abroad from July 1938 to January 1939, he addressed an audience at Chatham House on 21 February 1939 on the subject of 'world order', telling his audience: 'I am sure that a world government is the ultimate goal we shall reach.' The outbreak of war only hardened Curtis's commitment to the cause of world government, the only solution he believed would both win the war and win the peace.[25] Finally, Walter Layton echoed similar arguments when analysing allied war aims. While emphasizing his notion of a 'European association of nations', plans for disarmament and economic reconstruction, he was equally

[22] Murray, letter to the *Manchester Guardian*, 4 October 1938, and letter to *The Times*, 22 October 1938.

[23] Murray to Halifax, 8 November 1938, FO371/22512, W14847/3/98. The letter evoked some minutes but no response. See also Murray to Halifax, 22 October 1938, FO371, W14446/547/98.

[24] Basil Liddell Hart, *The Defence of Britain* (London, 1939), pp. 21, 79, 83–84. See also his letter to *The Times*, 10 November 1938.

[25] Lionel Curtis, 'World order', *International Affairs*, 18 (1939), p. 308, and his *World War: Its Cause and Cure* (London, 1945), p. 266. The latter was largely a compilation of these pamphlets which Curtis had produced in wartime, 'Decision, action', and 'Faith and works'.

clear that the world could not 'go on indefinitely from crisis to crisis [. . .]. The law of the jungle is at issue with the rule of reason'.[26]

It is evident, therefore, that the post-Munich thinking and contributions made by the principal participants in the Foreign Affairs Group suffered from the same deep divisions of opinion displayed during its meetings. Those who argued for an agreement with Germany at almost all costs continued to do so. Others continued their campaign for industrial and economic reorganization with even greater vigour. Some continued to press for a major rearmament campaign, with a few addressing the needs for a constructive peace policy and a revitalization of the League of Nations. Whatever view was espoused or propagated, it is also evident that the Foreign Affairs Group provided a vigorous forum for debate and discussion. Its prescriptions, plans and ideas continued to inform the thinking of participants.

It is ironic, however, that the Foreign Affairs Group spawned the formation of another pressure group which was able to report some moderate degree of success, though not in the sphere of foreign affairs. The bridge between the practical and the theoretical had always been of concern to Salter. So too from the outset of the meetings had been the question of civilian defence against air attack. Official planning for civilian defence focused later in the 1930s on the problem of aerial bombardment. From 1935 to 1938 the Air Raid Precautions Department of the Home Office took responsibility for planning and preparation. Meanwhile, public perceptions of the future nature of aerial warfare continued to be determined by worst-case scenarios from the outbreak of wars in China, Abyssinia, and Spain.

It was under such circumstances that Salter had taken the initiative in April 1938 to spearhead the formation of an air-raid defence group.[27] The Munich crisis, which served to highlight 'both the importance and inadequacy of ARP preparations', led on 1 November 1938 to the appointment of Sir John Anderson as Lord Privy Seal, with overall responsibility for co-ordinating civil defence.[28] On 7 February 1939 the Air Raid Defence League was publicly launched. Anderson lauded its formation and its non-party approach, as did an editorial in *The Times* that day, welcoming 'an organization which will be wholly

[26] Walter Layton, 'The allied war aims: a plan for European peace', *News Chronicle*, 2 November 1939. This was later published as a pamphlet.

[27] See above, pp. 147–148.

[28] Joseph S. Meisel, 'Air raid shelter policy and its critics in Britain before the Second World War', *Twentieth Century British History*, 5 (1994), pp. 301–319. For background, see Richard M. Titmuss, *Problems of Social Policy* (London, 1950), and Terence H. O'Brien, *Civil Defence* (London, 1955).

independent of the Government, yet ready to cooperate in every effort of the Government which its own expert opinion considers salutary and to suggest other useful efforts for the Government to make'. The *New Statesman* too congratulated the League for its determination 'to put some sense into our civilian defence'.[29]

The League publicized its objectives which were to secure protection for the civilian population against air attack and concentrate public interest on the issue through meetings, speakers, and relevant publications. As well, the League pledged itself to co-operate with local and central government, and encourage voluntary service. Salter was at pains to emphasize that, given Britain's strategic weakness in the air, it was vital to make Britain 'at least immune from the risk that a quick blow would knock us out'.[30] Lord Hailey, formerly of the Indian Civil Service, was appointed Chairman of the League, but the driving forces were Salter and Sir Ralph Wedgewood, Chief General Manager since 1923 of the London and North Eastern Railway Company.[31] Both were able to report in the following days on the 'intelligent enthusiasm' shown by the public response.[32] A high profile was maintained throughout the spring and summer. The League issued its first 'Bulletin' on 31 March and suggested that the protection of civilians required a combination of both deep and shallow (nicknamed the Anderson) shelters. This was followed, for example, by 'An outline of civil defence' on 28 April which was a detailed, constructive statement on the subject, and then on 14 June by 'The nature of the air raid threat'. The latter argued that a 'lightening blow' from the German *Luftwaffe* might not lead to the collapse of civilian morale 'provided that passive defence was organized now'. A sixth and apparently final 'Bulletin', 'The Warden Service: a study in ARP methods', targeted 'the system of public training against air attack'.[33] In July, however, the League complained that government

[29] *The Times*, 7 February 1939; *New Statesman*, 17 (11 February 1938), p. 198. *The Times* also mentioned that the new League would maintain contact with the Air Raid Protection Institute, whose president was Sir Oliver Simmonds, MP, 1931–1945. It concluded by listing a very impressive array of public figures, 'founder members', who had declared their support. As well, the League incorporated the National Association of Air Raid Wardens, who were to form a 'special section'. See Arthur Salter, 'The public and the air menace', *New Statesman*, 17 (18 February 1939), pp. 238–239.

[30] *The Times*, 8 February 1939.

[31] Wedgewood retired from this post on 3 March 1939. Three days later he accepted an invitation to stand as an independent candidate for Cambridge University at the next general election.

[32] See *The Times*, 11 February 1939.

[33] See *The Times*, 31 March 1939; *The Times*, 28 April 1939; Wedgewood, letter to the *New Statesman*, 17 (27 May 1939), p. 823; *The Times*, 14 June 1939; *The Times*, 30 July 1939.

policy was still defective: 'it is in general being translated far too slowly from paper into fact'.[34]

'Salter's Soviet' – in its two manifestations – thus had little influence on government policy or thinking with regard to international issues or civilian defence against air attack. Even with its excellent contacts in the policymaking establishment and the media, progress was slight. Rowse's obsession about the central role played by the Fellows of All Souls College in the formulation and implementation of appeasement, therefore, must be qualified. He admitted as much when he pointed out that the younger Fellows were opposed to appeasement. The Foreign Affairs Group at All Souls confirmed that generation gap. Additionally, the experience of the group illustrates that where, why, when, and how to make a stand, if at all, were the central issues at the heart of appeasement. Prime Minister, Neville Chamberlain had the utmost difficulties with these questions, and his were the responsibilities of power not debate. Debating appeasement at All Souls was no more successful.

The fifth bulletin, 'Food in war-time', was critical of the lack of co-ordination in preparing agriculture for war production; *The Times*, 10 July 1939.

[34] Sir Ralph Wedgewood, 'Gaps in civilian defence', *The Spectator*, 163 (7 July 1939), p. 7.

APPENDIX

PARTICIPANTS IN THE ALL SOULS FOREIGN AFFAIRS GROUP

Adams, William George Stewart (1874–1966) public servant; Fellow of All Souls, 1910–1933; Gladstone Professor of Political Theory and Institutions, Oxford University, 1912–1933; founder and editor *The Political Quarterly*, 1914–1916; secretary to David Lloyd George, 1916–1919; Warden of All Souls, 1933–1945; and then honorary Fellow, 1945.

Allen, Reginald Clifford, Baron Allen of Hurtwood (1889–1939) Labour politician; three times imprisoned conscientious objector, 1916–1917; Treasurer and Chairman, ILP, 1922–1926; director, *Daily Herald*, 1925–1930; supported 'national' labour group, 1931–1936; publications include: *Putting Socialism into Practice* (London, 1924); *Britain's Political Future: A Plea for Liberty and Leadership* (London, 1934); and *Peace in Our Time* (London, 1936).

Angell, Sir Norman (1874–1967) publicist and author of *The Great Illusion* (London, 1910); *Peace with the Dictators?* (London, 1938); *For What Do We Fight?* (London, 1939), and some thirty-five other books; Editor, *Foreign Affairs*, 1928–1931; Labour MP, 1929–1931; Nobel Peace Prize, 1933; memoirs, *After All* (London, 1951).

Arnold, Sydney, 1st Baron Arnold (1878–1945) Liberal MP, 1912–1921; joined Labour Party, 1922; created a Labour peer and appointed Under-Secretary for the Colonies, 1924; Paymaster-General, 1929–1931; resigned from Labour Party for its alleged pro-war policies, 1938.

Arnold-Forster, William Edward (1885–1951) with the Admiralty, 1914–1918; joined the Labour Party, 1917; strong supporter of the League of Nations and frequent contributor to *Headway*; secretary to Lord Cecil, 1929–1931; artist specializing in pastel landscapes; author of *Why We Have Failed to Disarm* (London, 1927); *The Disarmament Conference* (London, 1931); *The Blockade, 1914–1919: Before the Armistice – and After* (London, 1939), and *The New Freedom of the Seas* (London, 1942).

Barratt Brown, Alfred (1887–1947) Vice-Principal, 1921–1926, and Principal, 1926–1944, Ruskin College, Oxford; member of the Quaker Executive Committee, 1914–1918; twice imprisoned for his Christian pacifist views, first as a member of the No-Conscription Fellowship and then as a conscientious objector; books include *The Machine and the Worker* (London, 1934); *Great Democrats* (London, 1934); and *Democratic Leadership* (London, 1938).

Curtis, Lionel George (1872–1955) public servant and federalist; a founder of the *Round Table*, 1910; and of the Royal Institute of International Affairs, 1920–1921; Research Fellow of All Souls, 1921–1955; author of *Dyarchy* (London, 1920); *The Prevention of War* (London, 1924); *Civitas Dei*, 3 vols (London, 1934–1937); *Faith and Works* (London, 1943); *World War: Its Cause and Cure* (London, 1945); and *With Milner in South Africa* (London, 1951).

Fisher, Herbert Albert Laurens (1865–1940) historian and statesman; introduced Education Act, 1918; Liberal MP, 1916–1926; delegate to League of Nations Assembly, 1920–1922; Warden of New College, Oxford, 1925–1940; publications include *James Bryce*, 2 vols (London, 1927); *A History of Europe*, 3 vols (London, 1935), and *An Unfinished Autobiography* (London, 1940).

Hodson, Henry Vincent (1906–1999) Fellow of All Souls, 1928–1935; Editor, *Round Table*, 1934–1939, and *Annual Register of World Events*, 1973–1988; with Ministry of Information, 1939–1941, and Ministry of Production, 1942–1945; Assistant Editor, 1945–1950, and Editor, 1950–1961, *The Sunday Times*; books include *Economics of a Changing World* (London, 1933); *Slump and Recovery, 1929–1937* (London, 1938), and *The British Commonwealth and the Future* (London, 1939).

Hudson, Geoffrey Francis (1903–1974) historian, Fellow of All Souls, 1926–1954; with the Research Department, Foreign Office, 1939–1946; Fellow and Director of Far Eastern Studies, St. Antony's College, Oxford, 1954–1974; author of *Europe and China* (London, 1931); *The Far East in World Politics: A Study in Recent History* (London, 1936), with Marthe Rajchman; *An Atlas of Far Eastern Politics* (London, 1938), and *Fifty Years of Communism* (London, 1968).

Layton, Sir Walter, 1st Baron Layton (1884–1966) economist and newspaper proprietor; with Ministry of Munitions, 1914–1918; Editor, *The Economist*, 1922–1938; Chairman, *News Chronicle*, 1930–1950, and *Star*, 1936–1950; with Ministry of Supply, 1940–1942, and Ministry of Production, 1941–1943; published *An Introduction to the Study* *of Prices* (London, 1920); *Allied War Aims* (London, 1939); and *How to Deal with Germany* (London, 1944).

Liddell Hart, Sir Basil Henry (1895–1970) military historian and strategist; military correspondent, the *Daily Telegraph*, 1925–1935, and *The Times*, 1935–1939; adviser to Minister of War, 1937–1938; some thirty books include *Europe in Arms* (London, 1937); *The Defence of Britain* (London, 1939); and *Memoirs*, 2 vols (London, 1965).

Macmillan, Harold, 1st Earl of Stockton (1894–1986) publisher and politician; Conservative MP, 1924–1929, 1931–1964; minister resident at allied headquarters in North-West Africa, 1942–1945; Prime Minister, 1957–1963; author of *Reconstruction* (London, 1933); *The Middle Way* (London, 1938); *Economic Aspects of Defence* (London, 1939), which reprints *The Price of Peace* (London, 1938), and *Memoirs*, 6 vols (London, 1966–1973).

Murray, Gilbert (1866–1957) Regius Professor of Greek, Oxford University, 1908–1936; founder of the League of Nations Union and chairman of the executive council, 1923–1938; besides numerous classical studies, works include *The Foreign Policy of Sir Edward Grey* (London, 1915); *The Problem of Foreign Policy* (London, 1921), and *Liberality and Civilisation* (London, 1938); memoir – of sorts – in *An Unfinished Autobiography, with Contributions by his Friends*, Jean Smith and Arnold Toynbee (eds) (London, 1960).

Nicolson, Sir Harold George (1886–1968) diplomat, author, and critic; entered Foreign Office, 1909; married Victoria Sackville-West, 1913; with British delegation to Paris peace conference, 1919; served at Foreign Office and abroad, 1920–1929; National Labour MP, 1935–1945; governor of the BBC, 1941–1946; his numerous books include *Curzon, the Last Phase* (London, 1934); *Diplomacy* (London, 1939); *King George V* (London, 1952); and *Diaries and Letters, 1930–1962*, 3 vols (London, 1966–1968).

Radcliffe-Brown, Alfred Reginald (1881–1955) Professor of Social Anthropology, University of Sydney, 1925–1931, University of Chicago, 1931–1937; Fellow of All Souls and Professor of Social Anthropology, Oxford University, 1937–1946; President of Royal Anthropological Institute, 1939–1940.

Rowse, Alfred Leslie (1903–1997) historian; stood as Labour candidate, 1929, 1935; Fellow, and later Emeritus Fellow, of All Souls, 1925–1974; author of numerous books of history, politics, and reminiscences; the latter include *A Cornishman at Oxford* (London, 1965); *A Cornishman Abroad* (London, 1976); *A Man of the Thirties* (London, 1979); *Memories of Men and Women* (London, 1980); *Glimpses of the Great* (London, 1985); *Friends and Contemporaries* (London, 1989), *All Souls in My Time* (London, 1993), and *Historians I Have Known* (London, 1995).

Salter, Sir James Arthur, 1st Baron Salter (1881–1975) General Secretary, Reparation Commission, 1920–1922; director, economic and finance section, League of Nations, 1919–1920, 1922–1931; Independent MP, Oxford University, 1937–1950, then Conservative, Ormskirk, 1951–1953; Fellow of All Souls, 1934–1975; Gladstone Professor of Political Theory and Institutions, Oxford University, 1934–1944; Head of British Shipping Mission, Washington, 1941–1943; numerous books include *Recovery* (London, 1932); *The United States of Europe* (London, 1933); *Security: Can We Retrieve It?* (London, 1939); and *Personality in Politics* (London, 1947); reminiscences in *Memoirs of a Public Servant* (London, 1961), and *Slave of the Lamp* (London, 1967).

Toynbee, Arnold Joseph (1889–1975) Professor of Byzantine and Modern Greek Language, Literature and History, London University, 1919–1924; Director of Studies, Royal Institute of International Affairs, 1925–1955; Director, Research Department, Foreign Office, 1943–1946; Editor, 1924–1938, *A Survey of International Affairs*; numerous publications include *A Study of History*, 12 vols (London 1934–1961), memoirs *Acquaintances* (London, 1967), and the sequel *Experiences* (London, 1969).

Wint, Guy (1910–1969) author and Orientalist; accompanied Sir Arthur Salter to China, 1933; wartime work in India for the Ministry of Information; on the staff of the *Manchester Guardian*, 1947–1957; books include *The British in Asia* (London, 1947); *Spotlight on Asia* (London, 1955); *Commonsense about China* (London, 1960), and with Peter Calvocoressi, *Total War: Causes and Courses of the Second World War* (London, 1972).

Woodward, Sir Ernest Llewellyn (1890–1971) Fellow of All Souls, 1919–1944, 1962–1971; Professor of International Relations, Oxford, 1944–1947, and Modern History, 1947–1951; Editor, 1944–1955 of *Documents on British Foreign Policy, 1919–1939*; and author of *The Age of Reform, 1815–1870* (London, 1938); *Great Britain and the War, 1914–1918* (London, 1967), and *British Foreign Policy During the Second World War*, 5 vols (London, 1970–1976); memoirs *Short Journey* (London, 1942).

BIBLIOGRAPHY

Unpublished primary sources

The following collections provided the primary materials for this study:

Lord Allen of Hurtwood papers, Thomas Cooper Library, University of South Carolina, Columbia, SC. Much vital correspondence and printed materials.

Norman Angell papers, Bracken Library, Ball State University, Muncie, IN.

Lord Cecil of Chelwood papers, Department of Manuscripts, British Library, London.

Lionel Curtis papers: (1) Bodleian Library, Oxford; (2) Royal Institute of International Affairs Archives, Chatham House, London.

Paul Emrys-Evans papers, Department of Manuscripts, British Library, London.

H.A.L. Fisher papers, Bodleian Library, Oxford.

Foreign Office papers, FO371, Public Record Office, Kew, London.

Walter Layton papers, Trinity College, Cambridge.

Basil Liddell Hart papers, Centre for Military Archives, King's College, London, University of London. A major source for the activities of the group.

Harold Macmillan papers, Bodleian Library, Oxford.

Gilbert Murray papers, Bodleian Library, Oxford.

Harold Nicolson diaries and papers, Balliol College, Oxford. Helpful in many ways, including correlating participants with some of their views on foreign policy.

A.L. Rowse papers, Exeter University Library, Exeter.

Royal Institute of International Affairs archives, Chatham House, London.

Lord Salter of Kidlington papers, in the possession of the author.

J.A. Spender papers, Department of Manuscripts, British Library, London.

Arnold J. Toynbee papers: (1) Bodleian Library, Oxford; (2) Royal Institute of International Affairs Archives, Chatham House, London.

The author's enquiries regarding the papers of other participants produced these results:

William George Adams: no information.

Lord Arnold: There survives 'a very small collection of papers relating to Arnold's political career'; Cameron Hazlehurst and Christine Woodland, *A Guide to the Papers of British Cabinet Ministers* (London, 1974), p. 5. It later proved impossible to determine the fate of these papers. See *ibid.*, p. 29.

Will Arnold-Forster: 'I don't have any written source materials which might help you'; Mark Arnold-Forster [son] to the author, 23 June 1979.

Alfred Barratt Brown: 'I do not have any of my father's papers, which went either to Clifford Allen or to Geoffrey Crowther'; Michael Barratt Brown to the author, 19 July 1979.

Henry Vincent Hodson: 'My own pre-1939 papers were destroyed with most of my domestic possessions in a fire-bomb raid on London in 1941'; Hodson to the author, 2 August 1978.

Geoffrey Francis Hudson: no information.

Alfred Reginald Radcliffe-Brown: 'no papers of Radcliffe-Brown's have come to light'; R.G. Lienhardt [literary executor] to the author, 12 February 1982.

Guy Wint: no surviving papers; Freda Wint to the author, 13 February 1973.

E.L. Woodward: no information.

Official documents and publications

Documents on British Foreign Policy, 1919–1939, third series, II (London, 1949).

Documents on German Foreign Policy, 1918–1945, Series D, II (London, 1949).

Parliamentary Debates, House of Commons, fifth series, CCCXXIX–CCCLI (London, 1937–1939).

Parliamentary Debates, House of Lords, fifth series, CVII–CXIV (London, 1937–1939).

Secondary sources

This compilation is limited to some of the secondary sources cited in the footnotes, as well as a selection of relevant biographies.

Publications by individual contributors to the All Souls Foreign Affairs Group are largely detailed in the appendix, with additional relevant citations below.

Contemporary books and articles

Adams, W.G.S., 'Whither England?', *Southern Review*, 3 (1937), pp. 15–27.

Allen, Lord, of Hurtwood, *Peace in Our Time: An Appeal to the International Peace Conference of June 16, 1936* (London, 1936).

'A constructive peace policy', *Contemporary Review*, 152 (1937), pp. 11–20.

'1937 in retrospect', in National Peace Council, *Peace Year Book 1938* (London, 1938).

Angell, Norman, 'Can aggressor states be checked?', *Contemporary Review*, 152 (1937), pp. 521–529.

'British policy now – V', *The Spectator*, 161 (11 November 1938), pp. 800–801.

Arnold-Forster, Will, 'For what should national power be used?', in Geneva Institute of International Relations, *War Is Not Inevitable: Problems of Peace*, thirteenth series (London, 1938), pp. 225–256.

'Hans Litten', *New Statesman*, 15 (19 March 1938), p. 475.

Bevan, Edwyn, 'Collective security or collective defence?', *The Spectator*, 160 (24 June 1938), pp. 1136–1137.

Curtis, Lionel, 'World order', *International Affairs*, 18 (1939), pp. 301–311.

Hodson, Henry Vincent, 'Empire migration', *The Spectator*, 161 (5 August 1938), pp. 223–224.

'Eire and the British Commonwealth', *Foreign Affairs*, 16 (1938), pp. 525–536.

Liddell Hart, Basil H., 'We learn from history?', *London Mercury*, 38 (1938), pp. 112–122.

'The defence of the Empire', *Fortnightly*, 143 (1938), pp. 20–30.

'Military lessons from Spain', *New Republic*, 91 (4 August 1937), pp. 357–359.

Macmillan, Harold, *The Price of Peace* (London, 1938).

Murray, Gilbert, 'Sanctions', *Contemporary Review*, 152 (1937), pp. 135–141.

'Moral basis or power politics?', *The Spectator*, 161 (1 July 1938), pp. 11–12.

Nicolson, Harold, 'Germany and the colonies', *Fortnightly*, 142 (1937), pp. 641–648.

'The colonial problem', *International Affairs*, 17 (1938), pp. 32–41.
'After Munich', *Nineteenth Century and After*, 124 (1938), pp. 513–524.
Why Britain Is at War (London, 1939).
Rowse, A.L. 'The present and immediate future policy of the Labour Party', *Political Quarterly*, 9 (1938), pp. 13–30.
'Reflections on the European situation', *Political Quarterly*, 9 (1938), pp. 334–350.
Salter, Arthur, 'Food storage for defence', *The Economist*, 129 (2 October 1937), pp. 12–16.
'British policy now – II', *The Spectator*, 161 (21 October 1938), p. 643.
'The public and the air menace', *New Statesman*, 17 (18 February 1939), pp. 238–239.
Spender, J.A. 'British policy now – VI', *The Spectator*, 161 (18 November 1938), p. 839.
Toynbee, Arnold J. 'The issues in British foreign policy', *International Affairs*, 17 (1938), pp. 307–337.
'After Munich: the world outlook', *International Affairs*, 18 (1939), pp. 1–19.
'A turning point in history', *Foreign Affairs*, 17 (1939), pp. 305–320.
Wedgewood, Ralph, 'Air Raid Defence League', *New Statesman*, 17 (27 May 1939), p. 823.
'Gaps in civilian defence', *The Spectator*, 163 (7 July 1939), p. 7.
Woodward, E.L. 'From 1914 till now', *The Spectator*, 160 (1,8, 15, 22, 29 April 1938) pp. 575, 620–621, 664–665, 700–701, 740–741.
'Historians and the crisis', *The Spectator*, 161 (9 September 1938), p. 402.

Other books

Adeney, Martin, *Nuffield: a Biography* (London, 1993).
Allen, Lady Margery, *Memoirs of an Uneducated Lady* (London, 1975).
Amery, L.S., *My Political Life*, 3 vols (London, 1953–1955).
The Leo Amery Diaries, 2 vols, John Barnes and David Nicholson (eds) (London, 1980–1988).
Andrews, P.W.S. and Brunner, Elizabeth, *The Life of Lord Nuffield: A Study in Enterprise and Benevolence* (London, 1955).
Bond, Brian, *Liddell Hart: A Study of His Military Thought* (London, 1977).
Ceadel, Martin, *Semi-Detached Idealists: The British Peace Movement and International Relations, 1854–1945* (London, 2000).
Cell, John W., *Hailey: A Study in British Imperialism, 1872–1969* (London, 1992).

Cauveren, Sydney, *A.L. Rowse: A Bibliophile's Extensive Bibliography* (London, 2000).

Danchev, Alex, *Alchemist of War: The Life of Basil Liddell Hart* (London, 1998).

Gilbert, Martin, *Plough My Own Furrow: The Story of Lord Allen of Hurtwood as Told Through His Writings and Correspondence* (London, 1965).

Harris, Wilson, *J.A. Spender* (London, 1946).

Horne, Alistair, *Macmillan*, 2 vols (London, 1988–1989).

Hubback, David, *No Ordinary Press Baron: A Life of Walter Layton* (London, 1985).

Lavin, Deborah, *From Empire to International Commonwealth: A Biography of Lionel Curtis* (London, 1995).

Lees-Milne, James, *Harold Nicolson: A Biography*, 2 vols (London, 1980–1981).

McNeill, William H., *Arnold J. Toynbee: A Life* (London, 1989).

Marrin, Albert, *Sir Norman Angell* (Boston, MA, 1979).

Marwick, Arthur, *Clifford Allen: The Open Conspirator* (London, 1964).

Mearsheimer, John J., *Liddell Hart and the Weight of History* (London, 1988).

Medlicott, W.N., *Britain and Germany: The Search for Agreement, 1930–1937* (London, 1969).

The Next Five Years: An Essay in Political Agreement (London, 1935).

Nicolson, Nigel (ed.), *Vita and Harold: The Letters of Vita Sackville-West and Harold Nicolson* (London, 1992).

Ollard, Richard, *A Man of Contradictions: A Life of A.L. Rowse* (London, 1999).

(ed.), *The Diaries of A.L. Rowse* (London, 2003).

Overy, R.J., *William Morris: Viscount Nuffield* (London, 1976).

Rowse, A.L., *All Souls and Appeasement: A Contribution to Contemporary History* (London, 1961).

Appeasement: A Study in Political Decline, 1933–1939 (New York, 1961).

All Souls in My Time (London, 1993).

Simon, Ernest, *The Smaller Democracies* (London, 1939).

Stapleton, Julia, *Political Intellectuals and Public Identities in Britain since 1850* (Manchester, 2001).

Stocks, Mary, *Ernest Simon of Manchester* (Manchester, 1963).

Thomson, J.A.K.T. and Toynbee, Arnold J. (eds), *Essays in Honour of Gilbert Murray* (London, 1936).

West, Francis, *Gilbert Murray: A Life* (London, 1984).

Wheeler-Bennett, Sir John, *John Anderson: Viscount Waverley* (London, 1962).

Wilson, Duncan, *Gilbert Murray, OM, 1866–1957* (London, 1984).

Other articles

Aster, Sidney, '"Salter's Soviet"', in Michael Graham Fry (ed.), *Power, Personalities and Policies: Essays in Honour of Donald Cameron Watt* (London, 1992).

Brewer, Christopher, 'Arnold Toynbee and Chatham House', in Andrea Bosco and Cornelia Navari (eds), *Chatham House and British Foreign Policy, 1919–1945: The Royal Institute of International Affairs During the Inter-War Period* (London, 1994).

Crowson, N.J., 'Much ado about nothing? Macmillan and appeasement', in Richard Aldous (ed.), *Harold Macmillan: Aspects of a Political Life* (London, 1999).

Crozier, Andrew J., 'Chatham House and appeasement', in Bosco and Navari, *Chatham House and British Foreign Policy, 1919–1945*.

Kennedy, Thomas C., 'The Next Five Years Group and the failure of the politics of agreement in Britain', *Canadian Journal of History*, 9 (1974), pp. 45–68.

'"Peace in our time": The personal diplomacy of Lord Allen of Hurtwood, 1933–1938', in Solomon Wank (ed.), *Doves and Diplomats: Foreign Offices and Peace Movements in Europe and America in The Twentieth Century* (London, 1978).

Marwick, Arthur, 'Middle opinion in the thirties: planning, progress and political "agreement"', *English Historical Review*, 79 (1964), pp. 285–298.

Meisel, Joseph S., 'Air raid shelter policy and its critics in Britain before the Second World War', *Twentieth Century British History*, 5 (1994), pp. 301–319.

INDEX